CURRENT ISSUES BEFORE INDIAN ECONOMY

CURRENT ISSUES BEFORE INDIAN ECONOMY

I.D. GUPTA

ABHIJEET PUBLICATIONS
DELHI 110094

ABHIJEET PUBLICATIONS
2/46 Tukhmeerpur Extension
Delhi-110 094
Phone: 011-22960492, 65698474
E-mail: abhijeetpublication@gmail.com

CURRENT ISSUES BEFORE INDIAN ECONOMY

First Published 2009

ISBN 978-81-89886-84-4

PRINTED IN INDIA

Published by J.K. Singh for Abhijeet Publications, Delhi-110 094, Lasertypeset by Gaurav Graphics, New Delhi and Printed at Himanshu Printers, Delhi.

Dedicated to
The Spirits of

My Father and Mother

Preface

This book is a collection of thematic lectures, delivered in the Economic Conferences in India and abroad as well as in University Grants Commission's Refresher Courses in Economics conducted in various Central and State Universities in India, by the author. They also formed part of lectures to the students of Economics in the University of Lucknow in the post graduate classes where the author had been a Professor. The chapters in the book focus on the challenges of growth, development and social justice in the Indian economy, polity and society as well as on the changes happening in the world economy after the break down of the Soviet Russia and cessation of Communist or Socialist challenge to market economy system of Capitalism. The purpose of the writing is not to add one more book on Indian Economy, the area replete with voluminous books.

It was on the suggestions of my colleague Professors like Prof. Yashvir Tyagi, Prof. Mohammad Muzammil and Dr. Arvind Awasthi from my own university and others like Prof. A. K. Shrivastava, of the DDU Gorakhpur University who encouraged to pen down my lectures on challenging issues faced by the Indian economy, polity and society. I am grateful to all of them.

There may be some overlapping in the content of chapters as these are the independent lectures and deliberations at different forums and at different points of time. They are complete in themselves independently.

The endeavour is meant for students of research and post-graduate classes in economics and the related disciplines in India and abroad as well as for those appearing for higher level competitive examinations like the Indian Administrative Services, Indian Economic Services, Provincial Civil Services and the like and others interested in economic affairs.

I owe my gratitude to my wife Ananda who took all the pains in providing me every encouragement and support in completing this work, and my sons Rajiv K. Gupta, an MBA from Vienna School of Economics, Austria, Ashwini Kumar, an MBA from the European University, Belgium and Master of Management from University of Texas, USA and Ashutosh Kumar, a Roorkee Engineering graduate and an excellent thinker, and now an IPS, for discussions on various themes in detail from time to time. However, the errors if any are solely mine.

Lastly, I am thankful to Mr. J.K. Singh, the publisher of the book, who took all the pains in bringing out the book in the present form in a very short span of time.

I.D. GUPTA

Contents

PART FIVE:
CORRUPTION AND DEVELOPMENT

PART SIX:
GLOBALIZATION, DEMOCRACY AND DEVELOPMENT

PART SEVEN:
SUSTAINABLE DEVELOPMENT AGENDA

Introduction

Indian economy is facing multitude of challenges of development since Independence of the country in 1947. It is sixty years passed but some of the major problems are as gigantic as they were at the time of Independence, viz., the problems of widespread poverty, inequality and huge unemployment. Added to this, newer problems of corruption and black economy have taken great proportion, today. These problems transgress the field of economics to go deeper into political system and the social system and the functioning of their institutions. The period since 1971 is taken as epoch making when second generation in India took upon the Gandhian old guards. This was the time when political convulsions began after the death of Pandit Nehru in 1964 and subsequently time came when political consensus in favour of single political party were not to be taken for granted. The period was also regarded as the beginning of authoritarian regime under Indira Gandhi and criminals' entry into politics. Several factors, economic as well as others, for example, success of green revolution and subsequent enrichment of farm lobby, regionalism and casteism etc. are cited as the deciding factors. By seventies while the Gandhian or nationalistic values were going behind the newer values of materialism and rising ambitions and self-interest were seen to dominate the scene. The national character of the people was changing fast. Except during the times of war with China and Pakistan when we visualize the glimpses of patriotism, the common phase was quite different in other times. A new India was emerging giving rise to economic "dualism" in the country. During the eighties while the economy was growing at the rate of 5.5 per cent from the earlier 3.5 per cent per annum, there was a clear cut perception of the rising dualism. We find that where as the economy was growing at a faster rate, the inequality and poverty too was growing undaunted despite of the IRDP and Employment Generation Programmes.

The economy of shortages and controls during the sixties, while on the one hand, created a system of rationing and controls, it simultaneously created a system of black marketing and black money. The growth rate of black economy, subsequently, was higher than the growth rate of the national economy. In the coming years when this unholy alliance system got maturity it became prevalent not only in economic sphere but it also started entering the political arena to purchase mandate and became catalyst in making and unmaking of governments. By the nineties when Narasimha Rao was in power the dominant role of money and muscle power in politics was a common perception. Economic impact of these political developments was clearly visible in rising inequality in the society. We also mark a rise of a completely new Social Order in which all these things were accepted and accommodated by the society. This corruption tolerance of the Indian society and people was unimaginable. Not quite so long ago Gandhi and the people were fighting against the British evil design which had made the country drained and poor. Gandhi and his values of self-less politics were sabotaged in the newer India. The chapters in the present book attempt to catch these situations of economic and political compulsions and their inter connections. Part four, five and six of the book is an attempt to look into such difficult situations before Indian economy and polity. Part two and three are dealing with the generic problems of poverty, absolute as well as relative, and unemployment. Part one of the book is a commentary in brief on the performance of the economy and the structural changes in it. The first chapter is on the choice made by our nation builders in favour of an ideal economic policy for the country which could ensure speedy economic development and establish social justice. How the ideal of a socialistic pattern of society gave way to a market economy system is the area of analysis.

The chapters attempt to catch the ground realities faced by the Indian economy and attempt to analyse the difficult situations which led to the failure of our successive Five Year Plans during sixties and seventies, viz., the Chinese aggression in 1962 and four times war with Pakistan since 1947 up to 1998, as well as recurrent spell of droughts and floods. Unrelented growth of population added more to our difficulties with a growth rate of 2 to 2.5 per cent per annum causing a near stagnant growth of one per cent per annum per capita income during sixties and seventies. It was greatly responsible for rising unemployment and under employment. By the time we were crossing the eighties, one more India was added in terms of total size of population since 1947 and a few years later the actual size of population stood at over one billion starting from around 340 million in 1947.

The realities are hard. The eighties was also a watershed in history in the world when the USSR disintegrated and the Communist challenge to market economy system collapsed. We entered in to an uni-polar world. This was also the time when in India the Socialism was losing steam owing to people's 'weariness from planning' as the public sector undertakings were losing heavily and government services were, by and large, inefficient and corrupt. By the start of nineties country adopted widespread economic reforms and liberalization, marketization and privatization became the new catch words. It was a journey from an ideal of economic policy of a Socialistic Pattern of Society to a switch over to a market economy system, supposedly in the name of competition and efficiency. However, the daunting problems still remain with an enigmatic question mark as to how to protect the interests of those below the poverty line from the "Tyranny of the market" or of those leftover by the market. Market excludes those who have no money in the pocket from the commodity market. It also excludes those who are illiterate and untrained from the labour or the employment market as well. Hence the role of the government is being redefined in terms of "the facilitator" for development and a "trustee of the poor"

By the time it is all being discussed and analyzed, a social development perception is combined with the economic development agenda to give development a Human face. A pointer of Environmentalists towards sustainability of growth and safety of public life is being taken up in the part seven of the book.

One great change the common man of India is visualizing is about the quality and stature of our political leaders who make and unmake economic policy decisions for growth and development of the country. Decidedly, the perception is grounded on the calculations of the Election Commission of India and other agencies who state that a sizeable percentage of the elected members come from the shady or criminal background and still they are facing heinous charges of murders, loot and robbery and the like.

It is an awful situation when we talk of clean government in a situation where the three pillars of the democracy, the legislature, the executive and the judiciary are charged with corruption. Even the fourth pillar, the media is not unblemished. Who in this country is above suspicion where we can say 'Caesar's wife must be above suspicions' is a matter to be searched upon?

Another enigmatic question pertains to the weak governments in view of alliances owing to split mandates in elections. This "short termism" in politics has wider repercussions for economic policy making and development plans. These are the current challenges before the Indian economy and the society, in view of the author, which provide the subject matter of the book.

To refurbish the plan of the book, Chapter one attempts to present a brief account of India's journey towards a Socialistic Pattern of Society, based on the intentions of the Directive Principles of the State Policy as incorporated in the Indian Constitution. It attempts to pick up the moments of history under which the philosophy of justice, political, economic and social, was given a shape under our developmental plan objectives. Under what conditions the Mixed Economy was adopted as the path of development to proceed. Under which ideological perception Parliamentary Democracy system was chosen to run the government. Obviously we see the impact of Fabian socialism or state socialism of England in our policies.

Chapter two attempts to take account of the development experience of the past six decades and attempts to catch the nuances of the time.

Part two of the book is devoted to the study of poverty scenario in the country in the pre and post reform period. It contains two chapters which attempt to define poverty concepts and make a vivid description of rural and urban poverty in the country during the planning era and suggest development strategy to alleviate poverty in the light of current researches of Amartya Sen, the World Bank, Prof. Kalam, our ex-President and others. While Sen talks in terms of freedoms and unfreedoms to catch the concept of poverty, Prof. Kalam suggests PURA model of rural development based on three connectivities; physical connectivity, electronic connectivity and knowledge connectivity for the rural areas so that poverty could be eliminated from the rural areas and push to the town phenomenon is checked which has created tremendous problems in cities which have become unlivable.

Part three is devoted to the study of unemployment problem. Unemployment and poverty are related problems. It was considered on the Keynesian lines that employment is a function of income. And with higher growth rate of the economy unemployment could be eliminated. However, the reality is far from this theory where in India growth rate has risen but unemployment too has risen side by side. The current situation in India is sometimes called a state of jobless growth. The factors responsible for this state of affairs have been discussed in this part of the book.

Part four and five are devoted to the problem of parallel economy and corruption in the system. Part four, chapter six, is an attempt to look in to the genesis of black money economy in India and its stages of childhood to adulthood in the system. An attempt to perceive its networking, functioning, growth and its repercussions on economic development has been done. How it could be contained forms part of the suggestion in the chapter.

Part five is devoted to the advances made in theorizing the world wide phenomenon of corruption and rent-seeking and DUP activities particularly in Asian and African countries with or without democracy in polity. Chapter seven is on crime corruption and development in Indian economy. The paper was presented in the Indian Economic Conference in Jammu in its 83rd Conference in the year 2000.

Part six, chapter nine, is an area of current debate on democracy and development. How far democracy in polity is an ideal for rapid economic development or to what extent it limits the economic progress of the economy is the point of discussion based on the Indian experience. This paper was submitted to the International Conference of the IIDS in Fiji in the year 2005. Chapter ten is on developments happening in the world economy in the post-Socialist era—the era of globalization.

Part seven of the book, on Sustainable development contains four chapters which presents the viewpoints of J.K. Mehta and Gandhi. Both these papers were presented in Economic Conferences in the year 2002 and 2007. While Mehta's contribution lies in the area of wantlessness, Gandhi talks of righteousness in every walk of life. He talks of selflessness and sacrifice of individual wants for the sake of society. Chapter eleven was the paper for discussion in a National seminar in Osmania University, Hyderabad in 1997 which suggests for import of non-pollutive technologies instead of pollutive technology transfer. The paper on Vedic model of sustainable development was presented in the Banaras Hindu University in the Indian Economic Conference in 2004. It is chapter fourteen of the book.

PART ONE:
INDIA'S ECONOMIC POLICY AND PERFORMANCE

1

India's Economic Policy: A Journey from Socialistic Pattern of Society to Market Economy System

Today we have entered the 21st century or a new Millennium with a growth rate of economy around eight to nine per cent per annum but the scenario at the time of Independence of the nation in 1947 was quite different. On August 15th 1947 when the nation became Independent it was a nation divided into two parts with an unimaginable distress and chaos imposed upon the people. Hatred between two communities, bloodshed, and transfer of population in some parts of the country imposed unprecedented burden and sacrifices. India was a poor country. It was a bleeding nation. The task ahead was daunting to establish an order and lead the country on the path of development. An ideology was to be chosen which could lead to faster development and establish social and economic justice.

In the post World War II period the world economy have had two systems of economic policy. Most of the European economies were following the system created with Industrial Revolution since the nineteenth century, the market driven system of economic development or the Capitalist system. Industrial Revolution first started in Great Britain when machines began to dominate the production process and factory system was established. Power driven machines made revolutionary impact on production and scale of production moved towards large scale production from small scale man driven production process. The Industrial Revolution in Great Britain was based on two things, steel and coal. Steel made the machines and coal produced power. Subsequently several changes took place and cotton textiles, chemical and other industries started developing fast to transform the whole system. Income generation was unprecedented in history after the industrial system was established. With rising incomes in Europe levels of living significantly improved. The demonstration effect of Great Britain's success have had a large impact on other European economies and by and by Germany, France, Italy and other countries attempted to adopt the machinery driven factory system and a pattern of large scale production and foreign trade emerged.

Nineteenth century was also a period of great scientific advances. Intelligentsia class, particularly the scientists and engineers contributed a lot. During the second half of the nineteenth century scientific advances, inventions and innovations were taking place in Europe. As the system was gaining maturity the living standards of those countries that followed industrialization was going up and up. The emphasis of production shifted from agriculture to industry. And industrialization became a synonym of economic development.

The economists of the Classical school started justifying the emerging Capitalist system. Adam Smith, who is considered as the Father of Economics, has already published his *Wealth of Nations* (1776). He had advocated a policy of Laissez Faire in production and Free Trade in international trade. Laissez faire espouses that there should be no interference in the production process and exchange or market by the state. There should be perfect freedom. The basic decisions of the economy—what to produce, how to produce and far whom to produce—will be decided by the free market forces, they said. The Classicals believed in the "Invisible Hands' operating in a free market. They were the forces of demand and supply. Therefore, in a free market the forces of demand and supply determine the price which clears the market and maintains equilibrium. The price mechanism makes a balance between amount demanded and supplied in the market.

The economists believed that this system not only maintains equilibrium in the market at a particular price level but also ensures maximum profit to the entrepreneur and leads to development of the economy. Market also distributed incomes among different sections of productive factors viz., labour, land, capital and organization. In labour market the reward of labour is determined on the basis of the interplay of demand and supply. In money and capital market the same mechanism is adopted which maintains equilibrium between money and capital demanded and supplied via interest rate determination.

In brief, this is the crux of the Capitalist system.

However, as the capitalist system developed and was established it was soon realized that it has divided the society in to two parts or classes. That is, the labour class and the Capitalist class. The maxima of profit maximization which was the motive force behind entrepreneurial activities has driven the system to a Capitalistic exploitation of the labour class. And as the rule of the game was that the state has not to interfere in the production process or in the free play of the market and trade, the weak or the poor in the game was exposed to unopposed exploitation by the mighty and rich producer class.

Society and those intellectuals and people having concern to social cause who were watching the play of the capitalist market economy system, like Carlyle and Ruskin and others in Great Britain started raising voice against it. They raised voice against not only such type of exploitation but also against the science of economics as such which was termed as the bread and butter science and the Gospel of Mammon. This was the time when economics was defined as the 'science of wealth creation' and was least concerned with human welfare.

A more critical challenge emerged through Karl Marx who attempted to prove the injustices of the system which was exploitative and divided the society into the classes of the "bourgeois" and the "proletariat". Marxian challenge of industrial capitalism was not only on the lines of a theoretical criticism but it was a call for revolution to throw away the capitalist through revolutionary means by the united labour force. His "Communist Manifesto" appeared in 1848 which called for workers of the world to unite. It spoke "Workers of the world unite. You have to lose nothing but the chains. You have to win the world".

Karl Marx developed a theory of "scientific socialism" in which he espoused for a Socialist society based on egalitarian distribution of income and wealth of the nation. The main contention of Marx was that the wealth is solely created by the labour class with the help of the "free-gift" of nature and therefore, it belongs to the labour class. His analysis was based on the Classical Labour Theory of Value which says that the "units" of labour involved in the production of a commodity determines its value. Higher the hours of labour required for the production of a good, the higher is its value.

Marx challenged the theoretical tenets of Capitalist system and presented an alternative system free from exploitation and based on egalitarian distribution of income and wealth of the nation. His sense of justice stated "to each according to needs and to each according to abilities". Equality does not mean equal distribution. As the needs of the individuals and their qualifications differ so would be their rewards.

His catapulation of stages of growth presented Socialism as a stage in the fuller development of man and society under Communism. To Marx, in a Communist society, no state is required as people are already so enlightened that there is no place for injustices to exist.

In a world divided in between rich and the poor, 'haves' and the 'have-nots', Marx became an angel to the downtrodden. His words were gospels, his speeches astounding. Marx was aided in his attempt by Fredric Engel, who took up the battle against capitalism, with him and after him.

A new era dawned. Many countries of the world started following the theory of Marx and Engels. Workers in many countries started to unite. War against "bourgeois" started gaining strength. And even in the citadels of Capitalism Trade Unions were legalized. Social security measures started emerging and workers right to raise their grievances and get redressal were approved in many countries.

Several countries of the world, e.g., Russia, many of the East European countries and China and East Germany adopted this system of economic policy and became Socialist. The revolution in Russia in 1917 when Tsar was overthrown was the beginning of establishment of "Proletariat Dictatorship" or the government of the labour class (party). While "basic needs" coverage and employment to all were ensured by the state Private property rights of the individuals were abolished. All the resources and wealth of the nation belonged to the state with this change of the system. Developmental Planning in Russia achieved tremendous success and the Russian economy transformed itself into a big economic and military power.

The twentieth century witnessed two world wars, one during 1914-1918 and the other in between 1939-1944. It was also a period of "Great Depression" during 1929-1933 which greatly changed the perceptions of economic laws developed by the economists of the Classical school.

Nineteen thirties was a turning point in economic history when tenets of Classical theory were failing and were challenged and newer insights into economic theory were emerging. During Depression large scale unemployment emerged in the countries of the world. It was a period of continuously falling demand and prices. Producers were suffering unprecedented losses and were closing down. As a result unemployment was abounding.

Simpleton economic theories developed earlier by the Classicals based on pure and perfect competition in market and the operation of the invisible hands and price mechanism to bring equilibrium was unable to cope with the new complex realities of the world in the post First World war period.

This was the time when Keynesian Revolution came which diagnosed falling demand a result of falling incomes. While earlier thinking was that demand is a function of price, Keynes promulgated that demand is basically a function of income. His theory of employment stated that "employment is a function of income; larger the level of income larger the level of employment; lower the level of income lower the level of employment." And for increasing the level of employment he advocated a greater role of fiscal policy and state intervention. Pump priming the economy, cheap money policy and deficit budgeting and deficit financing became the tools of government to cope with the huge unemployment problem faced by the world community.

Classical tenet of perfect and pure competition was also challenged in 1933 when the works of Mrs. Joan Robinson and Joseph Chamberlain appeared separately. Their epoch making conclusions found that in reality markets are "imperfect". While one used the term "imperfect competition", the other applied the term "Monopolistic competition". There could exist in the market monopoly conditions or the conditions of duopoly or oligopoly. In each of the case market is far from perfectly competitive. These were the conditions of imperfect competition or monopolistic competition. And when the market is far from perfectly competitive, exploitation of the weaker partner in market becomes a possibility.

Karl Marx had earlier talked of "tyranny of the market" which resulted in the exploitation of the consumers and the workers in the commodity as well as in the labour market.

Therefore, it was established that market economy system based Capitalist model is far from ideal as it is may exploit the poor and may not distribute incomes and wealth in a just manner. Therefore, some sort of intervention is required to safeguard the interests of the weaker in the market. John Maynard Keynes was also prescribing State intervention to deal with the problems of unemployment and low incomes.

At the time India gained political Independence, there were, thus, two prevailing ideologies of development in the world. Both had their virtues and failures. India was a poor and significantly "drained" country. Her resources were earlier drained by the East India Company and later by the British rule. It is said that the success of England's Industrial Revolution was partly based on Indian raw material and resources and her vast market which was exploited through the network of railways. The urgent requirement of the country was to establish an order after the partition and lead her at the path of speedy development.

By now we have had the good and bad of both the prevailing ideologies. While Capitalist model was exploitative, the socialist model was regimentative and dictatorial. As India had opted for a Parliamentary Democratic system in polity the appropriate economic policy should have been democratic, non-exploitative and justice oriented. India opted for a Mixed Economic system or a Mixed Economy model, where in State sector leads the system supported by the private enterprise. For rapid development of the economy Planning was adopted on the pattern of Russia. The economy was divided in to public sector and the private sector. Their respective roles were assigned through the Industrial Policy Resolution of 1949 and later by the Industrial Policy 1956. It was the thinking then that India's mixed economy model would be a role model for the developing and poor backward economies of the world.

Indian nation adopted the Indian Constitution on 26th January 1950 and subsequently Planning was introduced in 1951. Planning in India was intended in the words of the government Resolution of March 1950 "to promote a rapid rise in the standard of living of the people by efficient exploitation of the resources of the country, increasing production and offering opportunities to all for employment in the service of community".

In December 1954 Indian Parliament adopted a resolution which contained the following clauses:

1. the objective of economic policy should be a Socialistic Pattern of Society; and
2. towards this end the tempo of economic activity in general and industrial development in particular should be stepped up to maximum possible extent".

The term Socialistic Pattern of Society was commented upon and elaborated in the Second Five Year Plan document and a long term strategy for economic advance was formulated based on this concept.

Socialistic pattern of society, essentially means that the basic criterion of determining lines of advance must not be private profit, but social gain, and that the pattern of development and structure of socio-economic relations should be so planned that they result not only in appreciable increases in national income and employment but also in greater equality in incomes and wealth. Major decisions regarding production, distribution, consumption and investment—and in fact all significant socio-economic relationships—must be made by agencies informed by social purpose.

The benefit of economic development must accrue more and more to relatively less privileged classes of society, and there should be progressive reduction of concentration of income, wealth and economic power. The problem is to create a milieu in which the small man who has so far had little opportunity of perceiving and participating in the immense possibilities of growth through organized effort is enabled to put in his best in the interest of a higher standard of life for himself and increased prosperity for the country. In the process, he rises in economic and social status.

> ".....The accent of the socialistic pattern of society is on the attainment of positive goals, raising of living standards, the enlargement of opportunities for all, the promotion of enterprise among the disadvantaged classes and creation of a sense of partnership among all sections of the community. These positive goals provide the criteria for basic decisions....."

The concept of socialistic pattern of society came out of the Directive Principles of the State Policy enshrined in the Indian Constitution. Two of the Articles, Article 38 and Article 39(a), (b) and (c) were cited in the resolution of 15th March 1950 by which Planning Commission on India was set up.

Article 38 states: "The State shall strive to promote the welfare of the people by securing and protecting, as effectively as it may, a social order in which justice, social, economic and political, shall inform all the institutions of national life."

Article 39 prescribes: "The State shall, in particular, direct its policy towards securing:

(a) that, the citizen, men and women, equally, have the right to an adequate means of livelihood:

(b) that, the ownership and control of the material resources of the community are so distributed as best to sub serve the common good;

(c) that the operation of the economic system does not result in the concentration of wealth and means of production to the common detriment.

The contemporary thinking in determining the lines of advance decidedly had Gandhian impression. Economic development means development of the poor and the downtrodden. The emphasis on social gain, common good, community approach of life, and lesser positioning of personal gains and private profit reflect our Indian community culture.

Clearly the thinking of our leaders was that Democracy in politics and Planning in economics would serve the best interest of Indian masses. Greater role of State in encouraging development was taken from Japanese example and the prescription of Keynes. It was a quest for the optimum. Nevertheless, the things were more "idealist" than practical as the time proved later on.

The Nehruvian model of development, however, had a clear departure from Gandhian model based on rural development, cottage and village industries and self-sufficient villages, lesser role to machinery and large scale production in factories dominated by machines. We clearly visualize Nehru's predilections for industrial development and large industries. Nehru, our the then Prime Minister, was highly impressed with the performance of Russian Plans for development and their performance. We clearly see his leftist bias in his actions.

When our country got political Independence the daunting task was to move to the path of speedy economic development to remove poverty, destitution and widespread unemployment. India lived in its villages as in reality more than seventy per cent of the population was living in the villages and earning their livelihood from agriculture and allied industries. Therefore, raising rural incomes through enhancing agricultural productivity and production was the challenge. It was also necessary to remove the hurdles and roadblocks from the path of establishment of economic and social justice. In this direction attempts were made in two directions: first in the direction of tenancy or land reforms and other in the direction of Community Development Projects.

The main areas of the Land Reforms were three: abolition of intermediaries, tenancy reforms and consolidation of holdings. Further tenancy reforms had three areas, viz., regulation of rent, ceiling on land holdings, and ownership rights to the tenants. This was to remove rack renting which had made the Indian farmers in debt for generations together. Further the motto was to provide land to the landless cultivators or the "Land to the Tiller'. Through ceiling on land holdings and consolidation of holdings in different States attempt were made to make the size of holdings economic. Co-operative farming also formed the part of agenda. Besides individual attempts were also made by Vinoba Bhave and Jai Prakash Narayan in the direction of Bhoodan and Gramdan movement on voluntary basis by big land owners so that land could be made available for farming to the landless agricultural labourers.

The objectives of Land Reforms were two fold: raising farmland productivity and removing injustices from the agrarian system which had emerged owing to past agrarian structure.

The other attempt to transform rural life was the start of Community Development Projects and later National Extension Services. This started in 1952 when the whole country was divided into above 3200 Development Blocks. For each development block a package programme was initiated under the supervision of a team of experts and officials. Block Development Officers (BDOs), Assistant Development Officers (ADOs) and Gram Sevaks were appointed to take care of the development work as per the local and situational needs of the area. It was an attempt to select the area and target it and provide financial and physical resources like quality seeds, know-how, agricultural tools and machinery, irrigation, expert advice and the like. Cooperatives were already strengthened to provide credit to the farmers. It was a time bound approach of a medium term of period. After the Block had completed the stages it was put under National Extension Service for two years. This was the map of rural development.

The flag bearers of economic policy so established under the Socialistic Pattern were the Five Year Plans which started in April 1951. Already the Industrial Policy Resolution (1948) was adopted by the Indian Parliament which had demarcated the areas of the public and private sectors. The greater task of nation building was given to the public sector and 'basic and key industries', development of infra-structure, and what became popular phrase the "commanding heights of the economy" became the exclusive responsibility of the State. Private sector was given a complementary role to assist the nation building. Areas of different industries were assigned and demarcated for private investment.

However, the investment climate was not clear owing to initial inhibitions and shyness of private capital investment was clearly visible for fear of nationalization. Foreign capital too remained shy. No sooner the Prime Minister and the Finance Minister had to alleviate this fear by their statements in the Parliament and at other forums that the government had no intention of nationalization and private capital is welcome and its safety would be the responsibility of the government. It was also assured to the foreign capital that there would be no discrimination with them and they would be free to repatriate their capital and government would provide them all freedom. The assurances worked and capital started coming in.

The First Five Year Plan (1951-56) was basically a ground work for real start of planning and industrial development. Its objectives were less ambitious and moderate. The thrust was on agriculture and rural development besides rehabilitation of large number of refugees who had come from Pakistan. It was also attempted to develop cottage and small scale industries and make villages self-sufficient as per Gandhi's wishes. The Plan was successful in achieving the targeted growth rate.

With the start of the Second Five Year Plan in 1956, the Industrial Policy was given a concrete shape as per the initial experiences in the field and areas of public and private sectors crystallized more clearly. The Second Plan laid emphasis on development of basic and heavy industries and large scale industrialization as per the predilections of Pandit Nehru. It was based on Mahalanobis's two sector model, viz., investment goods and consumption goods. This model was a variant of the earlier Harrod Domar model of the First Plan and more or less followed the 1928 Soviet model of Feldman. Starting from the initial two sector model covering labour and capital inputs, the Mahalanobis model developed the basic strategies of the Plan.

By the time fifties passed and the Third Five Year Plan began in 1961, the circumstances were largely different from what they had been for the Second Plan. "There was a financial crisis, a foreign exchange crisis and a food crisis. Foreign opinion (related to external resource mobilization) was critical of India's 'over-ambitious' plans which allegedly 'emphasized welfare' at the expense of efficiency and reduction of economic inequalities at the cost of rapid economic development." The atmosphere was thus discouraging for large scale expansion programmes for projects with long gestation periods and for ambitious resource mobilization.

However, nothing seriously daunted the framers of the plan in the Planning Commission. The Third Plan aimed at 5 per cent per annum increase in national income, self-sufficiency in food grains and optimization of production of other crops, expansion of basic industries like steel, chemicals, fuel and power, establishment of machine building capacity to promote industrialization, sustained increase in employment and manpower usage, equity in distribution, and reduction of disparity in income and wealth.

The Plan faced unforeseen misfortunes in the form of regular floods and droughts, acute power and transport shortages and aggression on our national borders by China in 1962 and Pakistan in 1965. This led to sharp hike in defense expenditure and development relegated. The country was in low self-esteem after the defeat at the hands of China in 1962.

It was apparent even at the conclusion of the Third Plan

that it had failed in nearly every sector, and that 'we (had) all but lost our Plan'. It was said: The experience of the Third Plan shows that the strategy was too long term, too vulnerable to shortfalls in aid and excesses of political pressure, and above all too sensitive to food scarcity and inflation.

This was also the time when the nation lost Pt. Jawahar Lal Nehru on 27th May 1964.

The years 1965-66 and 1966-67 were the periods of severe droughts. When Lal Bahadur Shastry was the Prime Minister of the country after Nehru it faced another aggression from Pakistan on our borders. By this time country was facing severe food crisis as a result of fast growing population and decreased supply of foodgrains. "Jai Jawan and Jai Kisan" was the slogan given by Shastry. Country's self-esteem returned with the victory over Pakistan's aggression.

The sixties was a period of calamities and were very crucial in deciding the fate of Indian economy. Lal Bahadur Shastry, the then Prime Minister of the country passed away in Tashkent after the negotiations were complete with Pakistan, in January 1966. Indira Gandhi came to power. Besides, severe droughts in the country interruptions were visible in external assistance. The original draft outline of the Fourth Plan prepared in 1966 under Ashok Mehta had to be abandoned on account of the pressure exerted on the economy by two consecutive droughts, devaluation of rupee in June 1966 and recessionary condition in the economy. A "Plan Holiday" was declared. India witnessed a bitter situation during Indo-Pakistan war when it's so called allies refused to supply essential equipment and raw materials for its economic development. It was therefore, decided that the Fourth Plan would be stalled and 'the interregnum would be filled by Annual Plans'.

Thus there were three Annual Plans for 1966-67, 1967-68 and 1968-69 respectively. The Annual Plans were meant to clear the deck for launching the Fourth Five Year Plan. It was natural that the crisis in agriculture earmarked by serious food shortages, the relative emphasis should have been focused on agriculture. It was in fact during the inter plan years that the whole of our "new agricultural strategy—widespread application of new high yielding varieties of seeds, the extensive use of fertilizers, the exploitation of irrigation potential, soil conservation—was put into effect during the drought years when the plan was supposedly at standstill".

Sufferings create the ground for success and bring back valour. Either you exist or you are destroyed. Extreme hardships of early sixties brought about the killing spirit for survival. Success of the Green Revolution was the outcome of the new strategy. Concerted efforts were made to open agricultural universities and agricultural research centers which developed short duration, high yielding varieties of wheat, paddy and other cereals. Farm machinery was put into more use. Varieties of seeds from Mexico, Canada and Japan were brought and developed. This brought about an impressive success in foodgrain production, especially wheat and rice.

In the wake of uncertain conditions of foreign aid an inward looking strategy of growth in the form of import substitution was adopted to lessen our reliance on foreign capital and foreign capital. The Fourth Five Year Plan began in 1969. Much preliminary work and many approach papers and multi platform dissensions went into the preparation of the Fourth Plan.

The basic strategy of the Fourth Plan is called the Gadgil strategy. It has a number of facets, viz., the New Agricultural Strategy as the main underpinning, indicative industrial planning as in France, and a new policy on both foreign aid and foreign trade.

The Agricultural strategy was based on the 'package programme' and use of 'short-term high-yielding varieties of major cereals', as stated earlier too. Under indicative planning, the Fourth Plan visualized that industrial production would increase by 8 to 12 per cent annually. It was also believed that it would be possible to raise exports by about 7 per cent per annum and to reduce net foreign aid to the level of 1969-70.

The strategy, however, did not give up the heavy industries programme. According to Gadgil, iron and steel, cement, engineering goods, and metallic products were to be produced in the future both for home consumption and exports.

For some time long term planning had to be virtually suspended. Country moved in to the direction of intensive agricultural programmes. Banks were nationalized in 1969 for the social cause of providing credit to the farmers and the unemployed and the loaning criteria was changed in favour of productive asset and income creation basis rather than fixed asset basis. It was called social control of banking. Initially the number of banks was 14 then six more banks came under it.

The Fourth Plan set out two principle objectives: "growth with stability" and "progressive achievement of self-reliance". The Plan aimed at 5.5 per cent rate of growth in national income and the provision of national minimum for the weaker sections of the community.

The Fourth Plan got off a flying start. The first two years were indeed promising. There were bumper and record crops and also excellent industrial production. There after things went steadily wrong. There was serious failure in energy and transport sectors, a disastrous failure of monsoon, and the Indo-Pak war of 1971. From around 1972 the inflationary spiral caught on the multiplier. Meanwhile the population explosion and rise in unemployment continued unabated.

The economy of shortages and war with Pakistan created a situation of nearing double digit inflation. To control prices and ensure distribution rationing had earlier been introduced. With supply shortagess and rationing, black marketing of essential commodities crept into the system with far reaching impact. The Inspector Raj became apparent and an unholy alliance was created in between black marketers and the Inspectors. The natural outcome of this rampant practice of bribery was the emergence of black money and black economy, which in coming years made yet another alliance with criminals, musclemen and politicians. A very difficult situation arrived in the next few decades when almost the whole democracy was hijacked in the hands of corrupt politicians, bureaucrats and industrialists and other important persons in society.

The Fourth Plan could not achieve the targets and the growth rate of national income stagnated around 3.3 per cent against a target of 5.5 per cent., and owing to fast rise in population per capita income growth stagnated around 1.2 per cent per annum. The agricultural production increased by 2.8 per cent as against a target of 5 per cent. The industrial production rose at the rate of 3.9 percent against 8 per cent target.

The Fifth Plan was introduced at the time when country was reeling under veritable economic crisis arising out of a run away inflation, fuelled by quadrupling of petroleum prices by the OPEC cartel in 1973.

The approach of the Fifth Plan, a document prepared by the Minister of Planning, D.P. Dhar, was the blueprint on which the plan was eventually finalized. The two objectives of the Plan were removal of poverty and self-reliance. The earlier objectives of 'growth with stability', and 'equity in distribution' and reduction of disparity was put behind the curtain.

By now it was understood that merely by acceleration in the rate of growth of economy the problems of unemployment, under-employment and massive low-end poverty can not be removed. Therefore, a "Direct Attack on Poverty" strategy was developed. For removal of rural poverty Intensive Rural Development Programmes (IRDP) was vitalized. A Twenty Point Programme was initiated at the instance of Indira Gandhi.

In the area of employment generation, the Crash Scheme for Rural Employment, the Drought Prone Area Programme, the Small Farmers and Development Agency and Marginal Farmers and Agricultural Labour Development Agency were among the first to be introduced. They were followed, some years later, by the Employment Guarantee Scheme in Maharashtra and the "Food for Work" programme in other states. Most of these programmes sought to create employment for the poor while a few sought to provide them with assets for self-employment.

Let us recapitulate and add some important events of the period. We find that while the period of sixties is regarded a period during which there was a sharp increase in the incidence of poverty, as both the number of the poor and the proportion of the population below the poverty line registered a substantial rise, its later part was marked with vast scale political ups and downs in Congress party, the ruling single party majority.

The General elections of 1967 established that electoral outcomes could no longer be taken for granted and that the Congress party could no longer assume the support of the people. The Congress party was defeated, in almost every north Indian state, in the general election of 1967. The political consequence was a sharp erosion in the cohesion of the Congress party as dissent and discord led to its split in 1969 i.e., after Kamraj plan. It was, however, the decline of the Congress party that explained the rise of Indira Gandhi and not the other way round. Indira opted out of old congress on the voice of her inner conscience, as per her own version, and formed Indira Congress.

The period of late sixties and early seventies represented a watershed in an evolving situation and a continuum of developments. The political scenario that emerged, according to Deepak Nayyar, was characterised by two discernible changes. First, the ideology of nationalism had begun to wane. This was partly a consequence of the passage of time as the second generation came to the fore in Congress party. It was also related to the regionalization of politics that surfaced because the central leadership, after Nehru, was weaker. At the same time, politics in India witnessed the first revolts of the young, manifest in the Naxalite movement and the stirring among the dalits. Second, there was slow but steady erosion of the political consensus. The heritage of nationalism began to fade from the memories and the compulsions of political democracy came home to roost.

Indira Gandhi became a war hero after victory over Pakistan war in 1971 and in the forthcoming General election every Tom, Dick and Harry who got Congress ticket almost won the election and Congress came back to power.

Things were difficult, however, and very soon Indira Gandhi had to promulgate "Emergency" in 1975, exactly 22 June 1975 to March 1977, to contain revolting voices (of Jai Prakash Narayan, particularly) which called for a "Total Revolution" against the dictatorial regime of her. This was the period when the Fifth Five Year Plan was under way. The supporting voice to the call for revolution was seemingly gained from the large unemployed masses and poor or the "have-nots".

Although Indira Gandhi was successful in containing the attempt to dislodge her, the repercussions of the Emergency and the measures adopted to control population etc. ruthlessly thrown her out of power in General elections of 1977 when Janata Party government came to power under Morarji Desai. The other important persons were Chaudhary Charan Singh and Jagjeevan Ram.

The economic reason behind this rise of ambition was that the rich peasantry which had reaped the benefits of the Green Revolution wanted to taste the political power, too, besides economic power. And the Congress party was not able to attract them under their umbrella due to bickering and regionalism that had crept in the late sixties and early seventies in it.

The Janata Party led government rolled back the economic policies carried through by Congress led governments and particularly the policies of Indira Gandhi. As a result the Fourth Five Year Plan (1974-79) was terminated a year earlier in 1978. The government rejected the Nehruvian model of development planning strategy based on development of heavy industries and industrialization, although it had all the praise for planning as such. Reviewing the over all achievements of planning during the first five plans the Sixth Plan (Janata) draft mentions: "It is a cause of legitimate national pride that over this period, a stagnant and dependent economy has been modernized and made self-reliant".

The new government had held the view that Nehru model of development was responsible for growing unemployment, concentration of economic power in the hands of a few powerful business and industrial families, for the widening of inequalities of income and wealth and for mounting poverty.

The Sixth Plan sought to reconcile the objectives of higher production with those of greater employment so that millions of people living below the poverty line could benefit therefrom. The focus of the Plan was enlargement of employment potential in agriculture and allied activities, encouragement to small industries producing consumer goods for mass consumption and to raise the incomes of the lowest classes through a minimum needs programme.

However, over-ambitions and inner bickering started soon emerging in the party as a result Morarji Desai, the then Prime Minister, dismissed Charan Singh from the cabinet. But soon he had to take him back due to the pressure inside the party. Subsequently Charan Singh became the Prime Minister of India in July 1979.

The policy adopted in 1977 lived too short, a period of about two years to have a durable impact on the industrial profile of the country. With the fall of the Janata government and resumption of power by Congress party in 1980 with Indira Gandhi as the Prime Minister, the government reconstituted the Planning Commission and formulated an altogether new Sixth Plan to cover the period from 1980 to 1985. It was again to restore the basic tenets of the Industrial Policy 1956 and Nehru model of development.

When the Sixth Plan was launched the country was facing difficult conditions. The Plan itself rationalized: the acute inflationary pressure which have prevailed since March 1979, the progressive deterioration in the first three years in the functioning of such critical sectors as power, coal, railways and steel and steep rise in petroleum prices... have already affected the overall growth prospects, India's balance of payments has deteriorated significantly.... with a very difficult foreign exchange situation.

It was against this background that the Sixth Plan was launched in order to achieve a ten-fold objective. These objectives were: to significantly raise the national income, to modernize technology, to reduce poverty and unemployment progressively, to speedily develop the energy sector, to improve the quality of life of the people and to reduce inequalities in income and wealth. The remaining objectives, also equally important were: to promote balanced regional development, to control the growth of population by promoting Family Planning, to promote ecological and environmental improvements and to elicit the widest possible popular participation.

The Sixth Plan was visualized as the first phase in a series of perspective plans. The perspective covers a spectrum of fifteen years from 1980-81 to 1994-95. According to the Plan, "this development perspective visualizes accelerated progress towards the removal of poverty, generation of gainful employment and technological and economic self-reliance".

While an annual growth rate of 5.2 per cent was envisaged for the gross national product (GDP) a 3.3 per cent rise per annum was contemplated for income per capita.

However, India's NNP during 1980-85 registered a growth rate of 4.7 per cent per annum and per capita income 2.5 per cent.

Political leadership gets a jolt when Prime Minister Indira Gandhi was assassinated on 31st October 1984. A national mourning continued for days and days. Rajiv Gandhi was sworn in as the next Prime Minister.

Soon after resumption of power in 1884, the Prime Minister Rajiv Gandhi had brought about a sea change in terms of liberalization of licensing policy in favour of large business houses, particularly in terms of making them free from the provisions of the MRTP Act and the FERA. To help them, import policy too had been liberalized in subsequent years.

Discernible trends were evidenced in 1980s in the economy. It was realized that Indian economy is in too much chains and an allegory was used that the Indian economy is a caged tiger. By now the air of Socialism started depleting as the country was experiencing recurrent failures of white elephants of economy, the public sector enterprises. Government or the State services had become delayful, inefficient and corrupt. And people started feeling some sort of "weariness from Planning". There was anger against the Inspector Raj which had become a synonym of inefficiency and corruption. Although attempts to reduce poverty and the number of population below the poverty line were made and they had got some success too, no perceptible dent was visible as the population more than doubled in the thirty years since Independence. Unemployment was staggering and a substantial number was added to the labour force every year. Inflation was unabated and galloping and corruption in government offices rampant. Even the Prime Minister Rajiv Gandhi realized that only 15 per cent of the govt. allocation reaches the beneficiary.

Rajiv Gandhi era is taken as the beginning of liberalization era in Indian economy. By allowing large industrial houses licenses for substantial expansion government was attempting to fulfill the objective of raising production at rapid rate.

The Sixth Plan almost achieved its target in terms of growth of GDP except for the last year (1984-85) of the Plan when many parts of the country faced severe famine conditions and the agricultural output was less than the record output of the last year. In words of the Seventh Five Year Plan (1985-90, Vol. 1, P 1) "on the whole the Sixth Plan has been fairly successful in sustaining and further strengthening the impulses for growth, modernization and social justice."

The Seventh Plan (1985-90) was being visualized as a vehicle for prosperity and social justice with a focus on the eradication of poverty creation of wider employment opportunities, larger availability of food grains, and increased income per capita. Other crucibles of the Plan follow from these basic objectives. Thus the focus was on food, work and productivity besides regional balance.

Estimates prepared by the National Sample Survey indicated that 36 million people crossed the poverty line between 1977-78 and 1983-84. Nevertheless, poverty was substantial at the end of 1983. As per the World Bank estimates, in January- December 1983, 45.31 per cent of rural population and 35.65 per cent of urban population, making for 43 per cent of total population lived below the poverty line in India.

With the combined efforts of IRDP, National Rural Employment Programme (NREP), and Rural Landless Employment Guarantee Programme (RLEGP) it was expected to reduce poverty substantially during the Seventh Plan. These programmes were expected to generate 2458 million man days of additional employment (9.04 million standard person years) in rural areas. For the removal of urban poverty considerable emphasis on improvement in the living conditions of slum dwellers had been laid down in the Plan.

However, when the Seventh Plan was in progress political uncertainties developed in 1988 and Rajiv Gandhi recommended for dissolution of the Parliament in October 1988. Prior to it seven opposition parties had formed National Front with V.P. Singh as convener, who had earlier resigned in April 1987 on Bofors gun purchase issue from the cabinet. In the election, Janata Dal came to power and V.P. Singh formed the Ministry on December 2nd 1989 with the support of BJP and the Communists. Now the country had moved in coalition politics and short termism of tenure which had wider meanings for economic policy decisions.

On economic front the Seventh Plan was a success and stagnation of economy was broken. The NNP at factor cost registered a growth rate of 5.5 per cent during 1984-85 and 1989-90. The per capita NNP, on average, grew at the rate of 3.5 per cent.

The Planning Commission had approved the Approach to the Eighth Plan under the Congress (I) government on September 1, 1989 but with the installation of National Front Government in December 1989, the Planning Commission was reconstituted and Mr. Ram Krishna Hegde was appointed as its Deputy Chairman. The Planning Commission prepared a new document "Approach to the Eighth Five Year Plan 1990-95, which was approved by the National Development Council on 19th June 1990'.

This was the time when to implement Social Justice agenda the report of Mandal Commission on reservation of the Other Backward Classes (OBCs) in government employment was implemented by the V.P. Singh government. Much hue and cry ensued its implementation. But it has come to be established. How far the motives behind it were pious or were for getting political mileage was difficult to delineate. Nevertheless it is certain that the country was being divided more firmly on caste lines, for whose alleviation Gandhi attempted for his whole life and after him Congress moved in this direction to create a caste-less society which had earlier divided the nation for thousands of years and was regarded as the foremost stumbling block in the national progress. As regionalism in politics had already entered for quite some time after the death of Pundit Nehru and the weakening of the Congress party after him, the division on caste lines opened a new Pandora's Box to be capitalized by the politicians as vote banks.

The politico-economic situation was moving in a different epoch when political mandate of the people was divided and it seemed, in future, it would be difficult to have a stable government of a party for full five years term. It was a start of "short termism" and instability in politics which had long term repercussions in economics and particularly in policy making and its implementation. The period of single party majority governments became a rare phenomenon in coming years and "Coalitions politics" period came into being in India.

V.P. Singh's minority government collapsed in November 1990 and on 10th November 1990 Chandra Shekhar, a Young Turk of Indira period, became the Prime Minister of the country with the support of Rajiv Gandhi's Congress party. The Planning Commission was again reconstituted with Mohan Dharia as Deputy Chairman who signed the Draft of the Eighth Plan on 31st May 1991.

Rajiv Gandhi, the ex-Prime Minister was assassinated in a public meeting, by deceit, in Sriperambadur in South India by a suicide lady terrorist and group having allegiance with Sri Lankan terrorist group, unhappy with Rajiv Gandhi and Indian support to the Sri Lankan (Ceylonese) government in containing terrorism, when he was the Prime Minister of India.

When Chandra Shekhar was the Prime Minister of India in 1990-1991, country's balance of payments position was in deep crisis and country's credibility in the world market had dipped so low that the government had to sell 20 tonnes of gold to ease the situation.

By this time world scenario had greatly changed as the USSR has by now disintegrated and the Communist challenge to Capitalism had ended. The current wave was in favour of market economy system. The developed economies of the world like that of the USA and others were in search of newer markets to sell their products to sustain their own economies as saturation had reached in their economies. Globalization was an imposition on the weaker economies of the world. The international institutions like the International Monetary Fund, the World Bank and the WTO, which has by now emerged after the GATT, were all espousing the cause of Capitalism for quite some long period as they were dominated by these very developed countries especially the USA. These Institutions were the self-appointed guardians of the developing economies and were interfering with their monetary, budget and trade policies and compromising their sovereign rights in lieu of providing financial help much needed by them to eliminate poverty from their lands.

Thus the market economy system had come to stay. So it was not the compulsion of the Indian economy to adopt Capitalism based market economy system in early 1990s rather it had been an imposition which our leaders had to accept under reluctance. Let us update on the political situation. The support to Chandra Shekhar's minority government was withdrawn by the Congress on June 21, 1991 and the government fell down. After the elections the Congress Party formed the government with other's support under P.V. Narasimha Rao. He introduced the agenda of market economy system and seemingly welcomed globalization and privatization by opening the economy trough liberalization of trade, investment and financial policies. This was to inculcate "efficiency" by way of competition in the economy. The catch word was "Economic Reforms" which was given to it to justify the acceptance of the opposite ideology than the erstwhile accepted ideology of Socialism. Notwithstanding, the acceptance of the new ideology, unresolved issues still remained to be pondered upon. They were the issues of redefining the role of the State and defining the role of the Market.

Government's role in economy was being redefined which was away from the Keynesian perception of a producer state. Now it was looked upon as a facilitator. It is also a trustee of the poor, because market excludes the poor. Even in a 'welfare State', the role of government can not be that of an entrepreneur or business man to work for profit maximization. Rather it is taken as a provider of cheap and efficient transport, communication and roads and other social goods and services at 'no profit no loss' basis or even at subsidized rates. The government has to take care of the weaker sections of the society and provide them essential educational and health services at cheaper rates than the market provides. Providing efficient communication network, quality roads, and cheap energy paves the way for development of the whole economy.

With the reduced role of the State and withering away of the philosophy of Socialism, the problems of economy were not over. Poverty and unemployment still remain the basic problems of the economy. During the Narasimha Rao period large scale liberalization of the economy was undertaken to globalize the economy to make it competitive. Several reforms in the trade sector and financial sectors were undertaken to implement it. Labour sector reforms are also pressed under the aegis of the WTO to pave way for private investments from overseas.

The change is symbolic to a new dawn in the Indian perceptions. Amartya Sen talks of freedoms and un-freedoms when he talks of poverty or development. Indicators like capabilities, opportunities, empowerment, vulnerability, deprivations, exclusions, voice-less-ness, and human rights have been now added to define poverty and hence development. In common parlance development today is defined in terms of human indicators of education, health care and economic provisioning represented by the level of income. It is much more than mere material achievements but a fuller and more refined acknowledgement of human values much needed for real development.

The debate over role of market and particularly free market had been a point of severe attack by the Communists. Their logic was that the market is a tool of the Capitalists for exploiting the poor. Markets exclude people as consumers or buyers if they do not have any incomes or sufficient incomes, which can be translated into purchasing power. This exclusion is attributable to a lack of entitlements. Such people are excluded from the consumption of goods and services which are sold in the market.

Markets further exclude people as producers or sellers if they have neither assets nor capabilities. People experience such exclusion if they do not have assets, physical or financial, which can be used or sold to yield an income in the form of rent, interest or profits. Even those without asset could enter the market as producers or sellers, using their labour, if they have some capabilities. Such capabilities can be acquired through education, training or experience. These capabilities yield an income in the form of wages. Hence, the people without capabilities, the poor, who can not find employment, are excluded from the employment market. It must be recognized that even people with capabilities or skill may be excluded from the employment or labour market if there is no demand for their capabilities.

Markets exclude people, both as consumer and producer or as buyers and sellers if they do not accept, or conform to, the values of a market system. The obvious example of such exclusion is tribal populations or forest communities in market economies.

Market may be more an unacceptable term for many who do not want to sell their capabilities for their inclination to a different value system. Like a University professor who does not accept tuition but offers free lectures as he believes that knowledge is not a salable thing or a commodity. An astrologer or a musician may be unwilling to charge a fee because of a different belief system that talents cannot and should not be sold. Much depends upon the belief in materialism and otherwise. While materialism is practical the renunciation of it is sublime.

The stagnation in Backward economies was explained in terms of a vicious circle of poverty where capabilities remained low or negligible due to lack of education and health care which again was due to lack of income. Therefore, the basic emphasis of development economics had been on raising the level of income.

With the introduction of globalization these issues emerged before the Indian economy and they still are enigmatic questions to be appropriately solved by the national leaders.

2

Performance of the Indian Economy in the Past Sixty Years: A Brief Review

Today India is rated as one of the largest economies in the world, measured in terms of purchasing power parity. In terms of Gross Domestic Product (GDP) growth rates, the country was one of the ten fastest growing economies in the world during the eighties, and moved up to eighth fastest growing economies during the period 1980 to 1998. During the last few years its growth rate is around eight to nine per cent and it is expected to touch double digit in near future. In the field of information technology the country is foremost supplier of computer engineers to the world and in other fields of medical, technology, engineering and management its brilliance is world renowned. However it is only one side of the picture. The other side of India is not so bright. Still there is large scale unemployment and particularly the unemployment of the educated youths, the most vocal class, and poverty is widespread. As per official estimates around 26.1 per cent of the population was below the poverty line in 1999-2000. Income disparities are widening. It appears, sometimes, that there live two India at the same time, one urban and elite and the other one rural and poor. It is a picture of economic and social "dualism". Industrial India has created "islands of development amidst ocean of poverty", some say, in the past sixty years.

However, the situation at the time of political Independence of the country in 1947 was quite different. The country was basically poor and drained of resources due to the policies of the British rulers who ruled the country for almost two centuries. The country was divided and due to that the gigantic problem of settlement of the refugees from Pakistan was before the country. Let us have some glimpses of the past so that it is not wiped out of the memory of the new generation.

Indian economy during the British rule presents a picture of near stagnation over a long period of time with a growth rate of 0.5 per cent for 1860-1945.

TABLE 1
GROWTH RATE OF PER CAPITA INCOME DURING BRITISH RULE

(Per cent, per annum)

1860-1885	1.1
1885-1905	-0.3
1905-1925	1.3
1925-1950	- 0.1
1860-1945	0.5

The low growth rate during the pre Independence years seems to owe its origin to the decline in per capita income between 1885 and 1905 and between 1925 and 1950. Occasional periods of stagnation are noticeable, e.g., the periods 1860-1865, 1930 to 1935 and 1945 to 1951.

The poverty and stagnation of the Indian economy was the result of apathetic British policies. Indian colony was used to supply raw materials to the Industrial Revolution in Great Britain and as a market for its manufacturing products. Railways helped in this design to penetrate in the far flung places of the country. Dadabhai Naoroji in his classical paper Poverty in India in 1876 emphasized that the "drain" of wealth and capital from the country which started after 1757 was responsible for absence of development in India. During the period of the East India Company an outright plunder in various forms was carried out.

Attempts to estimate per capita national income per head of population in India was a difficult matter in the words of Pandit Nehru (in *Glimpses of world History*, p. 726). "This is a difficult matter, and estimates vary greatly. Dadabhai Naoroji calculated it in 1870 as rupees 20 per head. Recent estimates (letter written on May 17, 1933 to Indira), have gone up to rupees 67, and even the most favourable , made by some Englishmen, do not go beyond rupees 116. It is interesting to compare this with other countries. In the United States of America the corresponding figure is rupees 1925 and even this has been greatly exceeded since: in Britain it is rupees 1000 per head. (A rupee at the present rate of exchange is equal to one shilling and six pence.)"

Thus in 1947 when the British transferred power to India, we inherited a crippled economy with a stagnant agriculture and a peasantry steeped in poverty. As Jawahar Lal Nehru puts it: "India was under an industrial capitalist regime, but here economy was largely that of the pre-capitalist period, minus many of the wealth producing elements of that pre-capitalist economy. She became a passive agent of modern industrial capitalism suffering all its ills and with hardly any of its advantages." (*Discovery of India*, p. 299).

India after Independence

As discussed in the earlier chapter Indian leaders have had a dream to take India on the path of speedy economic development and establish justice: social, economic and political. And to realize that dream we adopted a Mixed Economy which would be devoid of, it was thought, the shortcomings of the prevailing two systems in the world.

We desired of an ideal mix of Capitalistic competitiveness and efficiency along .with Communist discipline so that everyone's basic needs are taken care of. in free India. The system was to be free from Capitalistic exploitation and Communist regimentation. In politics Parliamentary Democracy was chosen, on somewhat British lines, through a Constitution which ensures liberty, equality and fraternity to the people. It was considered that Indian Mixed Economy with a democratic set up would be a role model for the upcoming independent countries.

Notwithstanding the sincere intentions of the stalwarts of the country, the realities were harsh. War with Pakistan over Kashmir issue in 1947 itself, rehabilitation of the large scale refugees coming across the borders, and push through reforms in the inert agricultural sector to bail out farmers from the burden of indebtedness, injustices of the system and poverty were the daunting challenges.

Indian Constitution was adopted on January 26, 1950 and the Industrial Policy Resolution was already declared in 1848 to demarcate the areas of public and private sectors. The government took up the responsibility of laying the base of development and the 'commanding heights of the economy' came under the direct charge of the state. Five Year Plans were adopted since 1951 on the pattern of Russian Plans. Zamindari and Jagirdari were abolished and subsequently privy purses to the erstwhile kings too were abolished in consonance with democratic norms of equity, equality and justice to make people the real power owners.

The first decade after Independence was the formative decade under which a framework of development was laid down. While the initial few years were the foundation building years the First Five Year Plan (1951-56) was also considered a preliminary plan which was not very ambitious and it was a success. The real start of planning in the country was from the Second Plan (1956-61). By the time the Parliament had already adopted in 1954 the norm of a 'Socialistic Pattern of Society' as the basic objective of policies. The Industrial Policy 1956 became the base of future development. The Second Five Year Plan was an industrial development plan, as at that time speedy industrialization was considered the only way of fast development. This plan was based on Mahalanobis two sector model and is popular as Nehru-Mahalanobis model. Nehru, then was considered, a 'modernizer par-excellence'.

Planning in a country lay its base on prevailing economic conditions, social requirements and people's ambitions and availability of resources—the factor endowments of a country, as well as on the present stage of scientific and technological advancement. In deciding the objectives of the plan these factors play important role. These factors are reflected in the objectives of the successive Five Year Plans in India which speak of the prevailing problems at the time of their formation. Indian planning, in fact, serves a multipurpose function through which, raising the rate of growth, self-sufficiency, modernization, poverty alleviation, reduction in inequality, and establishment of social justice, etc., are sought for.

It is necessary at this juncture to evaluate the progress of our development plans.

The sixty year period since Independence experienced many ups and downs and difficult phases. However, this could be divided in to three parts for evaluation: the period from 1947 up to mid 1970s—the period of slow growth of economy; the beginning of liberalization since 1980s and the period of somewhat higher growth rate; and the period of 1990s onwards—the period when reform started. This may also be categorized as the period of Gandhi and Nehru and the era of nationalism; the period of Indira Gandhi and Rajiv Gandhi; and the period of Narasimha Rao of "reforms".

Taking the entire period in to consideration, during the period 1950-51 to 2005-06, in absolute terms, the Gross Domestic Product at factor cost and at constant prices increased from 140.466 thousand crores to 2604.532 crores, that is, a raise of 18.45 times. The per capita National

Product, at constant prices, during this period registered a rise from rupees 3687 to rupees 20734, that is, an increase of 5.623 times.

Population of the country meanwhile increased from 359 million in 1950-51 to 1112 million in 2006. It is almost two more India added (to its original size) since the Independence of the country. It was realized during the sixties that India is adding one Australia each year, as around 1.2 crore population was added each year to the country's total population. Evidently with an explosive growth rate of population around 2.5 per cent per annum in free India and slow growth of economy at the rate of 3.5 per cent per annum, the period sixties and seventies remained a period of very slow per capita income growth around 1 to 1.2 per cent per annum. Evidently this was the period when poverty was high particularly in the sixties and seventies. Sixties had also been a period of not only high rural poverty it was also the period of high unemployment and under employment as well as food scarcity and high prices. Inflation rate was near double digit during the seventies owing to internal shortages and external shocks of OPEC price hike of petroleum products. This was also the era of rationing and controls which later on gave birth to black market economy and black money generation. The only redeeming feature was the widespread acceptance of the new strategy of agricultural development adopted since the mid sixties which later became successful in raising good productivity and food production. This was called the Green Revolution.

Coming to periodic analysis we find that the average annual growth rate of Gross National Product at factor cost, during the First and the Second Five year Plan was 3.7 per cent and 4.2 per cent at constant prices. The period of the Third Five Year Plan (1961-66) registered a very slow growth rate of 2.8 per cent per annum. The three Annul Plans (1966-69) showed a growth rate of 3.9 per cent per annum. During the Fourth Plan (1969-74) the growth rate was 3.4 per cent per annum.

An era of growth rate of five per cent and above started thereafter and the Fifth Plan (1974-79) registered a growth rate of 5 per cent per annum. The momentum continued during the Sixth Plan (1980-85) and the Seventh Plan (1985-90), barring 1979-80, the time of Annual Plan, due to shift and re shift of paradigm from Nehruvian to Gandhian and then again Nehruvian due to political change from Congress regime to change in favour of Janata party and then again in favour of Congress in 1980, when the average annual growth rate was 5.5 and 5.8 per cent.

During the beginning of the nineties the country was in deep crisis, basically the BOP crisis. The growth of GDP in the year 1991-92 was 1.1 per cent. The economy picked up thereafter as a result of structural adjustment programme (SAP). During the Eighth Plan (1992-97) the average annual growth rate of GNP was 6.8 per cent. The Ninth Plan (1997-2002), however, showed a growth rate of 5.5 per cent. Since the year 2003-04, the growth rate picked up and at constant prices it was 8.7 per cent in 2003-04, 7.4 per cent in 2004-05 and 9.0 per cent in 2005-06. During the year 2006-07 the GNP growth rate 9.4 per cent and the GDP growth rate was 9.2 per cent.

The target of growth rate in the Tenth Five Year Plan (2002-07) was put at 8 per cent per annum. This target, however, could not be achieved due to disappointing growth of 3.8 per cent in the first year of the Plan, and it remained at 7.6 per cent. This was made possible due to an average growth rate of 8.6 per cent in the four years of the Plan.

TABLE 2

AVERAGE ANNUAL GROWTH RATE OF GROSS NATIONAL PRODUCT AND PER CAPITA NNP

(At 1999-2000 prices) *(Per cent)*

	GNP At factor cost	*NNP per capita*
First Plan (1956-61)	3.7	1.8
Second Plan (1961-66)	4.2	2.0

Third Plan	(1961-66)	2.8	0.2
Annual Plans	(1966-69)	3.9	1.5
Fourth Plan	(1969-74)	3.4	1.0
Fifth Plan	(1974-79)	5.0	2.7
Annual Plan	(1979-80)	-5.0	-8.3
Sixth Plan	(1980-85)	5.5	3.2
Seventh Plan	(1985-90)	5.8	3.6
Annual Plans	(1990-92)	3.3	0.9
Eighth Plan	(1992-97)	6.8	4.6
Ninth Plan	(1997-2002)	5.5	3.5
2002-2003		3.9	1.9
2003-2004		8.7	7.0
2004-2005		7.4	5.7
2005-2006		9.0	7.4

Source: Economic Survey 2006-07.

2004-05 Provisional estimates.

2005-06 Quick estimates.

An analysis of the sectoral growth rate in the beginning of the twenty first century shows a disquieting trend in agricultural sector where growth rate of output was negative in the years 2000-01 and 2002-03 when it was -0.2 per cent and -7.2 per cent as compared with the previous year. In the year 2004-05 it was 00 per cent and in the year 2006-07 it remained 2.7 per cent. The growth rate of 6.3 per cent, 10 per cent and 6.0 per cent recorded in the years 2001-02, 2003-04, and 2005-06, respectively were, however, on negative or zero base of the previous downfall hence they should be treated with caution. This shows a situation of near stagnation in agriculture.

TABLE 3

SECTORAL REAL GROWTH RATES IN GDP AT FACTOR COST

(At 1999-2000 prices)

(Percent change over previous year)

Year	*Agriculture And allied*	*Industry*	*Services*	*Total GDP*
2000-01	-0.2	6.4	5.7	4.4
2001-02	6.3	2.7	7.2	5.8
2002-03	-7.2	7.1	7.4	3.8
2003-04	10.0	7.4	8.5	8.5
2004-05	0.0	9.8	9.6	7.5
2005-06*	6.0	9.6	9.8	9.0
2006-07**	2.7	10.0	11.2	9.2

Source: Economic Survey 2006-07.
* Quick estimates
** Advance estimates.

Low agricultural growth has serious implications for the 'inclusiveness' of growth. Furthermore, poor agricultural performance may complicate price stability with supply side problems in essential commodities of everyday consumption. There are evidences that prices of primary commodities, mainly food, have been on the rise in 2006-07. Wheat, pulses, edible oils, fruits and vegetables and condiments and spices have been the major contributors to the higher inflation rate of primary articles.

The poor growth rate of agriculture is attributed to low investment, imbalances in fertilizer use, low seeds replacement rate, a distorted incentive system and low post-harvest value addition.

Services contributed as much as 68.6 per cent of the average growth in GDP in the last five years between 2002-03 and 2006-07. The residual contribution came practically from industry. As a result, in 2006-07, while the share of agriculture in GDP declined to 18.5 per cent, the share of industry and services stood at 26.4 per cent and 55.1 per cent, respectively.

A Shift in Paradigm: From Socialistic Pattern of Society to Market Economy System

Although a need for change in the structure and elements of economic policies that were being followed since the beginning of the Second Plan had been recognized in the eighties, only mild reforms had been introduced till the end of that decade. In the form of some reduction in the rigour of controls and of allowing the market a little more play. Some little liberalization of imports had also been taken place. There was no general willingness to give up or alter in any substantial way the philosophy that was the foundation of the economic policy framework. Then in the midst of the grave balance of payments crisis of 1990-91, the decision was taken by the Narasimha Rao government to dispense with the old paradigm. It initiate far reaching reforms that would transform India from a controlled closed economy into a fairly open economy in which not only would the private sector have a much enhanced role, but the market would be given the prime role in the allocation of resources. Attempts were made for gradual opening up of economy so that the economy would become linked to the world economy to a substantial way. Major directions of reform were in trade sector and the financial sector and the popular words then were privatization, marketization and liberalization or globalization.

Initially the reforms, so called, were opposed from several quarters that it is a sell out at the hands of the US and the industrial giants or the MNCs. However, the favourable impact of these changes which came after an initial slump, from 1992-93 onwards as a result of structural adjustments undertaken, somewhat relinquished the fears. It was the thinking at that time that globalization and market economy system had, somehow, come to stay and there was no going back.

Evaluating the reforms, R.J. Chelliah says, "The most significant gain from the reforms so far carried out is the capacity to grow at a fairly high rate without running into balance of payments problems, provided of course, reasonably sound fiscal policies are followed." As Bimal Jalan has pointed out in 30 of the 36 years preceding 1990-91, we had some balance of payments problem or the other. Now it can be said that we have achieved self-reliance in one important aspect. We do not need to go to IMF at all, and can carry on even without World Bank loans.

While undoubtedly the major structural changes have benefited the economy, there is some genuine fear in some sections of the population that the direction of reform—greater role for the market, vastly reducing the importance and role of public enterprises and opening up the economy to foreign investment and MNCs—would adversely affect the vulnerable sections of the population and even erode the substance of our national sovereignty.

A major criticism of the liberalization process is that the higher growth rate achieved has no dent on poverty and unemployment. Discerning from the jugglery of percentage decline in poverty from above 44 per cent in 1983 to around 22 per cent in 2004-05, the fact remains that above 22 crore population is still below the poverty line.

In defense of reforms Chelliah says, "the reforms have not reversed or altered the trend of steady fall in the head count ratio since 1973-74. Also it is seen that economically better off states (in terms of higher per capita incomes) such as Kerala, Punjab, Haryana and Gujarat have lower poverty ratios. Fast growth is thus essential for reducing poverty and it does reduce poverty."

However, the economic reforms that accelerated growth could affect some poorer sections in the short run. Also, when substantial changes take place, there are gainers and losers. Hence the society (state) has to provide a safety net for those affected and also slow down or modify the reforms to a safeguard the interests of the vulnerable sections.

From the experience we might legitimately draw the conclusion that there is a trade-off between stability and growth in efficiency and productivity. Hence in pursuit of efficiency we should not expose ourselves to excessive instability by proceeding too fast with reforms in some directions.

On unemployment issue we find that the country had been facing a situation of 'jobless growth' for the past many years. At the one side where the production is rising fast the employment is not growing resulting in a situation of large scale unemployment. It is estimated that the number of unemployed has increased from about 8 million in 1983 to around 13.10 million in 2005 judged by usual principle status. The annual growth rate of employment in organized sector has shown a disappointing picture. During the period 1994-2004 employment in public sector decelerated by 0.80 per cent while in the previous decade it was positive at 1.53 per cent. The only sector where employment is growing is the private sector. But the total size of the private sector is too small as compared to the public sector hence the rise in employment opportunities in the organized private sector may be taken as "a storm in a tea cup". The major portion of the labour force is going in the unorganized and self-employment sector after the entry of MNCs and sophisticated labour replacing technology in the country since the reform.

It is a point to be noted that the share of agriculture in total employment which had been 61.67 per cent in 1993-94 has come down to 58.54 per cent in 1999-2000 and further to 54.19 in 2004-05. With the declining share of agriculture in GDP, the scope of absorbing substantial additional labour force in agriculture appears limited.

The slowing down of agricultural growth could be one of the main reason for the growth in unemployment rate besides the shift in favour of sophisticated technology and declining status of the public sector after 1991 being the other factors.

In the final analysis we may say that to sustain the

momentum of higher growth in the range of eight to ten per cent in future we shall have to take a few safeguards and that is not only in the field of economics but is also in the field of politics of the day having its impact on economic performance. One of the major crisis in the country stems from split mandate in polity. For quite some time in Indian elections the mandate is not clear which leads to "hung parliament". The government is formed by coalition, that is, by joining of different regional parties having different ideologies and areas of interest. The governments are formed on knife edge balance when a common minimum programme is formed with consensus. The disturbing fact is that in such a situation sometimes it is not the majority party or the parties with large number of members who decide the issue; it is the smaller groups, the marginalists, become more important in deciding major issues of national interest and the fate of the government.

Expressing his anguish at the failed consensus on Nuclear Deal with the US, in Indian Parliament, the Prime Minister says, "sometimes the resolution of problems acquires an excessively political hue, and narrow political considerations , based on regional or sectional loyalties and ideologies, can distort the national vision and sense of wider collective purposes."

Commenting on such piquant situations when the mighty governments in democracies are as helpless as they are today in India, the safeguard suggested by Chelliah becomes more appropriate when he says, " If the matter is left to the politicians alone , the reforms will not come up to the desired level....Intellectuals, professionals, or housewives, industry associations, NGOs and in fact the entire middle class should constantly apply pressure on governments to do what is good for the people in the long run. Without the active participation of the intelligent and informed electorate in public affair, through NGOs or otherwise, progress is likely to be much less than the country is capable of achieving."

PART TWO:
POVERTY IN INDIA

3

Challenge of Poverty in India

Poverty remains one of the most enigmatic questions in India even after sixteen years of economic reforms. Today poverty is defined not only in terms of income or subsistence or basic minimum needs. It is defined in terms of deprivations, denials, vulnerability, voicelessness, social identity, lack of fundamental freedoms, human rights coverage and so on. According to Amartya Sen, the Nobel Laureate, poor are denied of "fundamental freedoms of choice and action that the better-off take for granted". Poor people lack adequate food and shelter, education and health, deprivations that keep them away from the kind of life that everyone values. They also are often exposed to ill health, economic dislocation, and natural distress. And they are often exposed to ill treatment by institutions of state and society and are powerless to influence key decisions affecting their lives.

The problem of poverty is being discussed since the age of Plato. It had been an important question before Thomas Robert Malthus who wrote "The Essay" in 1798 on the problem and tried to locate the cause of poverty in growing population. There is a biological law of population, according to him, whereby men multiply faster than the growing capacity of mother earth. The pessimism that emerged in his time still haunts social scientists in populous poor countries despite the reversal of production trend after Industrial Revolution in the countries of the world.

The perception towards poverty differs in ancient and the mediaeval times. A quotation of the early sixteenth century from Discorci Politici of Fransesco Giuciardini says—

> "The poor are a part of the necessary furniture of the earth, a sort of perpetual gymnasium where the rich can practice virtue when they are so inclined."

This view represents the thinking of that time that poverty has always remained in the world and there is no hope that it could be abolished.

At the turn of the Twentieth century Neo Classical economist Reverend Phillip H Wicksteed wrote:

> "A man can neither be a saint, nor a lover, nor a poet unless he has comparatively recently had something to eat."

It had been regarded that to have a share in civilization one must first be granted the basic necessities.

During 1960s a quote from Lady Barbara Ward Jackson says,

> "If morals have any meaning at all, they must entail that the hungry are fed, the naked clothed, the homeless sheltered, and all the men given some little share in the world's great patrimony of knowledge and opportunity, of health and hope."

The agenda of New International Economic Order adopted by the United Nations outlined the same feelings. The subject matter of the NIEO veered round the removal of manifest injustices endemic in the present system of relationships between nations and people with a view to creating a new order in which life of dignity and well being becomes the inalienable right of all.

Accordingly, the existence and perpetuation of poverty is due to injustices prevailing in the system, which has given rise to inequality and dualism. To quote Jan Tinbergen, the Nobel Laureate, "The inequalities in the international system have given rise to two worlds and the disparities between them are growing. One is the world of the rich, the other the world of the poor, united by its heritage of common sufferings. A poverty curtain divides the worlds materially and philosophically. One world is literate, the other largely illiterate, one is industrial and urban, the other predominantly agrarian and rural, one consumption oriented, the other striving for survival. In rich world there is concern about quality of life, in the poor world about life itself which is threatened by disease, hunger and malnutrition. In the rich world there is concern about the conservation of non-renewable resources and learned books written about how the world should be kept in a stationary state. In the poor world there is anxiety, not about the depletion of resources, but about their exploitation and distribution for the benefit of all mankind rather than a few privileged nations, while the rich world is concerned about the impact of its pollutive activities on life support systems, the poor world is concerned by the pollution of poverty, because its problems arise not out of an excess of development and technology but out of the lack of development and technology and inadequate control over natural phenomenon."

He further writes, "we have today about two-thirds of mankind living—if they could be called living—on less than 30 cents a day. We have today a situation where there are about one billion illiterate people around the world, although the world has both the means and technology to spread education. We have nearly 70 per cent of children in the third world suffering from mal-nutrition, although the world has the resources to feed them. We have mal-distribution of the world's resources on a scale where the industrialized countries are consuming about twenty times more of resources per capita than the poor countries. We have a situation where in the third world where millions of people toil under a broiling sun from morning till dusk for miserable rewards and premature death without ever discovering the reason why."

Poverty has global as well as national or regional connotation. When we talk of world income inequality and find that about two thirds of the world population is miserably deprived of the basic things of life, then its dimension is global. And when we talk of a region or a country where the lower strata of the population is denied the basic things of life sustenance, then its dimension is limited to a region or a country.

The school of thought in Malthusian tradition considers poverty is due to excess or over population. When population of a country is far above the feeding capacity of the country a segment of population will remain hungry and poor. It could also be looked upon as a problem of low production and low productivity vis-a vis population size of the country.

The other school thinks it is a problem related with distributive justice. According to this view point inequality and exploitation in the system have given rise to poverty. Karl Marx emphatically argued that poverty is not an over population issue rather it is an issue of institutional and social injustice in the system where the dominating group ion the society usurps unduly larger proportion of the wealth created by the labouring population. Although he agrees that man's abilities differ and hence to an extent their rewards may also differ. The basic principle of justice is "to each according to his needs, and to each according to his abilities." But in the Capitalist system of production the element of exploitation divides the society into Bourgeoisie and Proletariat class where their rewards are indifferent of their needs and abilities, which are unjust. Therefore, poverty problem emanates from injustices in the system and that can not be abolished without abolishing the system itself.

More recently the concept of development has been modified to incorporate quality of life parameters and social sector indicators of health and education. Therefore the concept of poverty too has been refined. The United Nations Development Programme took initiative in devising measures of Capability Poverty and Human Poverty during the nineteen nineties. Income poverty is only one part of the picture according to them. Just as human development encompasses aspects of life much broader than income, so poverty should be seen as having many dimensions. The Capability poverty considers the lack of three basic capabilities: the capability to be well nourished and healthy (represented by the proportion of children under five who are underweight); the capability for healthy reproduction (represented by proportion of births unattended by trained health personnel); and capability to be educated and knowledgeable (represented by female literacy).

The human poverty extends the concept to other dimensions as well. Three indicators are included: the survival deprivation (represented by people not expected to survive to age 40); deprivation in education and knowledge (represented by adult literacy rate); and deprivation in economic provisioning which is a combined index of the indicators of population without access to safe water, health services, and under nourished children below the age five. Thus according to the UNDP, human poverty is more than income poverty. It is "denial of opportunities and choices most basic to human development—to lead long, healthy and creative life and to enjoy a decent standard of living, freedom, dignity, self-esteem and respect of others." This understanding of poverty perceives the poorest as active agents struggling against impoverishment. Therefore, eradication of poverty entails strengthening, what Amartya Sen calls, Capabilities of the poor, and simultaneously create opportunities in society to enable them to make full use of it. Strengthening capabilities, therefore, is crucial for helping the poor to confront and cope with not only a paucity of income but also a host of other adversaries as well, such as disease, disaster and discrimination.

The concept of human poverty in terms of human deprivation may take multifarious forms which include poor survival chances, unjust employment of children, child prostitution, bonded labour, hunger, environmental pollution, domestic violence, human rights violations, and social exclusion which arise out of caste and gender discrimination. A gendered approach to human poverty entails the recognition of gender inequality as an essential part of poverty.

Defining Poverty

There are two broad concepts of poverty: absolute poverty and the relative poverty. While relative poverty is measured in terms of inequality in distribution of income, absolute poverty is reckoned in terms of some kind of notion of subsistence considered appropriate to the circumstances of a country or group or countries concerned. In the less developed countries where incomes are low, absolute poverty is generally reflected mainly in inadequacy of food intake and the consequent under-nourishment on a mass scale, though the definition of subsistence appropriate to such countries might also include other essential minimum needs such as clothing, housing, fuel, light, education and health etc. In other words relative poverty arises entirely as a consequence of an unequal distribution of income irrespective of what the income level or the corresponding level of deprivation of the people at the bottom end of income scale might be. Absolute poverty on the other hand expresses collective view on deprivation in its somewhat physical manifestation. Thus any measure of relative poverty is, therefore, inextricably embedded in the measure of inequality, where a measure of absolute poverty primarily depends on an exogenously determined standard or poverty line, which represents a socially acceptable minimum level of living.

Poverty has been identified not merely with inequality but also with unemployment, Indian Planning Commission recognized "unemployment, under-employment, and low resource base of a multitude of producers, particularly in agriculture, are the principle causes of poverty." It is widely held in current literature that open unemployment in urban areas must be viewed as only one aspect, and not necessarily the most serious one, of the wider problem of under employment and poverty in developing countries.

There are, however, two major problems in defining the concept of poverty. The first relate to the problem of identifying the poor and second is the problem of measurement. It is worthwhile to quote Orshansky here who says:

"Poverty like beauty lies in the eye of the beholder"

and that summarizes one of the difficulties faced by those who would compare poverty in different settings. There have been a number of studies on the concept and measurement of poverty.

Rowntree (1901) was the first in Britain to consider in detail the problem involved in defining poverty. He stated that in Britain in order to get 'average nutritional requirement' the poverty line for a family of man, wife and three children was 17s 8p per week' made up of 12s 9d for food, 2s 3d for clothing, 1s 10dp for fuel and 10d for household sundries. A family was considered to be in poverty if its total earnings were insufficient to obtain the minimum necessaries for the maintenance of merely physical efficiency.

A study in the US in 1965 by Orshansky has given a similar definition of poverty on the basis of 'estimates of minimum food expenditure'.

In the words of Townshend "needs which are unmet can be defined only in relative terms to the society in which they are found. However, he does not accept the distinction between absolute and relative poverty or between basic and cultural needs, because, he argues that the needs which are believed to be basic or absolute can be shown to be relative. He, therefore, suggests poverty must be regarded as general form of relative deprivation which is the effect of the misdistribution of resources, and that section of the population whose resources are so depressed from the means as to be deprived of enjoying the benefits and participating in the activities which are customary in that society can be said to be in poverty". He argues that "possession by individuals and families of relatively low resources does not automatically mean that they are in poverty; but only if they are thereby unable to have the types of diets, participating in activities and have living conditions and amenities which are customary in that society".

Martin Rein (1970) says, "three broad concepts of poverty can be identified. Poverty can be defined as subsistence, inequality, and externality. Subsistence is concerned with the minimum provision needed to maintain health and working capacity......inequality is concerned with the relative position of the income groups to each other......The concept of poverty must be seen in the context of society as a whole......To understand the poor we must study the affluent.... Externality is concerned with the social consequence of poverty for the rest of the society rather than in terms of the need of the poor."

Dorothy Wedderburn (1974) stated that individuals, families and groups in the population can be said to be in poverty when they lack the resources to obtain the types of diets, participate in the activities and have the living conditions and amenities which are customary or are at least widely encouraged in the societies to which they belong. Their resources are so seriously below those commanded by the average individual or family that they are in effect, excluded from ordinary living patterns, customs, and activities. Wedderburn further stated that the literature both about poverty and inequality is closely related and needs be considered in turn. Although poverty is more than inequality the poor undoubtedly receive an unequal share of resources and any explanation of this fact must be related to the larger explanation of social inequality in general.

In view of Atkinson (1975) poverty line is necessarily defined in relation to social conventions and the contemporary living standards of a particular society, and in this way somebody in the United States may be adjudged poor even though he has higher income than the average person in India.

D.R. Gadgil (1965) stated that poverty is nothing but a standard of living below a certain minimum. He further stated that it has become usual since the publication of Rowntree to distinguish between two types of poverty:

i) primary poverty resulting from inadequate income; and

ii) secondary poverty caused by an "ignorant and careless housekeeping and other improvident expenditure" of an adequate income.

It is highlighted by Gadgil and correctly diagnosed that poverty is not only an income problem it is also a problem of improvident expenditure or wasteful expenditure and care-less house-keeping as well.

Writing about Poverty Alfred Marshall wrote in his book *Principles of Economics* that in his time in England there was a hard core of the urban poor who had little opportunity for friendship, who knew nothing of the decencies and the quiet and very little of the unity of family life and whom religion often failed to reach. While their physical, mental and moral ill health could be due in part to other causes as well, poverty was the chief cause.....Poverty led to stunted and degraded lives. The study of the causes of poverty was, therefore, *ipso facto* 'a study of the causes of degradation of a large part of mankind.' The time has come to question why such degradation should exist al all, "whether it was really impossible that all should start the world with a fair chance of leading a cultural life, free from the pains of poverty and stagnating influences of excessive mechanical toil."

While the above analysis helps us to reach the core of defining poverty, the newer attempts to define it in terms of Capability poverty and Human poverty focus on not only economic parameters of income or expenditure but take us to some more things of life pertaining to freedoms and un-freedoms and niceties of life required to lead a modern life. Amartya Sen in his book *Development as Freedom* writes about five distinct types of instrumental freedoms which could be regarded as the end as well as means to development. These are political freedoms, economic facilities, social opportunities, transparency guarantees and protective securities. Poverty could be seen as denial of these freedoms to an individual or a group of population.

Poverty and world income inequality may be traced in the background of international terrorism and drug trafficking. An enquiry into the economics of terrorism would explain that terrorism is flourishing in those very societies which are miserably poor and illiterate. Their economic and social infrastructure is so poor that they are depending for their survival on crime and terrorism. For example, Afghanistan's economy is surviving on poppy cultivation which is processed in Pakistan and its final produce of drug is supplied through Libya to other parts of the world including many African countries where drug menace is the highest. The money earned through drug trafficking is used for financing terrorism.

Measures of Poverty

The absolute poverty is measured on the basis of Head Count Ratio (HCR), and inequality or relative poverty is measured by Gini-Coefficient, whose value range from 0 to 1. Lorenz curve, plotted on the basis of Gini distribution, shows distribution of income among different percentile of population. The departure from the base of the curve shows the degree of inequality.

Head count poverty is measured on the basis of some norm of Poverty Line which is determined in terms of the value of consumption basket of food and non food items which provide a minimum subsistence for a person or a family as a whole. The minimum subsistence level of food items is determined in terms of the value of calorie intake and the value of subsistence of non-food items, e.g., clothing, fuel, light, education, health and housing etc. is determined on the basis of minimum human needs and other relevant factors within the society.

The value equivalent of such a consumption basket, of food and non-food items, of household on per capita basis is considered a dividing line, where those who earn or spend less than this value are 'poor' and those who earn or spend more than this figure are 'non-poor'. This is termed as critical poverty line.

There is, however, no consensus on the minimum per capita requirement of calories for a population, since a number of variables like, age, sex, body weight, occupation etc. affect the energy expenditure.

The concept of poverty line was first developed by Food and Agriculture Organization (FAO) in 1945. The joint expert group of FAO/WHO has recommended a minimum of 2223 calories per capita per day for the people in Asia and Far East. In India the national poverty level was worked out by a study group set up by the Planning Commission in July 1962 of which D.R. Gadgil, P.S. Lokanathan, and Ashok Mehta were the members. According to this study group consumption expenditure of Rs. 20 (at 1960-61 prices) was considered the bare minimum. Dandekar and Rath study have taken 2250 calories as the irreducible minimum or the cut-off point. Sukhatme paces the cut-off point for Indian population at 2250 calories. Indian planning Commission has defined a poverty line on the basis of 2400 calories per person per day for rural areas and 2100 calories per person per day for urban areas. The nutritional advisory committee of India has worked out a calorie requirement for India with reference to men and women at 2780 and 2080 calories respectively.

The Research and Planning division of ECAFE secretariat has assumed that for India, the minimum number of calories needed for keeping an average person in average health and well being is 2500 plus 80 protein units. Most of the studies conducted in India assumed that a reference man in India requires about 2250 calories per day.

The nutrition norm itself is subject to a number of limitations. Atkinson (1975) pointed out that there is no single 'subsistence' level which can be used as a basis for the poverty line. Even in the case of food, it is difficult to determine requirements with any precision. There is no one level of food intake required for subsistence but rather a broad range where physical efficiency declines with a falling intake of calories and proteins. Moreover, an individual's nutritional needs depend on the level of activity, an office worker requiring less than a farm worker. Thus precisely where the line is drawn depends, therefore, on the judgement of the investigator and the idea of a purely physiological basis for the poverty criterion is lost. Secondly, if nutritional requirements could be determined in terms of calories, proteins etc., there would still be problems arising from the disparity between expert judgement and actual consumption behaviour, not only due to lack of the dietary knowledge and uneconomic ways of spending by the poor families on food purchasing but also due to the eating habits which are profoundly influenced by social conventions. Thirdly, in case of non-food items there is an even greater degree of arbitrariness because the minimum needs norms and the other factors change from region to region due to climatic and social factors.

K.N. Raj pointed out that in a country like India in which a vast variety of items of food are available and the cost at which they are available also varies, conversion of expenditure data to their nutritional equivalent should be done rather cautiously, otherwise they can sometimes lead to odd results. Such caution is important because consumption of certain food items commonly used such as banana, coconut or groundnut tends to be under reported.

Amartya Sen modified the above poverty measure and took into account the following two factors:

1) one should be concerned not merely with the number of people below poverty line but also with the amounts by which the income of the poor fall short of the specific poverty level, and

2) the bigger the shortfall from the poverty level, the greater should be the weight per unit of that shortfall in poverty measure.

This measure is known as the Poverty Gap measure which measures the depth of poverty. Economists also use as indices of poverty Squared Poverty Gap—FGT index. Many of the economists in India challenge the poverty estimates by the official institutions of the government or the international agencies on the ground of reliability of data and deducing the results out of it. To quote Utsa Patnaik, "as regards poverty measurement the solution lies in using simple, direct and transparent indices of poverty and the minimum use of complex, indirect and opaque measures...Possession of Tangible assets, food grains absorption per head, whether the family resides in hard roofed structures, floor area occupied per family, yardage of textiles consumed, use of electric power, are the simple and crucial indices which will give a clear idea of poverty and its trend over time." She opines that poverty estimation should be entrusted to an independent body of academics, not to international financial institutions or to governments, which are parties interested in claiming success for their policies, and have by now amply demonstrated their lack of objectivity.

Estimates of Poverty in India

The basic assertion in the development theory laid exclusive emphasis on raising the level of Gross National Product as the performance indicator of economic development. This preoccupation with aggregate growth rates was prompted by the belief in the automatic and eventual "trickle down" of the benefits of development to the various strata of society. According to Hans Singer, it was assumed that, "the reduction of poverty could only be tackled after a certain level of GNP had been reached—first the cake has to be produced and made bigger before it could be equally distributed."

However, the experience of the less developed countries in the past few decades belied the hopes of 'percolation' thesis as the gaps between rich and poor were continuously widening at intra- national and international levels. Two assumptions have been made in the development theory in the seventies. Firstly, economic growth does not lead by itself to a proportionate increase in employment opportunities for those sections of the working population who do not have access to assets. Secondly, economic growth is not a sufficient condition for ensuring the improvement of consumption levels and employment status of the under privileged in a poor country and thereby improve the levels of living of the disadvantaged sections of society.

In Indian economy poor growth rate of around 3.5 per cent for quite a longer period of time, therefore, was not able to remove poverty from the land and improve the employment status or living standards of almost half of the population. According to World Bank estimates around 53 per cent of population in India during 1950s remained poor.

During the period of sixties several studies were conducted over rural and urban poverty in the country and they unequivocally propounded the conclusions that:

1) on the whole a substantial proportion of population, particularly, rural lived below the poverty line;
2) that although the percentage of population under the poverty line declined during the years the absolute number increased owing to rapidly growing population;
3) that a major chunk of poor in the villages were small farmers and marginal farmers and landless agricultural labourers besides village artisans and they belonged to lower strata of society, for example, schedule tribe and schedule caste; the most of the poor in urban areas are either unemployed or they are under employed;

4) that the major economic problem of the weaker sections in rural areas is not open unemployment but more than that low paid employment; that in the urban areas the problem of poverty is an over flow of rural poverty;

5) that most of the poor are either self–employed or are working in the unorganized manufacturing or services sectors of the economy.

The relevant point is of low paid job in case of wage employment and a low resource base in case of self-employment.

TABLE 1

INCIDENCE OF POVERTY IN INDIA

Year	*Poverty Ratio (Per cent)*			*Number of Poor (Million)*		
	Rural	*Urban*	*Combined*	*Rural*	*Urban*	*Combined*
1973-74	56.4	49.0	54.9	261.3	60.0	321.3
1977-78	53.1	45.2	51.3	264.3	64.6	328.9
1983	45.7	40.8	44.5	252.0	70.9	322.9
1987-88	39.1	38.2	38.9	231.9	75.2	307.1
1993-94	37.3	32.4	36.0	244.0	76.3	320.3
1999-2000	27.1	23.6	26.1	193.2	67.1	260.3
2007*	21.1	15.1	19.3	170.5	49.6	220.1

Source: Planning Commission, Tenth Five Year Plan (2002-07).

* Projected.

Table 1 shows that the poverty has declined from54.9 per cent in 1973-74 to 44.5 per cent in 1983, showing a decline of above ten per cent or around one per cent per annum. It further came down to 36 per cent in 1993-94. During the reform period the decline in poverty has been faster when it came down to 26.1 per cent in 1999-2000. The Planning Commission projected that poverty will decline further and it would not be more than 19.3 per cent in 2007.

It has been observed by the researchers that the pace of poverty reduction accelerated between 2000 and 2005 relative to the reduction between 1994 and 2000, (K. Sundaram, *EPW*, p. 3128, July 28, 2007).

TABLE 2

HEAD COUNT POVERTY RATIOS OF HOUSEHOLDS AND PERSONS

1993-94—2004-05 (per cent)

	Households			*Persons*		
	1993-94	*1999-2000*	*2004-05*	*1993-94*	*1999-2000*	*2004-05*
Rural	28.0	23.3	18.8	31.8	27.0	22.7
Urban	22.7	18.1	16.6	28.123.4		21.9
Poverty Line per capita	1993-94:		Rural:	205.84	Urban:	281.33
	1999-2000			327.56		454.11
	2004-05			356.30		538.60

Source: Planning Commission, quoted in *EPW*, July 28, 2007, p. 3128.

Table 2 shows that that the order of decline in poverty of the households between 2000 and 2005 has been of the order of 4.5 per cent in rural India and 1.5 per cent in urban India. The HCR for persons has been 4.3 and 1.5 per cent, respectively. The reduction of poverty in urban India was slower than that in the rural areas. The official poverty line for 2004-05 is Rs.356.30. However, economists like Utsa Patnaik find the calculations of the government, based on 61st round of NSS survey, unsatisfactory and estimate that in reality rural poverty is much higher than the official estimates based on the nutritional norms. There is clear evidence according to her, of a large and growing divergence over time between her direct estimates of poverty and the official indirect estimates (*EPW*, July 28, 2007, p. 3132). As per her study, for 2004-05 while the official estimate of rural poverty is 28.3 per cent, her direct estimate of persons below the poverty line is 87 per cent.

TABLE 3

ALL INDIA RURAL POVERTY ESTIMATE

1993-94 and 2004-05

Direct Estimate				
Levels of calorie intake per day	2400	2200	2100	1800
% of persons below specified level, 2004-05	87.0	69.5	60.5	25.0
% of persons below specified level, 1993-94	74.5	58.5	49.5	20.0
Required monthly per capita expenditure to access nutrition level in 2004-05, Rs.	795	575	515	342
Official Estimate				
Official Poverty Line (OPL)		1993-94		2004-05
Rs.		206		356
Calorie intake at OPL		1980		1820
Per cent of persons below OPL		37.3		28.3

Source: Utsa Patnaik, *EPW*, July 28, 2007, p. 3148.

It is evident from Table 3 that the percentage of rural persons not able to access 2400 calories at the all India level is 87 per cent up sharply from 74.5 per cent in 1993-94. The required spending to access this level is Rs. 795. The actual rise in poverty is even greater than anticipated, and poverty depth has increased more than during any previous period, not surprisingly given the pervasive agrarian depression and farmer/labour distress. According to Patnaik millions of persons have been pushed to a lower nutritional status. The average calorie intake in rural India has declined from 2153 to 2047 over the decade. Average daily protein intake has declined by 3 grams and average fat intake has risen by 5.5 grammes, both being small changes relative to large decline in energy intake.

The below 2100 calories percentage of persons is substantially higher at 60.5 compared to 49.5 in 1993-94 and the below 1800 calories percentage is 25, while it was 20 a decade earlier (Table 3). The absolute number of rural persons below 2100 calories has risen by 150 million, from 289 million in 1993-94 to 440 million in 2004-05. Those accessing below 1800 calories, the poorest of the poor, numbered 182 million by 2004-05 compared to 117 million in 1993-94, an increase by 65 million. Thus by taking a very low poverty line at which at most 1820 calories can be obtained, effectively the Planning Commission is designating as "the poor", only the poorest among the actually poor.

The study of Patnaik finds out that rural poverty has increased not marginally but markedly, in wide belt of states spanning the entire country, from Punjab, Haryana and U P to Gujrat, Rajasthan and Madhya Pradesh and from Bengal, Bihar and Orissa to Karnataka and Tamilnadu.

Report on Conditions of Work and Promotion of Livelihood in the Unorganised sector prepared by National Commission for Enterprises in the Unorganised Sector (NCEUS) based on government data for the period between 1993-94 and 2004-05, released in August 2007 reveals a shocking reality that 77 per cent of the Indian population is "poor and vulnerable", surviving on Rs.20.30 or less per day. According to it 79 per cent of unorganized workers, 88 per cent of SC/STs, 80 per cent of OBC population and 84 per cent of Muslims belong to the "poor and vulnerable group". The official poverty line is roughly Rs.12 per capita per day.

A staggering 394.9 million workers or 86 per cent of India's working population toil in the unorganized sector, which means they work without a social security cover. Nearly 80 per cent of these workers are among those who live on less than rupees 20 a day. The NCEUS chairman Arjun Sengupta says, "these are the discriminated, disadvantaged and downtrodden".

Analysing the relationship between poverty and vulnerability and the type of employment among unorganized workers, the report observed that 90 per cent of the poor were casual workers while only 10 per cent of the higher group was casual workers. Among regular wage workers, 66.7 were in the poor and vulnerable group while 33 per cent were from higher income group. And among the self-employed, 74.7 per cent were from the poor and vulnerable and 25.3 per cent came from the higher income group. The report highlighted that 79 per cent of unorganized casual non-agricultural women workers in the villages were illiterate. Dr. Sengupta observed that 'the illiterate have a very high probability of being poor or vulnerable, almost nine out of ten, and they are predominantly unorganized workers".

Human Poverty

Estimates of poverty that rely exclusively on income and consumption measures may fail to capture significant aspects of deprivation experienced by the poor. Therefore, a much broader multi-dimensional measure is required. Poverty is linked not only to material deprivation but also deprivation of human resources, social contacts, voice and power. Poverty is caused by lack of assets combined with low and uncertain returns to the limited stock of assets owned by the poor. Poor men and women suffer from poverty of private resources, access to public goods and services, and poverty of social relationships. The poor are thus a heterogeneous group, characterized by different forms of deprivation. Attempts to measure Capability poverty and Human poverty are steps in this direction, although still they are in formative stage and arc unable to reach the core of the objective of development itself. The objective of economic development in itself is in question to be captured by the materialistic indices alone.

The concepts of Capability and Human poverty have attempted to capture these things. The Human Poverty Index visualized by the UNDP comprises three types of deprivations, deprivation in health, knowledge and economic provisioning. Attempts have been made in India to calculate these values for different states.

TABLE 4
HUMAN POVERTY INDEX FOR INDIAN STATES: 1991-93

(Per cent)

States	*Health*	*Knowledge*	*Provisioning*	*HPI*
Andhra Pradesh	4.88	49.51	42.88	40.78
Assam	21.81	41.37	61.62	47.18
Bihar	19.48	57.25	64.40	53.60
Gujrat	16.75	33.91	38.63	32.33
Haryana	15.37	35.67	36.43	31.90
Karnataka	15.68	39.14	41.12	35.42
Kerala	5.14	8.47	33.22	23.19
Madhya Pradesh	25.34	49.77	52.52	45.60
Maharasthra	12.27	29.59	36.65	29.49
Orissa	22.33	44.08	56.92	45.42
Punjab	13.87	33.86	32.32	29.27
Rajasthan	19.88	54.70	51.82	49.96
Tamil Nadu	13.45	30.69	32.98	28.19
Uttar Pradesh	22.24	51.83	57.32	48.32
West Bengal	14.82	38.97	47.78	38.52
INDIA	17.99	42.69	48.70	40.49

Source: Chelliah, R.J. and Sudarshan R., *Income Poverty and Beyond*, pp.138-39.

The indicators used to measure the three main dimensions of deprivation included in the HPI for Indian states are given in Table 4. Health deprivation has been measured in terms of the probability of dying before age 40. Deprivation in knowledge is a composite indicator of the two variables, adult literacy, and percentage of children in the age group 6-14 years not attending school, with the former having a weight of two-thirds and the latter one-third. Deprivation in economic provisioning is in two parts, public and private. Deprivation in public provisioning is represented by the three indicators: i) percentage of population without access to health services, ii) percentage of population without access to safe water; and iii) percentage of population not living in electrified houses.

Deprivation in private provisioning has been represented by the percentage of children under four years of age who are mal-nourished.

The values of the HPI for the period 1991-93 are presented in Table 4. The Human poverty at all-India level is 40.49 per cent. It ranges between a low of 23 per cent for Kerala to a high of 54 per cent for Bihar. Among the three dimensions, the highest deprivation at all-India level as well as for fourteen individual states (excepting Punjab) is observed in the case of provisioning, with knowledge following closely. Health deprivation in terms of probability of death before the age 40 is found to be much lower. It is surprising that even in Kerala, as high a proportion as 33 per cent of population is deprived in terms of provisioning.

It has also been observed by Chelliah's study that relatively better economic status does not ensure lower deprivation in terms of basic capabilities.

There exists a close and inverse relationship between human poverty and human development. Human development has two sides. One is the formation of human capabilities such as improved health, knowledge of skills. The other is the use people make to their acquired capabilities for productive purpose. If the scales of human development do not finally balance the two sides, much human frustration emerge (UNDP, 1995). Human development is measured through Human Development Index (HDI) which is composite of three basic components: income, education and health as has been stated earlier, while human poverty is measured in terms of Deprivation Index (DI). Human development is possible either by raising the value of HDI closer to unity or by reducing the Deprivation Index (DI) closer to zero. Thus human poverty which is measured in terms of deprivation indices can be minimized through reducing the value of DI. As per definition (Sudhir Anand, Amartya K. Sen, 1994) the Deprivation Index (DI) lie between zero and unity. Closer the value of DI towards Zero indicates higher degree of quality of human life; while close the value of DI towards unity indicates acute human poverty.

Inter state human poverty in India in terms of income is expressed in form of per capita inter-state SDP deprivation indices. It has been observed that deprivation indices were zero for state of Punjab while in case of Bihar it was unity during the period 1981-2002, as per a study (by Gaur, A. K., 2007). The deprivation indices for economically poor states like U P (0.7958 in 1981 to 0.8580 in 2002), Orissa (0.7704 to 0.8617), M P (0.7496 to 7646) and hill stated like H P (0.5512 to 0.6949), J&K (0.5107 to 0.8775) and Tripura (0.7837 to 0.9437) have also risen during 1980-81 to 2001-02. Similar calculations have been made for educational deprivation and health deprivation. The empirical findings of the study are quite astonishing and shocking. For example, excepting education, average deprivation in terms of per capita SDP and Medical and Public Health, for twenty states has risen significantly during the period 1981-2002. Also inter-state variation in deprivation indices for all three parameters has increased during the period. Findings of the study further reveal that economic reforms did not affect to the existing structure of inter-state human deprivation during 1992-2002.

Why the Poor Stay Poor

The pertinent question that arises is why the poor stay poor despite the determination and planned development efforts in India for the past more than fifty years to eradicate poverty and unemployment Why not the colonial India's backlog of poverty been eradicated up till now when sixty years have already passed? Why the farmers are committing suicides in large numbers and the basics of life sustenance is not available to around forty per cent of the Indian population? Why the slums are existing in large numbers in every big city? Why potable water is not available to the large part of the masses? Why electricity is not available for 24 hours to the people? There are innumerable questions that challenge our vision of development. Is it lack of resources? Is it failure of distributive justice which resulted in rising inequality in the economy and society? Is it corruption and inefficiency of the government machinery? Is it lack of vision of our leaders and intellectual class who provide 'elitist' model of development? Is it Socialistic ideology which has failed? Why there is a dichotomy and 'dualism' in the economy?

Intellectuals of the leftist ideology analyse the situation—why poor stay poor—in terms of ownership of non-labour resources (assets) in the hands of a few, and in the market system. According to their thinking market as a social mechanism is propelled by the resource power and the operational rule is "to him who has more will accrue; from him who has not, even the little will be taken away". They argue that "market is a system based on private and unequal ownership of resources is an ally of rich and a terror to the poor". Even the nature's bounty to the mankind as 'free goods', such as land and water are privatized and sold as commodities. Further, the choice of technology is in the hands of the rich which favours them. The dynamics of socio-economic processes result from the interaction of the trio: i) privatization of non-labour resources and distribution of ownership of these resources; ii) nature and extent of market operations; iii) character of technology and production processes.

When Amartya Sen talks about entitlements to the poor and empowerments and freedoms he to an extent endorses a bit of the above despite Marx having been failed after seventy years of experimentation in the Soviet Russia. But even though egalitarianism having been failed before the forces of efficiency of the market mechanism and competition, the vast number of the poor world around still pose the question of justice in distribution of the wealth of nations in an equitable manner. But who will decide what is just and equitable for the people on the other side of the counter in the market is a big question to be answered.

4

Poverty Alleviation Strategy

Poverty is a major challenge in today's world where more than one billion people are living in poverty and destitution. They are mainly in the countries of the southern hemisphere, particularly in Asia, Africa and Latin American countries. Poverty at international level is measured in terms of $ 1 a day and $ 2 a day poverty line. Those who earn and spend $ 1 per day are taken as extremely poor. This measure was chosen for the World Bank's World Development report, 1990. It is measured in 1985 international prices and is adjusted to local currency using purchasing power parities (PPP). It has been recalculated in 1993 PPP terms at about $1.08 a day. According to World Bank report 1997, more than a billion people still live on less than US dollar one a day and nearly three billion on less than U S dollar two a day. In the Indian context , as we have seen in the earlier chapter, although the incidence of poverty has fallen (from nearly 54.9 per cent in 1973-74 to 26.1 per cent in 1999-2000), yet the absolute number of people below the poverty line has continued to rise due to the growth in population. In East Europe and Central Asia, both the incidence of poverty and the absolute number of people below poverty line have risen. In Sub-Saharan Africa, the incidence of poverty continues to remain at a high level. In a number of countries, the growth process has not been accompanied by a reduction in the extent of poverty.

Poverty alleviation policies have been suggested by economists and the researchers as well as by International Institutions like the World Bank and the like. Economists of the World Bank like Chenery and others suggested a strategy of 'Redistribution with Growth' during the seventies. It is a set of four approaches that can be used individually or in combination to increase the income of low income groups. The exact mix will depend on the economic and social structure of the country and the priority given to improving the welfare of the poorest. These approaches are:

1) Maximising GNP growth through raising savings and allocating savings more efficiently, with benefit to all groups in society.
2) Redirecting investment to poverty groups in the form of education, access to credit, public utilities and so on.
3) Redistributing income (or consumption) to poverty groups through fiscal system or through direct allocation of consumer goods.
4) A transfer of existing assets to poverty groups as in land Reforms.

We have seen our poverty analysis that maximizing GNP growth is not a sufficient condition for helping the poorest because of the weak income linkages between poverty groups and the rest of the economy.

As for the second strategy it may require some sacrifice of output in the short run in so far as returns on investment in human capital take longer to develop. To this extent this may involve a short run cost to upper income groups but these may also benefit in the long run as the productivity and income of the poor improve.

The scope for redistributing existing income on any scale in less developed countries while having some positive welfare effect in the short run is likely to be severely limited. Many of the countries are too poor for there to be any significant potential gain to the lower income groups from this strategy. There may be a high cost in terms of growth in the long run from its potential damaging effect on the incentives, savings and investment of the upper income groups.

The same stricture applies to asset distribution although in areas such as land ownership and security of tenure, some degree of asset redistribution may be an essential part of programme to make the rural poor more productive. But the preferred strategy is to divert a proportion of the annual investment resources of the rich towards the poor in this way altering the distribution of the increment to the overall capital stock.

Some economists have criticized the above strategy for being essentially an incrementalist strategy almost always to be pursued in an evolutionary way, (Leys, 1975). They argue that it offers no theory of political change and under estimates the resistance that the rich would offer to its policies. However, in defense of the strategy it has been argued that the four approaches of the Redistribution with Growth are generalizations of strategic options each of which if adopted at all might be applied in a more or less incrementalist and less or more radical manner, depending on time and situation, and no doubt, other factors too. But the essential point is that Redistribution with Growth is neither incrementalist nor radical but a framework for analyzing the inter connections between economic growth and redistribution.

Jean Dreze and Amartya Sen (1989) state that, it is possible to distinguish between two contrasting approaches to poverty alleviation. One approach is to promote economic growth. This would not only enable the population to take advantage of the potentialities released by greater general affluence but would also provide an improved basis for public support. This strategy is called "growth mediated security". The alternative approach called the "support-led security" consists of resorting to direct public support in fields such as employment provision, income redistribution, health care, education and social assistance so that destitution may be removed without waiting for an improvement in general level of affluence. Several interconnections between the two routes also have to be recognized in order to avoid a 'false total dichotomy'.

Sen in his later work further stressed that poverty is much more than lack of income. It is also lack of voice: people need avenues to express their needs or obtain redress. It is also lack of empowerment: people need the resources and authority to take charge of programmes meant for their benefit. And poverty is also lack of good governance people are worse off when officials are corrupt, unresponsive to local demands, and unaccountable.

As stated in earlier chapter Sen lists five dimensions of poverty: political space, economic space, social space, transparency and protective security. He views poverty as deficits along these five dimensions which limit the ability of people to develop their capabilities and function as empowered persons. Clearly these dimensions are overlapping. Higher income, for instance, often translates into greater social and political space, and rich countries often have greater government transparency and wider safety nets.

World Development Report 1990 looked at the issue of poverty and suggested that it could best be tackled as a joint venture by governments and markets. It felt that competitive open markets were the best way of promoting labour intensive employment and this could reduce poverty since labour was the main resource of the poor. At the same time an activist government was required to promote basic education and health, so that the poor could upgrade their human capital and become more productive.

During the 1990s the proportion of poor people hardly declined, save in east and south-east Asia and the absolute number of poor people went up. The greatest worsening was in countries constituting the former Soviet Union, despite ostensible opening-up of economies and high levels of literacy. These changes did not help when they were accompanied by collapsing governance and growing mafia rule or where Soviet era bosses continued as *de facto* autocrats despite supposed political reform. Even in case of India serious doubts were expressed over the market oriented reforms in their ability to address the problems of the poor by the markets. Rather the view still prevailing is that markets exclude the poor from the consumer as well as employment markets and that market as a capitalist tool widens the income inequality, that is, relative poverty. The situation of jobless growth in India in the last few years bears support to the finding and opens a case for government's intervention in market to safeguard the interests of the poor in both the markets.

The World Development Report 2000 puts forward a modified formula for tackling poverty. It is argued that major reductions in different dimensions of poverty are indeed possible through interactions of markets, state institutions and civil society. Actions are needed in three complementary areas:

1) promoting economic opportunities for the poor people;
2) facilitating empowerment by making state institutions more responsive to poor people and removing social barriers that exclude women, ethnic groups, and socially disadvantaged; and
3) enhancing security by preventing and managing economy wide shocks and providing mechanisms to reduce the sources of vulnerability that poor people face.

Promoting opportunity alone, through free markets and better education may not suffice. People need to be empowered through elections, decentralization to the grassroots, responsive administrations, an effective judiciary and good governance in general. Poor people need a greater voice in managing their future. This group belongs to the illiterate and less educated people of the scheduled class and scheduled tribes and other backward classes. They are mainly the landless agricultural labourers and small and marginal farmers and artisans with low resource base. It is paradoxical that democracy includes them for votes while markets exclude them owing to resource poor. Hence they need a voice. A special attention must be paid to reducing the vulnerability of the poor to adverse shocks.

When Sen views poverty as a deficit not only in income but in social and political space in governance and in security, a decentralized democracy, a crackdown on corruption, and beneficiary participation in economic development will reduce poverty independent of any income effects they may have. Increased empowerment, opportunity and security are all forms of poverty reduction in their own right. They are likely to reduce income poverty too in the due course, through an inclusive growth in real sense of the term.

Poverty Alleviation Strategy and Programmes in India

In India during late sixties it was increasingly realised that poverty, especially rural poverty is not reducing despite development and planning. That had been a hard time in economic history of India when economy was facing food crisis, foreign exchange crisis, aggression on its borders,, and natural calamities like droughts and so on. Population was rising at a fast pace and demand for food was increasing. The sixties and seventies were the period of severe inflation in the economy. Several studies were made on poverty during this period and it was understood that the basic cause of poverty is low productivity in agriculture and widespread unemployment. Since the inception of Planning in 1951 it was thought that Land Reforms along with Community Development and Cooperation would take care of rural development and eliminate poverty and injustices from the land tenure system. However, the realities were different. Land Reforms could not be completed and to a large extent they landed in to the quagmire of court cases and official corruption. Low investment in agriculture since the Second Plan owing to emphasis on industrial development resulted in lower food production. Hence the food prices began to rise. This led to further worsening of rural and urban poverty. The government decided to tackle the problem through Intensive Rural Development Programmes (IRDP) and employment generation programmes. The approach is known as 'direct attack on poverty' approach. Poverty removal *(Garibi Hatao)* had been the main plank of Parliamentary elections in 1971.

Indira Gandhi government initiated Twenty Point programme in 1976 for poverty removal. Besides "Food for Work" programme was introduced in 1977. Public distribution system had already come in vogue since the sixties. Small Farmers Development Agency (SFDA) and Marginal Farmer and Development Agencies (MFAL) had been in action up to the Fifth Plan. Their aim was to improve the economic conditions of the rural poor so that their incomes may improve. But these programmes did not cover the whole country and their operation overlapped. IRDP was launched in 1976 in 20 selected districts and from October 1982 it was extended to all the districts in the country. IRDP has been the major self-employment programme, with Training for Rural Youth for Self-Employment (TRYSEM) and Development of Women and Children in Rural Areas (DWAKRA) as its sub schemes. To provide employment in agricultural lean seasons and thus generate supplementary wage incomes public works programmes—the Jawahar Rozgar Yojana (JRY), and Employment Assurance Scheme (EAS)—are in operation. To streamline the existing PDS, a Targeted Public Distribution System (TPDS) was introduced in 1997. Under the scheme special cards are issued to families below poverty line (BPL) and essential articles under the PDS sold to them at subsidized prices. To alleviate urban poverty, the Nehru Rozgar Yojana (NRY) was introduced in 1989. To provide self-employment opportunities to the educated unemployed youth Prime Minister's Rozgar Yojana (PMRY) was launched in 1993. There are around three dozen programmes operating in the country at present. The recent and most important had been the National Rural Employment Guarantee Act (NREGA) which was passed by the Parliament in the year 2005. Under the scheme the government has to provide at least 100 days of guaranteed wage employment in every financial year at Rs. 60 to one person of each household.

Unlike wage employment programmes, which tend to be relief-oriented, the creation of self-employment opportunities through the provision of assets can make the poor economically viable. In practice, however, schemes for self-employment have operated like programmes distributing doles, and made meagre contribution to reducing poverty. There is a general feeling that only a very small percentage of funds allocated by the government for implementation of anti-poverty programmes reach the poor. There are following reasons for this: (1) multiplicity of programmes, (2) ineffective monitoring and evaluation strategy, and (3) lack of will to take punitive action against inefficiency and corruption.

Poverty Alleviation through Rural Development

The Human Development approach to poverty alleviation and employment generation focuses on capabilities enhancement through better nutrition, health care, quality education, skill training and better economic provisioning. However newer models of rural development have been suggested for poverty alleviation as India lives in the villages and around two thirds of its population not only live in villages but depend on agriculture and allied activities for their living. Hence any development programme neglecting the development of rural areas could not succeed. Twelfth President of India Dr. Abdul Kalam in his *India 2020—A Vision for the New Millennium* (1990), *Ignited Minds: Unleashing the Power within India,* (2002), and in Presidential Speeches, has outlined the idea of knowledge society that will transform India. He pushed through the idea of Providing Urban facilities in Rural Areas, known as the PURA model of rural development. It envisages employment generation as foundation for sustainable rural development. PURA speaks of three connectivities:

1) The physical connectivity of village clusters through quality roads and transport;
2) Electronic connectivity through tele-communication with high bandwidth fibre optic cables reaching the rural areas from urban cities and through internet kiosks; and
3) Knowledge connectivity through education, skill training for farmers, artisans and craftsmen and entrepreneurship programmes.

These three connectivity will lead to economic connectivity through strings of enterprises with the help of banks, micro credits and marketing of the products. Some of the productive employment generation schemes are bio-fuel production, waste-land development, water harvesting, bamboo mission, converting fly ash into wealth, cotton cultivation for garment manufacture, health care and village knowledge centre.

Gunnar Myrdal in his book the *Asian Drama* has suggested that the degree of success met by national strategy will depend on the extent we are able to create an adequate capacity to effectively absorb surplus labour, largely in the rural sector itself; and in some measure in industry, mining and infrastructure but with optimum productivity. It will also depend on how far we are able to stabilize and reverse the rise in population by adopting a bold and forthright programme of population control and family planning. Only in this way will the areas in unemployment as well as the annual additions to work force both sizeable go down, resulting in a higher income per capita and better standard of living.

Sen's vision look upon the poor as 'active agents' struggling for freedom from captivation and un-freedoms. This views that unless the poor themselves rise for the cause and come forward, the 'dole approach' would be too scanty and short-termist to fight out the genial and long term problems of poverty and injustices. The government agencies meant for the purpose , lack 'motivation' (to help) and hence they so often lack the vigour and fall into corruption and apathy. Therefore, the role of self-help groups and the Non Government Organisations (NGOs) are more befitting in the present context, provided they are with real intentions and are not fake or corrupt.

Governments as well as markets fail to deliver the goods sometimes. This was amply demonstrated as to why poverty could not be alleviated in India despite the operation of ten Five Year Plans and governments determination in the direction. The apprehension from 'market' has already been expressed in previous chapters as it is more likely 'not to address' the problems of poverty and unemployment rather it goes in the opposite direction for private entrepreneur's 'profit maximization'. In the situation we shall have to look for the 'Third Way' of people's co-operation, and institutions comprising of self-help groups, NGOs, Co-operatives, micro-finance agencies and so on.

Dr. A.P.J. Abdul Kalam unveiled a 'Developed India' vision model in terms of simultaneous growth in five development sectors—value adding agriculture and food processing, enabling infrastructure, optimizing educational opportunities and health care delivery systems, edging out in information and communication technology and self-propelling strategic dynamics, and the rural development 'connectivity' model in its impactional chain changes.

No study of future can ignore current social realities. To attain a "preferred future" we have to redefine our values, concepts and goals setting new social norms to judge and assess our national stock in all branches of life. Dr. Kalam asserts that "We must regain our broad outlook and draw upon our heritage and wisdom to enrich our lives. The fact that we advance technologically does not preclude spiritual development. We need to home grow our own model of development based on our inherent strengths. Progress is rapid whenever there is an efficient administrative set-up, a high level of education and minimum political interference in development activity. Development is a security-centric phenomenon—from poverty to food security, social security and there after national security. Action in five core areas—agriculture and food-processing, supply of electricity, education and health care, information technology and strategic sector—properly integrated, would lead to food, economic, social and national security. The key to success lies in connectivity. The education of education and health care will yield the benefits of smaller families and a more efficient work force. It is key to employability and social development. Improvements in the agricultural sector, including that of food processing, would lead to food security, employment opportunities and rapid economic growth. Growth in the information technology sector would assist rapid economic growth as well as play an important part in speeding up development. Electric power provides energy security so crucial for all sectors. The strategic sector has a direct impact on industry, sustaining growth and technological strength. For balanced development all the five areas are of importance."

Dr. Kalam assumes that knowledge is the primary production resource instead of capital and labour and a simultaneous expansion and diversification in the five critical core competence areas will transform (the existing India) in to a developed country by 2020. He suggested an annual GDP growth rate in the range of 9 to 11 per cent to reduce the poverty level to below 10 per cent. His vision of development has been converted in to a model by P.J. Gandhi, which is as follows:

$$GDP_{2020} = f\,(Pa, I, S, T) + \lambda N \ldots\ldots\ldots\ldots\ldots (1)$$

Where,

GDP = two digit growth of GDP in 2020

Pa = Growth of agriculture and food-processing industries

I = Physical infrastructural facilities

S = Social infrastructural facilities

T = Technology factors

λN = Constant growth rate of population.

Contrary to popular perception that size of population depresses growth in developing countries, in Kalam's vision the stock of human capital is considered as a growth potential propelling higher rate of socio economic growth. He also emphasized that mere utilization of resources of primary sectors: agriculture and food processing, would not bring the double digit growth of GDP by 2020, there is a need for value addition in this primary sector.

Dr. Kalam's vision of future India is imaginative and holistic as it talks of not only rural development it also holds the phenomenon of "push to the town" and rural migration by providing gainful employment in the rural areas itself, there by releasing the pressures of the cities and towns which are gasping. It addresses the problems of farmer's large scale suicides in the drought prone areas of the country by suggesting inter linking of rivers and solar farming for electricity generation, besides PURA and its connectivity. Use of Information and Communication Technology (ICT) is one of the areas of core competence and wealth generator. ICT can be used for Tele-education, Tele-medicine and E-governance to promote education in remote areas, healthcare, and also transparency in the administration. Finally he talks about Critical technologies and Strategic industries, viz., nuclear technology, space technology and defense technology to lead India in the 21st century as great power.

REFERENCES

1. Amartya Sen, *Development As Freedom*, Oxford University Press, 2000.
2. *Economic Survey, 2006-2007*, Government of India.
3. Myrdal, Gunnar, *The Asian Drama*.

4. Gaur, A.K., An Inter-State Analysis of Human Poverty, in *Poverty in India: Global and Regional Dimensions*, K. Nageswara Rao, (Ed), Deep and Deep, New Delhi, 2005.
5. Gandhi, P. Jagdish, Abdul Kalam's Developed India Model, in *IEA 87th. Conference Volume*, pp. 272-279, 2004.
6. K. Sundaram, Employment and Poverty in India 2000-2005, *EPW*, No. 30, July 28, 2007.
7. Patnaik,Utsa, Neoliberalism and rural poverty in India, *EPW*, No. 30, July 28, 2007
8. Bagchi, K.K., *Employment and Poverty Alleviation Programmes in India*, (Ed.), Abhijeet Publications, Delhi, 2007.
9. Tinbergen, Jan, *Reshaping the International Order.*
10. Chelliah, R. J. and Sudershan, R., *Income Poverty and Beyond*, Social Science Press, New Delhi, 1999.
11. Gupta, I.D., Employment Generation through Rural Development in Uttar Pradesh, *UPUEA Economic Journal*, Vol. 2, No. 1, 2006.

PART THREE: UNEMPLOYMENT IN INDIA

5

Employment Strategy for India: Realities and Challenges

India is emerging as a fast growing economy in the global scenario today. And the coming age would be of India and China as world powers, it is claimed. However, the biggest challenges are widespread unemployment and sizeable poverty.

Planners of India's future, at the time of Independence in 1947 have had the dreams of economic independence and freedom from want, ignorance and squalor. They dreamt of a Socialistic Pattern of Society in which the economy would be free from Capitalistic exploitation as well as Communist regimentation.

The realities were harsh and the economy could not grow at a faster rate and realize the targeted rate of growth of five per cent per annum as pronounced in its Five Year Plans till the eighties. The rate of growth of population around 2.5 per cent per annum posed another supply side pressure in the labour market.

Besides, several wars with Pakistan and with China in 1962 dragged the economy backwards. Natural devastations in the form of droughts posed severe challenges from time to time at regular intervals. During the sixties economy faced severe food crisis along with the already existing foreign exchange crisis. Inflation touched double digit during sixties and seventies due to internal shortages and worldwide petroleum price hike. Failure of land reforms in raising agricultural productivity was evident. The country had to adopt vigorous programmes for raising rural productivity. These programmes were called the New Strategy of Agricultural Development, which later brought the so-called Green Revolution. Resultantly high productivity was marked particularly in wheat and paddy production and the economy was able to come out of the food crisis.

By the same time it was also realized that despite positive growth rate economic inequality is rising and poverty and unemployment is posing a really big threat to the economy and the then Prime Minister Mrs. Indira Gandhi chalked out a two pronged strategy for poverty alleviation: vitalizing rural development through Integrated Rural Development Programmes and Employment Generation Programmes.

By the eighties it was also realized that Indian economy is in too much chains and it needs liberalization and lesser controls by the bureaucracy. Global wave too was favouring the same air. The USSR was at the verge of disintegration and Communist challenge to market economy system was dissipating. This brought a newer perception after the dissolution of the USSR was complete. Globalization, privatization and marketization formed the ingredients of economic reforms before the countries who were erstwhile in socialist influence and the other Less Developed Countries. With this also started withering away of the State's role in economic affairs, including employment generation and its role as 'trustee of the poor'.

India's innovation of the concept of Socialistic Pattern of Society which was considered a role model for other developing countries stated fading in the newer economic atmosphere of competition and efficiency during the nineties and faced with severe balance of payments crisis India had to chalk out a new Industrial Policy based on liberalization and global competition on 24th July 1991.

Even after the initiation of the economic reforms Indian economy faces grim challenges of a sizeable population below the poverty line and a very large number of unemployed mass, including educated unemployed. This not only poses only economic problem but it generates at a bigger plane social tensions, crime and terrorist/naxalite upheavals.

In economic literature of the recent past it has been observed that the problem of open unemployment is only a tip of the iceberg. The real problem of poverty has had its roots in vast scale under-employment and disguised unemployment and in low wages paid to the workers. The new situation in post-nineties has opened the vistas of casual, contract and other forms of unprotected labour employment. With the limited role of the State and weakening position of trade unions the problem has taken newer shapes and nuances.

The Indian economy today faces challenges in the labour market from both the sides: the supply side pressures generated from a growth rate of population around two per cent (exactly 1.93 per cent) and the 'army of the unemployables' generated through India's educational system; and the receding demand owing to technological advance and the adoption of the sophisticated technology by the Multi-Nationals and bigger industrial houses to face competition, particularly from low wage economies like China. As a result, despite the growth rate of above or around 6 per cent the growth rate of employment remained sluggish in the manufacturing sector. The employment elasticity of growth here touching a low of 0.16 as per current estimates. Growth rate of employment in agriculture and allied sector, which has erstwhile been biggest employment sector, has saturated and there is a near stagnation.

Outsourcing by the United States of America and other rich economies owing to cheaper labour in China and in India and India's advantage currently due to its English speaking youth may be a purely temporary phenomenon as China has stated training its youth in English language.

And in even sophisticated labour market of information technology the boom may burst within a few years.

The new strategy for employment generation will surely have to face these newer challenges presented by the global competition and market economy system.

This paper is in three parts: with this first part of introduction what follows is a brief data analysis and then in the next section employment strategy and suggestions have been taken care of.

PART-2
CURRENT SCENARIO

As per Government of India data, as on September 2002 number of job seekers, registered with 939 Employment Exchanges, was of the order of 4.16crores out of which 70 per cent were educated above 10th standard.

Maximum number of jobseekers registered was in West Bengal (6.3 lakh) while minimum were at Union Territory of Dadra and Nagar Haveli (0.06 lakh) and in Arunachal Pradesh (0.2 lakh). The placement was maximum in Gujarat.

The Economic Survey 2002-03 shows a rate of unemployment of 7.32 per cent while the total number of the unemployed is 26.58 millions.

The Tenth Five Year Plan depicts a backlog of 35 millions and aims at providing 10 million jobs per year during its tenure 2002-05.

Employment in the organized sector as on March 2001 was 27.8 million, out of which public sector employment stood at 19.1 million, that is, 69 per cent of total employment. Private sector employment stood at 8.7 million.

Rate of growth of employment, on current daily status, declined from 2.7 per cent per annum in 1983-94 to 1.07 percent in 1994-2000 periods. The decline in the rate of growth of employment was associated with a comparatively higher growth rate in Gross Domestic Product, indicating a decline in the labour intensity of production.

In the organized sector there was a marginal decrease in employment in the year 2001 as compared to year 2000. Employment in the public sector declined by 0.9 per cent while private sector employment increased by 0.1 per cent.

TABLE 1

EMPLOYMENT AND UNEMPLOYMENT (CDS BASIS)

(Persons Year)

(Million)

	1983			*1993-94*			*1999-00*		
	Rural	*Urban*	*Total*	*Rural*	*Urban*	*Total*	*Rural*	*Urban*	*Total*
Popn.	546.61	171.59	718.20	658.83	234.98	894.01	727.50	276.47	1003.97
L Force	204.18	57.15	261.33	255.38	80.60	335.97	270.39	92.95	363.33
W force	187.92	51.64	239.57	241.04	74.80	315.84	250.89	85.84	336.75
Un. Rate	7.96	9.64	8.30	5.61	7.19	5.99	7.21	7.65	7.32
No. Un	16.26	5.51	21.76	14.34	5.80	20.13	19.50	7.11	26.58

Some of the other important findings emerging from the 55th National Sample Survey Round (1999-2000) are:

1. The decline in the rate of growth of employment was associated with a sharp decline in the rate of growth of labour force.
2. The absolute number of unemployed as well as the incidence of unemployment (unemployed as percentage of labour force) Increased during this period.
3. The decline in the overall growth rate of employment in 1994-2000 was largely attributable to a near stagnation of employment in agriculture. As a result, the share of agriculture in total employment dropped substantially from 60 per cent in 1993-94 to 57 percent in 1999-2000.
4. Employment growth in all the sub sectors within services (except community, social and personal services) exceeded 5 per cent per annum.
5. As has been the trend in the past, the share of casual labour in total employment has gone up.

TABLE 2

ANNUAL GROWTH RATES

(Percent)

	1983-1994			1993-2000		
	Rural	*Urban*	*Total*	*Rural*	*Urban*	*Total*
Popn.	1.79	3.04	2.00	1.67	2.74	1.95
Labour Force	2.15	3.33	2.43	0.96	2.40	1.31
Work Force	2.40	3.59	2.70	0.67	2.32	1.07
No. Unemp	-1.19	0.49	-0.08	5.26	3.45	4.74

It is worthwhile to note that only a small percentage (8 to 9 per cent) of the total work force of the country is employed in the organized sector. While employment growth in the private organized sector significantly improved n the 1990s, the growth of employment in public sector was negligible. Since the public sector accounts for more than two-thirds of the total organized sector employment there was slow down of the over all growth in organized sector employment.

To quantify some of the above observations we notice that:

Employment elasticity of output has gone down from 0.52 over the years 1983 to 1993-94 to 0.16 over 1993-94 to 1999-2000. This decline in the employment elasticity is observed in most sectors except transport, financial services and real estate.

Employment in the organized sector had been hardly 8.34 per cent, of which public sector accounts for 5.77 per cent and private sector only 2.58 per cent in the total employment generated.

Under organized manufacturing, the employment generation potential of the private sector is seen to be higher than of public sector manufacturing, but it hardly constitutes 1.5 per cent of the total employment in the country and 16.5 per cent of total manufacturing employment.

The main employment generating activities identified today are:

1. Agriculture and allied activities;
2. Trade, restaurants and hotels including tourism;
3. Some of the social sectors like education and health;
4. Small and medium enterprises, mainly in the rural non-farm sector; and
5. Transport and communication.

Agriculture and allied activities, account for 57 per cent of India's total employment. Between 1983 and 1993-94, its employment elasticity was as high as 0.70 and now in the later period of 1993-94 to 1999-2000; it has come down to 0.01.

We also visualize large scale inter state differentials in the unemployment scenario.

Some of the other major important findings emerging are:

Marginalisation of Trade Unions in the post reform period. And the supportive role of State is no longer available and it is more likely that the State will come to the rescue of the employers than labour.

The entry of Multi-Nationals and their demand to amend some of the labour laws particularly the Industrial Disputes Act provisions relating to lay-off and retrenchment are likely to erode further the State support to Trade Unions.

In the background of these realities it is increasingly becoming difficult for the State to adhere to the Article 43 of the Indian Constitution whereby it states that, " The State shall endeavour to secure, by suitable legislation or economic organization or in any other way, to all workers, agricultural, industrial or otherwise, work, a living wage, conditions of work ensuring a decent standard of life and full enjoyment of leisure and social and cultural opportunities".

The objectives before the State during the First Five Year Plan had been " to bring about welfare of the working class and the country's economic stability and progress".

The Second Five Year Plan suggested for " creation of industrial democracy as a pre-requisite for the establishment of a Socialist society ". This was in the background of the acceptance by the Indian Parliament in 1954 the paradigm of " Socialistic Pattern of Society " as policy objective.

However, the change of perceptions during the last five decades and faced with newer realities and nuances the New Economic Policy announced in mid –1991 spoke of " industrial restructuring " besides accepting liberalization and global pressure in favour of market economy system and increased role of private entrepreneurs, instead of public hands, in shaping the future scenario of the economy and its labour market.

The process of industrial restructuring, which started in 1985-86, has also led to a shift in management strategies. Some of the new strategies adopted by management are:

1. Reduction in permanent work force;
2. Organization of the bulk of production through ancillary units;
3. Employment of casual, contract or other forms of unprotected labour;
4. Shift of production facilities to the backward areas where labour is both cheap and not unionized;
5. Signing of agreements with individual workers by bypassing Trade Unions; and so on.

The new management strategies have created the following situations:

1. An atmosphere of job insecurity among workers
2. Curtailment of Trade Union action
3. Strike becoming a less effective weapon for Unions
4. Increase in the frequency of lockouts declared by management.

It has been observed that between 1985 and 1991,

number of man-days lost due to lock-outs has been greater than those lost due to strike, excepting the year 1986.

The important thing observed is that there has been a gradual shift of employment from the organized to the unorganized sector during the past 10-15 years. Within the organized sector the proportion of contract and casual labour has increased significantly. Casual wage employment increased from 28.4 per cent in 1977-78 to 31.2 percent in 1987-88. Industrial restructuring followed with economic reforms is bound to accelerate this trend.

Government of India's Economic Survey (1993-94) noted that "the restructuring of industry in response to internal and external competition is an urgent necessity." However, this will inevitably cause reductions in the number of presently employed persons in the organized industrial sector.

It would be a hard task before the Government to keep the promise " in order to have a human face, restructuring must be accompanied by certain measures that ameliorate its bad effects".

PART-3
THE STRATEGY

India is a country of villages. "Nearly 700 million people of India live in the rural areas in 600,000 villages. Connectivity of village complexes providing economic opportunities to all segments of people is an urgent need to bridge the urban rural divide, generate employment and enhance rural prosperity", says Dr. Abdul Kalam, the President of India in his recent address in Vijnyan Bhawan.

As migration from rural sector to the urban areas in search of job is the main source of exacerbating unemployment, there is an urgent need to check this trend. As per the Todaro model, rural urban wage differential is the basic cause of this migration. The other Dual Economy models, such as, Lewis depict of subsistence sector and organized industrial sector where the wages are kept low in the latter on the basis of low wages prevailing in the former. The subsistence sector is a surplus labour sector. To check this rural exodus there is an urgent need to generate high wage employment in the rural sector itself. This could be done through vitalizing the rural sector and via Providing Urban Amenities in the Rural Areas (PURA). PURA envisages the employment generation as the foundation for sustainable development.

Dr. Kalam speaks of three connectivities in this regard: the physical connectivity of village clusters through quality roads and transport; electronic connectivity through tele-communication with high bandwidth fibre optic cables reaching the rural areas from urban cities and through internet kiosks, and knowledge connectivity through education, skill training for farmers, artisans and craftsmen and entrepreneurship programmes. These three connectivity will lead to economic connectivity through starting of enterprises with the help of banks, micro credits and marketing of products. Some of the productive employment generation schemes are bio-fuel production, wasteland development, water harvesting, bamboo mission, converting fly ash into wealth, cotton cultivation to garment manufacture, health care and village knowledge center.

Amartya Sen, the Nobel Laureate is of the opinion that eradication of poverty entails strengthening the "capabilities" of the poor and simultaneously create "opportunities" in society to enable them to make full use of it. Strengthening capabilities, therefore, is crucial for helping the poor to confront and cope with not only a paucity of income but also a host of other adversaries as well, such as disease, disaster and discrimination.

The Human Development approach to poverty alleviation and employment generation focuses on capability enhancement through better health care, quality education and better economic provisioning, e.g., access to safe drinking water, better sanitation etc. Power generation and quality roads are already on the top agenda of the Government today. Without these economic and social provisioning the attainment of most basic things of Human development—"to lead long, healthy and creative life and to enjoy a decent standard of living, freedom, dignity, self-esteem and respect of others" is no longer be possible.

What country needs is generation of large-scale employment in and around the villages. This could be done on the pattern of Japanese model of development based on small-scale industries equipped with modern techniques supported by the State. Ludhiana model of development is an example in itself, which has changed the shape of Punjab's economy. There is much scope in this line. Besides agro-processing, quality packaging and marketing units have enough scope of labour absorption.

To deal with the problems of unskilled workers who amass the unorganized sector, basically rural sector, what is needed is to develop skill development programmes for the illiterate and semi-literate manpower, where poverty is concentrating most. This poorest of the poor group consists of tribals, agricultural laboures belonging to backward classes of the society and others. The establishments of Industrial Training Institutes (ITI), and Polytechnics who impart knowledge to the lesser-educated, such as, quality carpentry, masonry, electrical works and at even lower levels of construction workers who know nothing, a small duration training programmes and providing them with certificates can bring about a sea change in their lot as well as minimize the hassles of those who give them job.

As is evident from the data above, the strategy of public sector employment generation of the sixties has gone dated and the agriculture sector's viability in this respect is also saturated the current and future generations may find hope only through private sector and self-employment. The private sector employment has its own complexes as the only objective there is profit maximization, which more often than not remind of Capitalistic exploitation of the post Industrial Revolution phase. The motivational factors are different in public sector and private sector employments. Besides, while the former has been providing permanent and secured jobs for the lifetime apart from other social security measures the one is the provider of temporary and casual jobs.

Any discussion regarding employment market would be incomplete without taking into consideration the population factor and the education planning and policy points of the country. It is a sigh of relief that the growth rate of population has shown tendency of coming down. It has come down to below two per cent. With the spread of literacy and opulence it is further hoped that favourable trend will emerge and supply side pressure will ease in future.

Regarding choice of technique we cannot talk of obsolete labour intensive or intermediate technology for the manufacturing sector at this stage. In the present situation of the global competition resorting to the old would not be a wise survival strategy. India has moved ahead on the basis of sophisticated information technology and there could be no going back. The same competency needs to be spread to manufacturing and other sectors of the economy.

An Incomes Policy too is needed for the country to reduce or at least prevent a widening of the gap between earnings of the modern sector and the rest of the economy. However, it would be a difficult task owing to diminishing role of the government in the production sector, as it is going to be today, in the market economy system.

New realities are emerging and we hope the intelligentsia in the academia would find solutions, as ever, for it, in the future.

PART FOUR:
BLACK ECONOMY IN INDIA

6

Black Economy in India

A nation is known by its people's character. The countries which have ruled over the world in the past centuries have had something basic in the character of their people. National character is a sum total of the character of its people. Character is constituted on the basis of the attitudes, traits and attributes, and functioning embodied in a man. However, one possesses the good and the bad both in him and how he will respond to a particular event at a particular time and in a particular situation depends how he thinks about it. Man behaves differently over a particular stimulus in different times and at different places. As he is a complex personality, therefore, he is unpredictable and his behaviour in future can not be predicted. Stephen Hawkins says as the behaviour of a man is unpredictable hence the future can not be foretold.

In reality, in each one's psyche there is a continuing war between good and the evil. The dominance of the good or bad traits in one defines him.

It has also been found that the character of a man, sometimes, has an undulating surface representing the presence of ups and downs on the point of ethics or morality depending upon the situation and his thinking or interpretation of the situation. In some scriptures it has been described as godly forces and the devil's forces. One is coloured in white in our imagination while the other is painted as black.

Any action which is regarded by society as unethical or immoral is taken as belonging to the realm of Satan who is an emperor of the darkness and black; and the action which is upright and pious is taken as belonging to the realm of the gods and its colour is white. Purity, light and whiteness are the attributes of godliness. When we apply this concept to the earnings of a person then what is earned through any clandestine deal and is kept in hiding away from the sight of the government and the society is taken as black earning. Money being black or white owes its origin in these concepts.

India at the time of political Independence was overflowing with idealism in its people. Nationalism was in the life and blood of almost everyone in the society. However, as the time gone by the self-less ness and righteousness in life started disappearing from many of the people in society.

Sixties and seventies of the last century were the hard times for the country when it was struggling with 'food crisis' and the 'foreign exchange crisis'. Rationing was introduced and controls were tightened so that each one of the population could get a proper minimum to his mouth and could sustain the onslaught of current drudgeries of life. Rationing and control breeded black marketing as they represent the supply shortages to the demand. This gave rise to black money generation in the markets of the essential commodities. So was the case with foreign exchange market. Many scholars diagnose this situation a result of a very high marginal rate of income taxation and very strict foreign exchange regulations. At the time of Indira Gandhi the peak rate of Income tax was 97.5 per cent.

In the beginning the number of those involved in black marketing and smuggling was small. However once getting a 'taste' of easy money coming in without being caught with the connivance of some of the officials which were in charge of controlling these very practices, the number started growing . A "spoil system" started emerging to protect the illegal practices and the persons involved in these activities.

India is a country with overwhelming poverty. And poverty is a fertile ground for germination of criminal activities and crime starting from petty thefts to smuggling of foreign exchange, drugs, and the like. The ground level workers or the so called agents or the 'carriers' of smuggling of drugs and other things are the poor people without having sufficient or respectable means for survival at their disposal. They are active across the international borders. By this logic those living in sufficiency are, by and large, pro status quo in the society and they are against change. They belong to the middle class. And in any society where the middle class is in large proportion that society is treated as a healthy society. And in societies where the middle class is thin and there are two classes, of the rich and the poor, the society is unhealthy and prone to disturbances and even violence. The examples of Bihar and the North East in India where poverty is highest the criminal activities and Naxalism_ a revolt against state or the existing social order, is also of high order. This is also one of the reasons behind migration of the rich and the super rich from Bihar to the other states for their survival and safety. This may be the logic behind the migration of the youths of Punjab, Gujrat, Andhra, and Kerala etc. towards USA, Canada, England and other European countries. Poverty or insufficiency leads to migration in most of the cases. This is also true to rural migration and 'push to the town' phenomenon.

It is said that India is facing the problem of black money since the Second World War. The war period was a period of shortages of food and essential articles. However, in the Independence period the above mentioned periods of sixties and seventies may be taken as the start of menacing proportions of the black money and black economy.

As per the Wanchoo Committee "the term black money is generally used to denote unaccounted money or concealed income and/or wealth as well as money involved in transactions wholly or partly suppressed."

It is generally taken as hidden money/wealth earned through illegal gratification by businessmen or politicians or others without being reported to tax officials/authorities. These days many of the big Indian politicians, Chief Ministers and bureaucrats are facing criminal charges of disproportionate assets accumulation to their known sources of income. There is flood of such cases in the post nineties.

Whenever the economy faces supply shortages of the essential commodities there emerges a system in 'black' where things are available at a 'premium' to a selected few. Subsequently the premium system gets maturity at the hands of the guardians who share the benefit acquired out of it. A whole network emerges under the patronage of some big politician or the mafia muscleman.

Confusion prevails over the definition of black money which sometimes takes the flow aspect and sometimes the stock aspect of money. By definition money is round and it is also flat. While income is a flow concept wealth is a stock concept. We may estimate the amount of black money circulating in the economy as well as take account of the wealth accumulated through such clandestine deals.

Estimates of Black Money

In India Nicholas Kaldor had attempted seriously, for the first time, a computation of how much black money circulates in the economy. As his calculations involved many assumptions particularly in regard to the disorganized sector, Kaldor himself postulated that his estimates were tentative and should be interpreted with caution.

Kaldor, soon enough discovered that tax evasion and black money was deep and extensive. He concluded that 'if his estimates were anywhere near truth, tax evasion was of the order of rupees 200 to 300 crores.

This was a far cry from the more or less official estimate of only 20 to 30 crores, as voiced by the Board of Revenue of the Government of India (speeches in Parliament of the Union Minister of Finance 1956-57 Budget).

The Direct Taxes Administration Enquiry Committee, 1958-59 admitted the existence of 50 crores of black money in the economy.

Calculating further on Kaldor's estimation it was estimated that in 1958-59 around 400 crores black money was available in the country. While one third of it was in the hidden storage the rest two third was in circulation.

The Direct Taxes Enquiry Committee, known popularly as Wanchoo Committee after Justice K.N. Wanchoo, a Supreme Court Judge, submitted final report in 1971 on tax evasion and black money in Indian economy. As per Justice Wanchoo's definition, black money symbolized money which had been earned by violating the provisions of law and even social conscience, and which is kept secret and unaccounted for.

In later research and writings and in official and non-official references, black money covers a subterranean economic phenomenon which inter alia, sustains the black market and smuggling underworld through largely or wholly irregular deals and transactions not reflected in books of accounts.

A huge black money infrastructure extends its sphere of influence in black market and clandestine international trade, and thwarts growth, planning, price stabilization, public revenue and investible surplus.

The DTEC emphasized the dual nature of the Indian economy—an official economy functions on the basis of the official monetary system, involving open transactions financed through identifiable sources of funds generating ascertainable income and wealth; on the other hand a parallel economy functions in open and secretive competition with the official economy.

A parallel economy is at war at every stage with the government's monetary, banking and fiscal policies. "A secretive, defiant, and an unscrupulous element in our society provide the parallel economy with its blood for sustenance." It involves a complex range of undisclosed deals and transactions pushed through secretly with unaccounted sources of funds, generating in the process income and wealth which escape official estimation (Final Report DTEC, 1971).

TABLE 1

ESTIMATES OF BLACK INCOME IN INDIA

Nicholas Kaldor	1953-54	Rs. 200 to 300 crores	
Wanchoo Committee	1961-62	Rs. 700 crores	(4.4 per cent of NY)
(1971)	1965-66	Rs. 1000 crores	(4.2 per cent of NY)
	1968-69	Rs. 1400 crores	(4.2 Per cent of NY)
Rangnekar	1961-62	Rs. 1150 crores	(7.2 per cent of NY)
	1965-66	Rs. 2350 crores	(8.2 per cent of NY)
	1968-69	Rs. 2833 crores	(8.6 per cent of NY)
	1969-70	Rs. 3080 crores	(8.4 per cent of NY)
NIPFP (1985)	1975-76	Rs. 9985 to 11870 crores	(15 to 18 per cent)
	1980-81	Rs. 20362 to 23678 crores	(18 to 21 per cent)
	1983-84	Rs. 31584 to 36784 crores	(18 to 21 per cent)
SB Gupta (1992)	1980-81	Rs. 50977 crores	(41.7 per cent)
	1983-84	Rs. 85208 crores	(45.8 per cent)
	1987-88	Rs. 142297 crores	(51.7 per cent of NY)

Figures in brackets are per cent of the national income of the respective year.
Source: As stated in the text.

Table 1 shows the various study results about the spread of black money in the economy.

It is pertinent to note that while the black money as per Kaldor's estimates was a little above four per cent during the sixties it was around eight to a little less than nine per cent as per Rangnekar's estimates during the same period. However, as per the National Institute for Public Finance and Policy's report in 1985 the extent of black money was around fifteen to eighteen per cent during seventies and around eighteen to twenty one per cent during the early eighties.

The estimation of S B Gupta are an eye opener which state that the extent of black money in the Indian economy was as high as 41.7 per cent in 1980-81 and it rose sharply to 45.8 per cent and then to 51.7 per cent in 1983-84 and 1987-88 respectively. The growth rate of black money is higher during the later period depicts that the Indian economy is knee deep in black waters and the water level is persistently rising. Details of the two later studies are worth analyzing to understand the problem more carefully.

TABLE 2

ESTIMATE OF BLACK INCOME GENERATED IN INDIA

(Rs. crores)

Source	*1975-76*	*1980-81*
1. From Gross Personal Income	3741	9813
2. Under-reporting of output	3318 to 4978	5713 to 8750
3. Under-registration of immovable property	2256	3664
4. Leakages from public sector Investment	335 to 503	720 to 1071
5. Leakages from private corporate investment	169 to 253	217 to 325
6. Under-invoicing of exports	139	235
7. Total Black Income	9958 to 11870	20362 to 23678
8. GDP at factor cost (at current prices)	66370	142271
9. Black Income as Per cent of GDP	15 to 18 per cent	18 to 21 per cent

Source: Aspects of Black Economy in India, NIPFP.

Table 2 brings out the details of the sources of black money generation in the economy. It highlights the evasion from personal income as the highest source of black money generation. Then it is the under reporting of the output to evade excise duty and other taxes on output. It indicates towards the connivance of tax authorities and the businessmen which is a growing menace. After the two big sources of tax evasion comes the under reporting of registration value on immovable property and thereby evading taxes on the true value of the property. Again it points towards the connivance of the tax authorities who choose a fast buck for themselves, instead of submitting the revenue to the national accounts.

The DTEC in its final report has submitted that, 'Black money and tax evasion, which go hand in hand, have also the effect of seriously undermining the equity concept of taxation and warping its progressiveness. Together they throw a greater burden on the honest tax payers and lead to economic inequality and concentration of wealth in the hands of the unscrupulous few in the country.'

TABLE 3

BLACK INCOME GENERATION IN INDIA

(In crores of Rupees)

Source	*1980-81*	*1983-84*	*1987-88*
1. Income tax evasion	14665	22319	34329
2. Corporation tax evasion	393	743	1030
3. Black gains in real estate	5260	9089	18847
4. Excise duty evasion	4333	6815	10951
5. Custom duty evasion	1463	2424	5953
6. Black Income from smuggling	1200	7000	12000
7. Black Income from exports	1007	1466	2361
8. Evasion from state taxes	5674	8447	16131
9. Black Income from public expenditure			
a) States	4093	5682	11850
b) Central government	1861	3102	4950
10. Black Income from private corporate investment	531	1010	1724
11. TOTAL	50977	85208	149297
12. GDP at factor cost (at current prices)	122226	185991	294408
13. Black Money as per cent of GDP	41.71	45.81	50.71
14. GDP at factor cost : Agriculture sector	46649	67498	92379
15. GDP at factor cost: Non-Agr. Sector	75577	118493	207029
16. Black money as % of Non Agr. Sector	67.45	71.91	72.11

Source: Black Income in India, SB Gupta, 1992.

Table 3 is more revealing. Prof. Gupta bifurcates the total GDP into agricultural and non agricultural sectors and attempts to show that leaving the agriculture sector aside the black income generation is rampant in the non agricultural sector. During the eighties the extent of black money was around 72 per cent. of the Gross Domestic Product of the country. The black money generation rate in the economy shows an annual average compound rate of 16.54 per cent during 1980-81 to 1987-88.

Income tax evasion is the highest followed by black gains in the real estates deals. Evasion from State taxes and the smugglings were the other big sources of black money generation during the eighties.

Although attempts to liberalize the economy started since· the eighties and since early nineties many of the controls and regulations on foreign exchange were done away with the introduction of economic reforms there is no definite sign of slackness in the black money generation in the economy. It might have put a dent on the smuggling and foreign exchange market as many of the things which had come through the smuggling are now available in the market and foreign firms have entered into the economy at a big scale and the foreign exchange availability has taken an easy proportion due to large foreign exchange reserve in the country, the habit of the officials and the businessmen and those involved in earning fast buck in the past is not easy to be left out easily and reformed, even when there is no supply shortages in the economy as were felt during the sixties and seventies. Rather we find definite signs of maturity of the black system which has come to control the different things in the political market as well besides controlling the things in the economic market. It is a very dangerous situation of economics entering into the politics of the country. There were marked signs of these exposures during the Narasimha Rao period during the early nineties when money bags were descending New Delhi to purchase votes of the Parliamentarians to stabilize the ruling government. Later politics shows signs of much more cases of role of money entering into political arena. When the market of economics enters into the politics and when politics enters into the market of economics and profit maximization becomes the sole motive behind political activities, the downfall becomes limitless, say the visionaries.

Causes of the generation of Black Money

There may be several causes which lead to the creation of black money but definitely the two could be considered the most important. One is very high marginal rate of Income taxation and ambiguous and cumbersome laws; and the other the economy of shortages and controls and slow growth rate of the economy accompanied with inflation rate of above and around eight per cent. This was the case in sixties and seventies. Inflation is still around five per cent in the economy. Multiplicity of regulations and controls add to creation of a situation of tax avoidance and black money generation. In a populous country with high rate of population growth, adding approximately the size of Australian population each year, the size of demand generation is very high in Indian economy which outweighs the supply many a times, resulting in shortages and price escalation in the market.

The other point to mention is the change in society's attitude towards earning income. Gandhian view of earning through 'fair means' which guided the society for long, is diminishing in the wake of consumerism in the country. The change in cultural values in Indian society is evident since the seventies of the last century. People who earn money and create wealth by whatever means are regarded respectable in society unlike in the earlier time. This generates a demonstration effect in society where the limits of right and wrong means of earning became blurred.

The Wanchoo Committee had concluded that "The implication of 97.75 per cent income tax is that it is more profitable at a certain level of income to evade tax on Rs. 30 than to earn honestly Rs. 1000. We will not be surprised that placed in such a situation it would be difficult for a person to resist the temptation to evade taxes. And, so long as the marginal rates of taxation are confiscatory it would be difficult to convince the public that tax evasion is anti-social."

The high rate of taxation and too many regulations provide enough inducement to the businessmen, traders, and the middlemen for manipulating them for their benefit. Prevalence of corruption, and bribery on the part of businessmen and slowness and red tapism on the part of public officials, are to a great extent the by-products of these two major causes.

Black money requires for its protection, proliferation and expansion services of organization composed of musclemen, touts and brokers to combat the forces of law and order, on the one hand, and on the other hand there are the requirements of income tax advisers or chartered accountants to suggest ways and means to get the things done with ease. The situation above narrated not only creates such organizations it also provides contact men who negotiate favours from top bureaucracy and political bosses through bribes of black money. This system developed into a self-propelling model in India which developed an altogether new culture of black money in the country. It was a dawn of new era of development of the other type, development of a few and certainly not the development of the masses.

Effects of Black Money on the Economy and Society

Black money not only has economic impact in loss of revenue to the government but it disturbs the moral fibre of the society and the economic system as a whole. Money in an exchange economy runs like blood circulation in the body of a human being. There is a circular flow in the economic system where by production of the country is distributed in the form of rewards to the five contributors, viz., land, labour, capital, organization, and enterprise. And when something spurious runs through the system, it disturbs the whole system like spurious blood ruins the whole system of the body.

As stated earlier black money generates through tax evasion and violation of economic regulations wherein the real amount is not declared and is kept in hiding. This is used in bribery and graft to regulatory authorities and/ or enforcement agencies to save tax and to perpetuate the system of further black money generation.

The amount of black saving or unaccounted income is used for conspicuous consumption of domestic goods as well as foreign goods. As the conspicuous consumption does have a widespread demonstration effect this brings in an undesirable impact on society's consumption pattern which is often socially less valuable. The longing it creates in the 'cleans' lead them to run after undesirable channels of earnings. The corrupt means of earning once undertaken to fulfill newly created wants leads the person towards an insatiable realm of competitive desires. As the number of such persons becomes large, the society moves on a slope of consumption pattern which has no stop. This conspicuous consumption pattern encourages smuggling of goods from foreign countries when the domestic economy is by and large, regulated and controlled.

Thus whereas the black money results in loss of revenue to the government exchequer as a consequence of tax evasion from direct and indirect taxes, the conspicuous consumption and its demonstration effect tilts the consumption pattern in favour of the rich and the elite classes at the cost of encouraging the production of articles of general good and mass consumption. A rise in the overall consumption in a less developed economy leaves less resource for investment in priority areas.

Black savings are mostly invested in 'real estate' and in business. Some time it is deposited in foreign banks. There are examples in India of politicians and others having Swiss Bank accounts. Diverting resources in real estate is easy as there is enough scope to undervalue the real cost. According to Wanchoo Committee the ratio of white and black in land and building deals in Bombay was 60:40. Now it is estimated that this ratio has come to 40:60 in recent years. The cases of connivance of registration authorities and builders and other buyers are very common all over India. Diversion of black savings in to land has pushed up the prices of land because of speculative purchases of land by black money operators. As a consequence middle classes are priced out in the purchase of land or houses. We also visualize a phenomenon of over pricing of building and flats by the builders in big cities by private builders. There appears no relation between the actual cost of the building or flat and its sale price. The price quoted is very high than the 'just' price. Price in a market, as per Classical economists is cost of production plus normal profit, where normal profit is the amount "just sufficient for the firm to stay in the industry". In the present context of a sellers market it is what could be squeezed out from the buyers irrespective of the actual cost. It is a case of "Tyranny of the Market" where common man is pushed out of the market.

On macro level black liquidity frustrates the attempts of the government to control excess demand through monetary measures. Monetary policy could control only the regular channel while a parallel black channel is out of reach of the monetary policy. Similarly the tax policy too is unable to control the black channel. Tax avoidance leads to lower turn out to the government treasury which prompts further taxation only to be borne out by the honest tax payers who are already taxed. This brings resentment among the tax payers. And when the taxes are high even honest tax payers attempt to shift to dishonest channels to avoid excessive taxation. When the tax officials too are involved in this process of mutual gratification, a vicious circle is created where more and more people become corrupt. The net result is further accentuation of already existing inequality in economy.

When the black money enters the political arena through party funds or otherwise to be used for purchasing votes in elections and buying elected representatives for making or unmaking of government after the elections then a new story of downfall of democracy begins. In further developments economy moves in the direction of Directly Unproductive Activities (the DUP activities) when political leadership only acts as a mouthpiece of big business to seek favours for the big businessmen who voted them to power, in the name of national interest or productivity.

The Remedy

It is difficult but not impossible to come out of the menace of black economy or lessen its extent to a minimum provided there is a firm determination on the part of the government and people in society. Although it is difficult to root out the evil when it has entered the psyche of a larger group of the people in society for a longer period of time, the civil society can put its weight on the righteous path through sustained efforts. A change in circumstances which gave rise to the evil can make a change in thinking of those involved in it. And liberalization and globalization in Indian economy since the Nineties have had a change in the situation.

The suggestions may be given on the lines of:

1. Rationalization of tax structure and removal of unnecessary controls.
2. Breaking nexus among businessmen bureaucrats and political leaders.
3. Making stringent laws for black money operators and those supporting its cause.
4. Check on political funding by businessmen and industrialists.
5. Reward to honesty and compliance.
6. Quick judicial awards to delimit delays.

The menace of black money originates in shortages and high to very high marginal rate of taxation. That was the case of the past. As the tax rates have come down in Indian economy and now the income tax rate is around 30 to 33 per cent from 95.5 per cent, the perception is changing. Further the Indian economy is growing at the rate of 8 to 9 per cent per annum in the past many years breaking its barrier of slow growth of three per cent of thirty years almost, a change is expected. With growing incomes there is scope to rationalize the Income tax rate to further lower it to not more than 15 to 20 per cent. The law should not be cumbersome as it is today. It was drawn in early sixties and has become dated. Why not make an income up to two lakhs free from any tax. An income up to five lakhs be under 10 per cent category. Similarly the income up to 10 lacks be under 20 per cent category and above it be taxed at the rate of 30 per cent. It is an old system of ancient India when Manu prescribes to tax 15 per cent of the produce of the farmer by the king. In the later period too that has been the extent of tax imposed by popular kings. If one sixth of the income is taken by the government there would be no grudge among the people. So should be the case with other indirect taxes. A lower tax regime would encourage its compliance and bring honesty in the system. At the same time it will root out corruption.

The next step would be to break the nexus among industrialists, big businessmen, bureaucrats and politicians supporting the evil cause. A large sum of black money circulates among these channels from clerks to the higher officers in bureaucracy who make favour to the businessmen.

Political funding is used to favour big industrialists and businessmen with policy measures which may not be in the interest of the masses and the general public. Black money plays a king maker's role in elections and then in government formation. The masks of welfare society, socialism and social justice used by various political parties appear farce before their real intentions to come to power to make money and enjoy the benefits of power.

While stringent laws and their strict enforcement are the need of the hour, there should be awards for the honesty. In a new situation in India where the persons in private employments are reaping a high to very high salary ranging between seventy thousands to a lac and above per month, a salary structure for the civil officers in Indian bureaucracy who come through a very hard selection process, ranging between ten to twenty thousands per month appears a mockery. Even in British Raj it was the opinion of one of the Viceroys that "it is not worthwhile for civil officers to give them more powers and let them live in penury". Many countries in the world award their honest officers immaculately and pay them a premium for being honest in service. This needs to be done to root out corruption from the bureaucracy.

Other suggestions ask for more raids and seizures on black marketers and black money operators and quick judicial punishments. People's cooperation may be sought in this regard where the neighbors may be required to report the matter to the appropriate authorities. The awareness is emerging in present Indian society towards zero tolerance of corruption and it is a healthy sign. Media's role too is positive in this direction in highlighting the things.

Many of the things will change in the near future with the sustained growth of Indian economy in the range of nine to ten per cent evidenced for quite a few years and alleviation of poverty and coming out of an age of sufficiency for the masses. As poverty is the root cause of many an evils, its alleviation may bring out a positive change in society provided we learn to satisfy ourselves with righteous means of earning our living.

PART FIVE: CORRUPTION AND DEVELOPMENT

7

Crime, Corruption and Development in Indian Economy

India is termed as one of the most corrupt countries in the world. At the same time, it is said India is set to be a super power in the Twenty-first century. While Indian economy is recognized as one of the less developed countries whose prime characteristics are low per capita income, low living standard, lower productivity levels and so on so forth its efficient manpower pool is world recognized. She is one of the largest suppliers of engineers, doctors and other technical personnel. Now there is a rush for trained engineers in computers and information technology. So where do we reconcile amidst these cross currents?

It is not only India but Transparency International has recognized China, Philippines and so many other countries of world as highly corrupt. Is upsurge of crime and corruption a global tendency? Is it going to be discussed at par with inflation—which at one point of time was recognized as a short–term local market disequilibrium phenomenon? Classicals never discussed it and even Keynes left it as one of the phenomena after attainment of full employment in his inflationary–gap analysis. Even then world economies faced and are facing both inflation and unemployment in most developed countries after the two world wars.

This chapter attempts to analyze the setting and crystallization process of corruption vis-a-vis planned economic and social development in India in the past fifty years. It seeks to answer the basic questions of development for what and development for whom. It also seeks to analyze the degeneration that has set in the country and attempts to find its ideological background. The developments in development theory regarding corruption is one of the areas of search. Briefly in the last sections it puts its impact on economy and attempts to find out the way-out in its concluding section.

The agenda of corruption is being discussed since Plato and even before him while discussing "sins" of the citizens. We have to recognize it as part and parcel of life, an essential truth, which emerges and had been emerging in the mind-set of people since ages. The point of discussion ought to be the sustainable level of corruption that a country could bear and the levels which are not reacting with proactive and productive forces of economy.

Leaving aside corruption for the moment we may take up the concept and meaning of development itself, which is changing overtime, as also the relevance of development for different classes of society. Development is a complex phenomenon that tends to resist analysis cast in simple, aggregate terms. Development economies, by and large, remains a "young" branch of economics, one which still grapples with the problem of finding a stable identity. As a result the focus of study has shifted, time after time, and old "truths" have had to be re-examined.

Defined in terms of aggregates or rates of changes in national production, to quality of life, to human development, to attainment of human rights and civilized life, to poverty alleviation, to gender justice and gender empowerment, to sustainable development, to social sector development and human face of development, to maintenance, of "core values" of society it has been encompassing concrete to abstract levels of longings, hopes and aspirations of different nation and peoples. Still the agenda may be unfinished.

Is development a tool for attaining certain ends? Then could we fall in line with Gandhi or Tilak in stressing or obvaiting purity of means and purity of end? This could only answer development for what and how. The third answer development for whom will automatically come then.

The development of a country depends on the ideology that she follows as also on the character of its people—the inner qualities and disqualifications of its citizens. These are two things. India had been intellectually superior or spiritual giant in the past, its Brahmins owe their allegiance to God and His realization to them dominated their thought process in prescribing a path of development based on "simple living and high thinking" for centuries. Indians least bothered for material acquisition and had given no weight to amassing wealth, for the higher thing to attain humanity. Relieving people of their sufferings. This had been in true sence the philosophy of life. They believed in karma philosophy—of cause and result, embodied in Indian way of life.

With the advent of Moughuls and the English and their cultural cross currents and moreso in the post-industrial revolution era the emphasis shifted towards material acquisition and "standards" of living based on material things of life. There was a changed prescription for alleviation of human sufferings.

Our emphasis of development shifted from wantlessness and minimizing wants to maximizing wants and how to attain new peaks of material acquisition.

At the cross roads in Indian history after our political independence we were confused over acceptance of value systems: whether Indian or western and students in universities and seats of higher learning ere taught lessons in line with western vision of development.

Nehru's ideological predilections and his vision of India, however, put India on a path of mixed economy. The objectives of economic planning and policies being attainment of socialistic pattern of society.

Nehru's socialist leaning was not out of context, in view of excellent soviet exploitation (of labour and consumers) as well as socialist regimentation which almost negated civilized values so avowedly fought and won through French Revolution and Lincoln's crusade against slavery.

Planning in India was intended, in the words of Government Resolution of March 1950 "to promote a rapid rise in the standard of living of the people by efficient exploitation of resources of the country, increasing production, and offering opportunities to all for employment in the service of the community."

In December 1954, Parliament adopted a resolution which contained the clauses: "the objective of economic policy should be a socialistic pattern of society; and, towards this end the tempo of economic activity in general and industrial development in particular should be stepped up to maximum possible extent."

It also declared that the "basic criterion of determining lines of advance must not be private profit, but social gain."

Article 39 of the Directive Principles of State Policy declared "that State's policies would ensure that operation of economic system does not result in the concentration of wealth and means of production to the common detriment."

The intentions were clear (although we adopted a western vision of development).

Now it is time to review the progress. How we performed? And where we erred?

Indian economy was divided into public and private sectors; public sector was assigned commanding heights and economy started growing through planned efforts. The overall rate of growth of GDP had been 3.7 percent per annum uptill 1980s thereafter is escalated above 5 percent.

Despite severe set backs in the form of three wars of 1962, 1965 and 1971 and droughts in late sixties the performance was not unsatisfactory, if not impressive.

However, due mainly to massive population growth, (which doubles the population in every 25 years according to Malthusian projection), in India most of our growth targets started belying hopes and a system of 'regulated economy' and shortages of food and foreign exchange which began after Second Five Year Plan contributed to a system of black money economy and degeneration of moral values started setting in the system.

It took some years uptill 1970s and then it got matured from an infancy stage of 1960s—the years of food crisis. The second element of development, the character and quality of the vehicles of growth, as mentioned earlier, now becomes important. We have to analyse what are basic constituents of character of people and in totality nation, and its driving force. And who constitute the functional part of the "people". The vocal among the people, the urban elite, the upper twenty percent segment of population, or who form important or functional part of people? Because it is he or they who speak takes away the (due or undue) share—the fruits of development. I mean to say, in this case in a free system (democratic) development share goes to them who form functional part of people i.e., the men who matter.

If we could define the basic traits of character we could get into its motive force and read the "mind-set" of the larger part of the people. We have to get into the factors which corrupt the psyche of people.

Defining "mind" which drives one to work, we can say it is an interplay of thoughts, emotions and intellect. Man is supposed to be superior to other living beings due to its development of mind. Brain is the physical counterpart though which mind works. Hence, it is direction of mind in a particular way through intellect or reason which makes man superior to other animals. Reasons contains emotional outbursts and that makes man superior and civilized.

Factors which made its people (most or few) corrupt over the years needs to be analyzed. It is amply clear that economic events cannot be explained in isolation and we shall have to find its roots in social and political developments in the country as well, during this period.

In India particularly since the "food crisis" in early sixties and beginning of rationing and control regime things started moving from had to worse. With rationing and control emerged black market system which started growing under "Inspector raj". Officials in power—the empowered ones—started misusing their authority. Such was the allurement of black or 'easy money' in the form of bribe that forces employed to combat corruption fell prey to corruption itself.

The lure to become rich quickly in a starved country like India has a 'demonstration effect'. We observe that while during the fifties only court clerks and octroi posts were recognized for accepting petty grafts, over the years almost all public institutions fell prey to earning easy money. Whether it is police, tax, municipal, public works, railways, electricity, telephones, forest department or even it is judiciary everywhere corruption pervades. We cannot single out the government department where it is non-existent.

There was a change in ethos. Society over the years legitimized and accepted it. Those who were indicted earlier in society for getting through corrupt means were exonerated and being powerful with money power became respectable.

This could not have been possible unless and until protection had been granted to the 'players' by the godfathers. Over the past three decades in every street and corners 'toughs' emerged protected by local mafias which again were protected by police and political godfathers. The local market of corruption later developed into state, national and international syndicates. We shall revisit the Indian scenario.

Recent works in development theory brought to light that in the Third World Countries of Africa and Asia the political system has started moving from democracy to Kleptocracy. Kleptocratic or predatory state has been defined as a political system where brigandage constitutes the predominant form of power and the ruler or elite are those who are specialists in violence. Economists like Douglas North even defines the state as a praetorian entity with a comparative advantage in violence and it uses this advantage to specify property rights in a way which favours the ruler and the group supporting him, i.e., the state easily becomes predatory.

Margarate Levi argues that all states are predatory in principle. It is only the existence of a number of constraints on government behaviour that prevents predation from being practiced in some cases.

With the criminalization of politics and increasing influence of money (black money) the Indian political and economic scenario since seventies present a picture of the above described predatory character where the ruler or the ruling clique uses the state apparatus to maximize his or its private net revenue. One of the main problems of a ruler or a party in such a state is how to remain in power, for without power these is no income.

Douglas North opines that one method of predation is the use of 'ideology' Typically ideologies entail norms and values which run counter to self interest, and what is more, ideologies are often created with this very purpose in mind: to make citizens of a country loyal to its rulers and their official proclaimed goals (seldom real ones). In this context ideology serve to make citizens do something contrary to what they actually want. A functioning ideology increases the legitimacy of the sitting regime in the eyes of the public. Framing the things in an ideological get-up can be easily done by the 'elite' which is subservient to the ruling class. The group of intelligentsia in and around the government machinery and administration can easily make the things 'presentable' and 'marketable'. The slogans of 'Garibi Hatao' in seventies Mandal divide in the name of 'social justice' in 1980s were all merely diplomacy of terms. The inner objective was clinging to the seat of power.

We observe changes in the politico economic scenario of the country in subsequent decades after the attainment of independence forties and fifties—the Gandhi-Nehru period—reflected a value system embodying Gandhian philosophy of sacrifice and selflessness. Obviously the freedom struggle was fresh in the mind set of the people. The policies were tuned in the direction of attainment of a 'socialistic pattern of society' and nation's well-being superseded individual's well being.

By the seventies many of the premises had changed and as a result of rationing and control regime developed a parallel system in the economy vitiating the value system of fifties and in politics during Indira Gandhi–Sanjaya era Criminalisation of politics started setting in. Disappearance of work culture in public sector and in permanent government jobs made the system sick. The country was swiftly moving from Gandhian self-lessness norm to a materialistic and 'self' before nation philosophy. The rat race for becoming rich by any means became preponderant. Obviously, the distributive justice was at a jeopardy and income and wealth inequalities began to widen. It was observed that despite the three four Five Years Plans around 40 percent of the population were below the poverty line. Equations started changing and society found neo-rich classes of industrialists bureaucrats and a few others flourishing with 'easy money'. Uptill now as stated earlier those with acquired riches by corrupt means were regarded condemned in the society. Later on society started accepting it and money and muscle power started dominating every scene. This was the time when old generation of people was replaced by next-generation who were born and brought-up in peace time free India.

Narasimha Rao period 1990's was marked with political corruption and scams. The very forces which started setting in during the earlier period were crystalised and plundering of nations' wealth became systematic. Many of the ministers, bureaucrats and those in power and positions left no stone unturned in fulfilling the duties of their inner self (Kleptocracy). In one of the discussions during a seminar one of the famous historians estimated that plundering of nations wealth during free India and those kept in Swiss Bank accounts far exceeds the wealth plundered by Mahmud Gazanavi, and the English. Had this not happened the country were not poor.

By now criminal-police-politician nexus has come of age and the infant is grown up. Black money pervades this nexus and, as said earlier, lubricated the estimated in 1953-54 by Nicholas Kaldor while talking of Indian Tax Reform that the size of unaccounted income was six percent of GDP or 600 crores. Wanchoo Committee's final report in 1971 put it at 4.2 percent. Rangnekar estimated it at 7 to 9 percent. Recently NIPFP has estimated the size of black money economy at Rs. 40,000 crores. Some opine that the amount involved is as much as 20 percent of the GDP of the economy. Suraj Bhan Gupta put the size of black money at over 50 percent of GDP in 1987-88 (1,49,297 crores). It is stated that the annual rate of growth of black money is higher than the annual growth rate of GDP.

Direct tax Enquiry Committee in its final report (1971) had recognized "Black money and tax evasion, which go hand in hand, have also the effect of seriously undermining the equity concept of taxation and warping its progressiveness. Together they throw a greater burden on the honest tax payer and lead to economic inequality and concentration of wealth in the hands of the unscrupulous few in the country".

Now we may look into the system that has developed over the years. As started earlier, crime, corruption and black income requires for its protection, proliferation and expansion a service of organization composed of musclemen, toughs, touts and brokers to combat the forces of law and order, on the one hand and on the other hand there are tax advisers, consultants and chartered accountants in the pay role of black money operators. Then there are contactmen who negotiate favours from top bureaucracy and political bosses through bribes of black money.

We may also look into this process from another angle. The politics of black money has eroded the moral fibre of Indian polity and society. Musclemen and criminals are fed by political parties to capture booths and thus elections are becoming more and more of a farce. National policies re, therefore, being bent in favour of the big business under there pressure of black money. Big subscriptions to party funds during elections is an example Thus, it is the parallel economy which does back seat driving (remote controlled driving), while the political leadership only acts as a mouthpiece of big business to justify the abolition of controls or introduction of dual system of price in the name of productivity or national interest.

As stated earlier too, the malignant growth of corruption in Indian is eroding value system of society. Virtues such as honesty, hardwork and sincerity are undermined. This has serious consequences for economy, political system and society. The virus has multiplied at a tremendous rate. In a recently concluded press meet one of the DGP's in U.P. remarked candidly about increasing political interference and corruption in the IPS cadre. "Honest police officers are being systematically sidelined while the corrupt are getting crushy postings", said the Director General." When I joined the cadre, only five officers out of 175 were known to be dishonest. They were singled out and ostracized. But now there is a dramatic rise of this tribe and this is cause of concern lamented he. "Law and order in U.P. is deteriorating over the last one decade and this can be attributed to social and political changes. The nexus between student leaders and criminals has contributed to this and politicians are also responsible for the phenomenon", he diagnosed.

Police patronizing criminals (and criminal activities) and then political leaders patronizing police and criminals through political interference in the working of combative machinery have become common practice. Researches have shown that many of the criminals themselves have become politicians. And many elected leaders and ministers have criminal cases pending against them.

Divided on caste lines since Mandal divide in 1980s the things have become more complicated. Parties for getting majority in elections have invited and given party tickets to known dacoits and there is a competition to outnumber the rival party by any means. Fro in a democracy it is the number and weight of personality that counts. Persons with higher degree of nuisance-value have high rating of eligibility in the matter. Recurrent violence in council houses of many states (whether it is U.P., Bihar, Andhra or Maharasthra) speaks volumes about the quality of incumbents and their culture.

The situation has reached to such proportions that every lucrative police post is auctioned, every lucrative seat in almost all the government departments are auctioned to biggest bidders. There are rates of appointment from peon to the higher posts. Every public department has developed percentage system. The contractor passes on the premium and gets the payment. System is smooth with 'honesty of thieves' in dividing the loot.

Even educational institutions are now not free from the menace. There are operating rackets from admissions to the award of degree. This is not to touch upon the fake universities and colleges running on donations. So called student leaders and corrupt officials and clerks of the Universities and Colleges in remote areas are live demonstration of admission to copying to degree rackets. Even Vice-Chancellors—the god of local academia—of many reputed universities have been indicted for being involved in money rackets and appointments scandals. They have either been arrested or vigilance enquiries are pending against them.

Politics is the best refuge of scoundrels, said a thinker. It makes one 'above law'—and immune to punishment. This explains why politics has become so lucrative.

Development of crime and corruption has have insurmountable impact on economy and society. First and foremost you cannot correctly estimate the size and volume of your own economic activities and therefore your policy formulations may be, in most of the cases, misdirected. Then, the scarce national resources being put in for poverty removal go waste in the 'leaking bottles'. The huge public fund diversion for the purpose in Plans is being usurped by bureaucrats, netas, mafias and middlemen flourishing on the corrupt system. Again this heavily hampers the equitable distributions of income and wealth. Inequitable income distribution again leads to social tensions besides economic tensions. Growth of crime too is partly attributed to unjust income distribution. This also explains why the lots of the landless, small and marginal farmers and those identified below the poverty line have not improved despite sustained planned efforts for fifty years. Was the planning meant for 'trickle down' or 'trickle up'? We can easily identify which classes have gained over successive decades and through what means. Hence, there is a need for a cogent incomes policy and tax system based not on recorded incomes only but on expenditure levels. The exercise has to be worked out by the government and ways and means could be suggested by the economists gathered here in the conference.

In the last section of the paper coming to the "way-out" we may suggest that there may be three dimensions of the solution. One pertains to ideological clarity, second related to strengthening the institutions which inculcate value system and prepare civilized and responsible citizenry for future and third concerns with the combative machinery and evolving systems which eliminate opportunities for corruption.

The paper has mentioned in earlier parts about the ideological confusion in defining goal of economic policies. And there it mentioned about lack of direction mainly after the acceptance of globalization, privatization and marketisation as economic reform measures since 1991. We know that India cannot refuse the pressure of international forces but atleast we can find out our own solutions to protect our national identity and people of the country particularly the common man and those below the poverty-line. Again the question to be answered is development for what and for whom. Our economic policies cannot afford for long catering only to 'elite' and upper twenty percent segment of the population.

Since the problem has emerged from the 'mind-set' of the people in India (due mainly to disregarding real Indian character and philosophy of life) hence the solution has to be searched there. We are living with Western ideology in formulating our economic system which will never suit the psyche of the people in true sense and is bound to be derailed.

India is a home of some major religions of the world. She has also democratic form of government. Both, people's involvement with religion and democratic polity, are major constraints on speedier growth. However, the rate of economic growth cannot be a true measure of well-being in the Indian setting. Development of non-material resources has also to viewed as a vital component of social advancement. This implies that India does not have to be in the market for full scale liberalization.

Just as our planned mixed economy was unique we will have to look for an alternative path within. 'Leaders of great nations cannot afford to be puppets'. Affirming faith in Socialism on the occasion of the recently held celebrations of the 50th anniversary of the founding of Communist China President Jiang Zemin spoke of "socialist modernization" emphatically repudiating *laissez–faire*.

In view of India's large cultural diversity and involvement of her people with religion and a value system bequeathed by an ancient civilization, her development strategy cannot avoid "explicitly dealings with values".

Solution to today's problems does not lie in either capitalism or socialism. Changes in the past fifty years and particularly growth in technology has recently led to a drastic redefining of the relative roles of State and Market and such a re-definition need not be a uni-directional retreat on an across-the-board expansion. World has seen the futility of either of the two systems and hence even in market economy countries national leaders are talking about the "Third-way". To quote Tony Blair, the British Prime Minister, "I have always believed that polities is first and foremost about ideas. Without a powerful commitment to goals and values, governments are rudderless and ineffective, however large their majorities. Furthermore, ideas need labels if they are to become popular and widely understood. The "Third-way" "is to my mind, the best label for the new polities which the progressive centre-left is forging in Britain and beyond".

"The Third-way stands for a modernized social democracy, passionate in the commitment to social justice and the goals of the centre-left, but flexible, innovative and forward-looking in the mean to achieve them."

It is opportune time for India, whose democracy is matured one, to rethink about the so called reforms and decide what policies would best conserve the contents of welfare state. What would be best way in the interest of masses? Obviously we will have to go back to the middle path of mixed-economy in its new form. Redefining the role of market and state and a new mix of the mixed economy is the need of time. The discussions in academia should be on this point.

And here again we will have to discuss the path of "rationalizing wants". Our scarce resources should decidedly go into the production of those goods which are "needed most" by "most people". In deciding and re-directing the consumption pattern of Indian economy we will have to distinguish between "legitimate consumption" and otherwise.

The next step in dealing with corruption and development issue would be strengthening the institutions:

where family comes first and next to it the schools (upto universities) where our young generation is prepared to face the world and make it on ideal place to live and grow. Many of degeneration that we find in society today is due to the weakening of these institutions. There was an old saying "as the kind so the people". Now it is "as the people so the king" for it is a democracy – the people's government.

The point here is what are the forces which are responsible for degeneration of these institutions. We may mention one among them the massive growth of population over the years. One of the Swedish Economists was of such and opinion that he had not awarded the university degree unless students believed that source of all the problems is population growth.

We visualize crowd and crowd everywhere in schools, in colleges, in universities, on roads, on railways, on buses, in hospitals. How can we compare Indian living standards with those of Switzerland and Sweden and compare with them in Human Poverty Index ranking.

Correct the atmosphere of homes and schools, the school of thought will automatically develop in right direction. We talk about student leader-criminal nexus and politicians patronizing them. Why we allow student Unions in colleges and universities at all? May be they are the democratic institutions. But is it the right place where they have set in? Most of the student leaders are indiscipline, ruffians and toughs. The more or excels in breaking glass-pans, furniture, burning buses, pelting stones on vehicles, intimidating and beating teachers the best suited he is for student cause. The students cause—to allow their admissions by obviating rules, not to attend classes, freely copy in the examination halls and if failed in the examination get a pass degree in connivance with corrupt clerks and officials of universities. Time has come when not only we have to discuss Electoral Reforms we will have to discuss the legitimacy of allowing student unions in Universities. They are the degenerating force (in society) under preparation. Why not reform begin there and salvage the universities and colleges to breath in free and fresh air?

Assess the role of electronic media in deciding their role in our cultural degeneration by invading our home frontiers. We may use and develop this institution in expressing mature public opinion and starting debate over complex issues. This has started showing signs in analyzing budgets, election and other things.

Talking about institutions we may explore the role of media in responsible investigative journalism and the institution of public interest litigations (PIL). It is a new invention of the past few years which expresses maturity of the public opinion. Hope in true sense lies with it and there seems to be light in the dark tunnel in these forms.

Our discussion must address the issue of judicial reforms in weaning out corruption from there and in particular evolving quick punishment system in cases involving corruption.

Again talking up political corruption issue we see no point in harping on improving the moral fibre of our leaders or exhorting our voters not to elect corrupt leaders. It may help to legislate that persons with a criminal record or an established record of corruption should not be eligible to stand for any public office. But beyond that, the moral fibre of a nation or group or a class hardly changes over the short-run, and if it does, it is only if our families became more principled and our so called saints less opportunistic and more gifted at persuasion.

The next dimension of the 'way-out' would be strengthening the combative machinery dealing with cases of corruption and reducing tax rates. We have come out of the phase of high marginal income tax rate. Three four years back they have been moderated. Still it needs to be reduced so that the allurement to tax evasion is reduced. People should not be burdened to the level where they revolt to become dishonest. To my humble suggestion income tax rates should be streamlined to 10, 15 and 25 percent for the existing slabs. What is required this to bring in more and more people in the tax net and as stated in the text earlier we should replace taxation on income with a suitable expenditure tax. So is the case with commodity taxation. This will go far in containing black money generation.

One of the basic psychological points in mind is that people with equal status are not taxed equally. It is only the salaried class whose income is reported pays tax rightly. The others equal to and above his income status in other profession either pay no tax or pay a meagre amount not disclosing their real incomes. Another point is why pay taxes at all, on hard earned income, when government machinery is corrupt and inefficient in catering the results and huge sums are wasted on uneconomic ceremonial pomp and show, wastages on politicians security and their useless foreign visits. Can a poor country afford for long their ministers, MPs and MLAs flaunting in luxurious air-conditioned class when most of the townships and villages are reeling in darkness?

We have to think how the combative machinery of vigilance and police be given more teeth in fighting with gangs, and mafia syndicates.

Now it is time to conclude and open this debate before academia. In the concluding lines we may suggest that we will have to develop a transparent system everywhere in administration and to remove corruption from offices we may take the help of technological advancement and put the data and record on internet so that it could be available to all and "babu-raj" be given farewell. Heartening example has been set by Andhra Chief Minister. We could also think in the direction of getting younger ministers, Chief Ministers and administrators replacing those tired ones living in past. We may introduce a bar of 65 (or 70 year) as it is in all public institutions and judiciary.

Our young generation finding no jobs here flee to USA and other countries of Europe. Why can't we stop this brain-drain of trained personnels? This enormous flow of human capital is not being utilized by us. If they can convert waste into gold elsewhere why can't they do it here?

Ultimately the responsibility comes on the shoulder of matured public opinion and persons in academia. This could not be done by only newspaper columnists. Universities have to come out in directing the country on vital issues. I conclude by quoting that

"Battle of Waterloo was won on the playfields of Eton".

REFERENCES

1. Douglas North in Lundahl, Mats, The Economics of Kloptocracy: Some Reflections on Under-development and the Predatory States, in *Development That Lasts,* Kartik Roy et. al (Ed.), New Age International (1997).
2. *Times of India,* July 31, 2000.
3. *India Today,* July 31, 2000, Chancellors of Vice, p. 57.
4. Manmohan Singh, H. K., Rethinking Reforms: Back to the Middle Path, *The Indian Economic Journal,* Vol. 47, No. 3, Jan-March 2000, pp. 19-30.
5. Blair, Tony, New Politics for a New Century, *Indian Fiscal Journal,* Vol. IX, Nos. 1-3, Jan-March, 2000, p. 11.
6. Reddy, Y.V., State and Market: Altering the Boundaries and Emerging New Balances, *The Asian Economic Review,* Vol. 41, No. 3, Dec. 1999
7. Gupta, I.D., Development And Environmental Imperatives of Sustainable Development: India's Options, in Satyanarayan, B. (Ed.) *Social Sciences and Planning for Sustainable Development,* Himalaya Publishing House (1998).
8. Patel, I.G., *Economic Reforms and Global Change,* McMillan India Ltd. (1998).

8

Corruption and Rent Seeking in Less Developed Countries: An Indian Perspective

Economic growth is dependent upon factor endowments of a country, the rate of investment, the capital-output ratio and the level of technology. Besides non-economic factors, e.g., the philosophy of life or attitude of people, institutional arrangements, political system and administrative efficiency are the important factors, which lay the frame within which development takes place. In brief, we may visualize it basically as an interplay among economic, social, and political forces and the institutional set up. How for these forces gain momentum or are deterred by corruption is the topic of analysis in the paper.

Corruption has never been absolutely absent from public life and institutions. But its proportion varied historically and geographically. It had been endemic in the system since ages like cough, cold and fever which showed some level of disturbance (disequilibrium) in the system to be cured by usual pathology and medicine, meaning there by that their remedies too were always present in the form of police, intelligence and judicial institutions. However, of late it has become cause of concern owing to deeper proportions and penetration it has taken in the system, infringing upon and distorting the institutions and forces of growth and development, in many of the Less Developed Countries where growth is the basic priority to remove poverty—absolute and relative—and establish social and economic justice.

Part one of the paper begins with brief observations of Kautilya and other scholars, the second attempts to analyse the things in economic framework, the third deals how even in democracies corruption is prevalent, the fourth attempts to know what went wrong in India, and the next tries to suggest the solution.

Four decades ago a political scientist Colin Leys asked, "What is the problem about corruption?" Following a line from Machiavelli, Leys argued that corruption has its functions, even its benefits. Under awful conditions, bribery and its close relatives may be socially and not just privately beneficial. Political Scientist Samuel Huntington remarked, "in terms of economic growth, the only thing worse than a society with a rigid, over centralized, dishonest bureaucracy is one with a rigid, over-centralized, honest bureaucracy".

Herein we attempt to look at the good and bad points of corruption from the viewpoint of economic development. For the purpose we take corruption in its rather limited meaning defined as "abuse of public power for private benefit". In other words it refers to a transaction between two individual or parties, in which a person with accumulated political and/ or bureaucratic power demands and accepts cash or some favour in return for rendering a service or showing a favour to another. Hence it may assume monetary or non-monetary form.

Two contrasting aspects of corruption and their role in economic development are observed in economic literature. One takes corruption as grease for the wheels of development machinery, the other regards it sand which disrupts the functioning of it. Several authors have pointed out that some corruption might be desirable (Leff, 1964). First, it works like a piece rate for government employees (a bureaucrat might be more helpful when paid directly). Second, it enables entrepreneurs to overcome cumbersome regulations. The observations are based on findings at different stages and span of time in different countries. The overriding message, which flows from the latter view, is that systemic corruption distorts incentives, undermines institutions and redistributes wealth and power to the undeserving. When corruption undermines property rights, the rule of law, and incentive to invest, economic, political and social development are crippled. Even Huntington pointed out that "a society in which corruption is already pervasive, however, is unlikely to be improved by more corruption."

The agenda of corruption and moral turpitude is being discussed since Plato or even before him. Dating back the fourth century B.C. in India Vishnugupta (Kautilya) stated "forty" ways of embezzlement by the government officials. His two oft quotations are "just as it is impossible not to taste honey or poison that finds itself at the tip of the tongue, so it is impossible for a government servant not to eat up, at least a bit of king's revenue". After analysing this human tendency of temptation he points towards the impossibility of detection by stating that "just as fish moving under water can not possibly be detected either as sipping or not sipping water, so government servants employed in the government work can not be found out (while) taking money (for themselves)".

Kautilya found out the root of corruption in human psychology wherein he compared human tendency with that of a horse, who appears to be noble and silent while pegged to a place but starts showing its true nature when attached to a chariot. So is the case with persons who, when not in job, appear to be honest, sincere and noble but once assured of a permanent employment and given reward start revealing their true colour (by assuming innumerable forms to abuse the power of authority).

Recent decades have seen the fallout of corruption on political and economic life of many of the top world leaders and even the economic system of communism is stated to have fallen prey more to corruption than to its inner or in-built ideological weaknesses. What to say of Ceausescu of Romania or the top leadership of Soviet Communist Party, Japanese Prime Minister and so on so forth? It reminds of the in-built social corrective system through its pervasive awareness or enlightened public opinion where consciousness is raised about the existence and harms of corruption. In many countries there seems to be a sea change in public opinion, as elections are increasingly fought in terms of what to do about corruption. Research is moving beyond perceptions of corruption to the studies of where in government and markets the vulnerabilities to corruption lie. We need to learn and do more in a next stage of anti-corruption activities. What can be done if consciousness raising and prevention have failed, if corruption has become the norm, and if political-will cannot be counted on? How can systemic corruption be subverted?

In economic framework we could conceive of a position of corruption in a demand supply or market analogy, where the man in authority sells public good or is a service Provider. We could think of two situations, one corruption without theft and the other corruption with theft. The figures one owe to Shleifer, A. and Vishy, R. (1993).

Figure A :Corruption without Theft

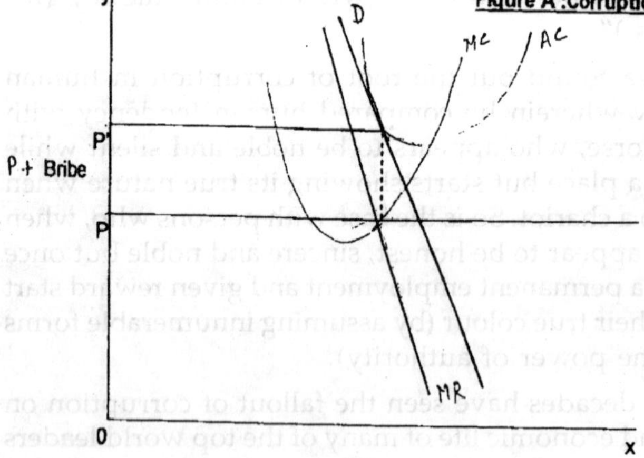

In Figure A, OP is the official price of the good. It is a monopoly market where the authority to sell lies with the public official who sets the price OP′ instead of OP. OP is the marginal cost to the official and given the demand curve D he gains a margin of P′ P as bribe. In the situation government receives the OP price and the rest is usurped by the official.

Figure B :Corruption with Theft

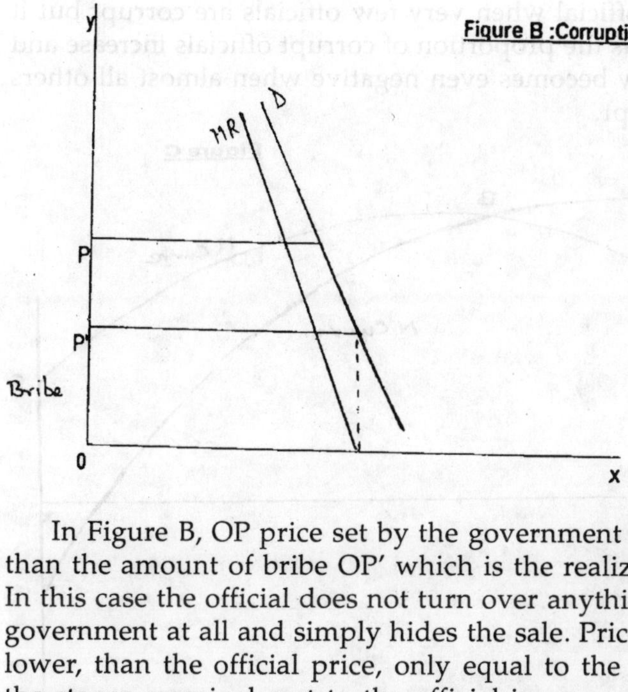

In Figure B, OP price set by the government is higher than the amount of bribe OP′ which is the realized price. In this case the official does not turn over anything to the government at all and simply hides the sale. Price may be lower, than the official price, only equal to the bribe. In the stance marginal cost to the official is zero.

We may also think of a situation where in a system of governance some people are honest and others corrupt. In the first stage only a few are corrupt then as time passes the "demonstration- effect" and other factors lead to more and more people becoming corrupt and subsequently corruption becomes systemic.

In Figure C (drawn after Bardhan, 1997) the distance between origin and any point on the horizontal axis represents the proportion of a given total number of officials (or transactions) that is known to be corrupt, so that the point of origin is when no one is corrupt and the end point is when everyone is corrupt. The curves M and N represent the marginal benefit for a corrupt and an honest official respectively for all different allocations of the remaining officials in the two categories. The way N curve is drawn the benefit of an honest official is higher than that of a corrupt official when very few officials are corrupt but it declines as the proportion of corrupt officials increase and ultimately becomes even negative when almost all others are corrupt.

Figure C

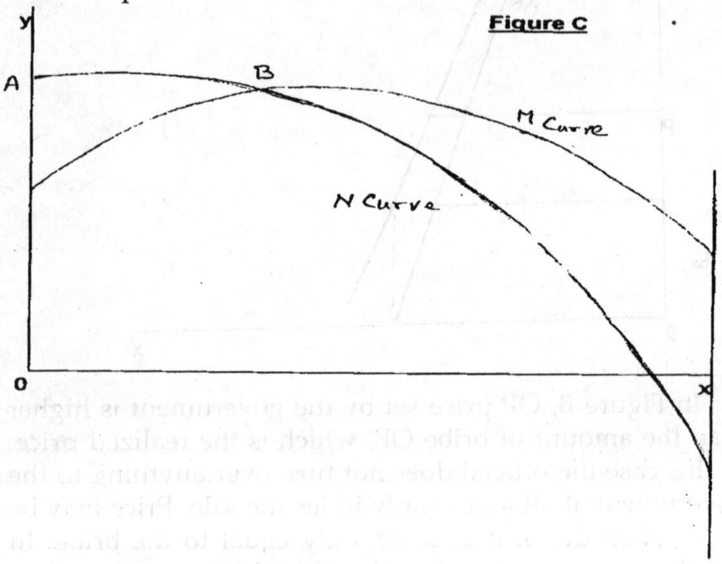

The M curve goes up at the beginning when more and more officials are corrupt (for, the marginal corrupt official lower reputation loss when detected, lower chance of detection, lower search cost in finding a briber etc.), but ultimately declines (when the size of bribe is bid down by too many competing bribers, for example,), even though at the end point the payoff for a corrupt official remains positive.

In the figure there are three equilibrium points A, B and C. A, and C are stable, but B is not. At point A all are honest and it does not pay to be corrupt. At C all are corrupt, and it does not pay to be honest. At B any given official is indifferent (between being corrupt and honest) but if only one more official is corrupt it pays to be corrupt; on the other hand if one fewer is corrupt, the marginal official will chose to be honest. So the initial conditions are important: if the economy starts with (or gets jolted in to) a high level of corruption it will move towards the high corruption stable equilibrium C; if the initial average corruption is low the economy gravitate towards the honest equilibrium A. The diagram illustrates in an elementary way how two otherwise similar countries (both in socio economic structure and moral attitude) may end up with two different equilibrium levels of corruption; also, how small changes may have a large impact on corruption if one starts out at points close to B.

The above analysis directs our attention towards the conditions in which the marginal official falls prey to corruption. Even administrations with relatively little corruption at the outset easily end up in a situation where majority of the public servants are corrupt. An important determinant of whether a bureaucrat will be corrupt or not is whether he thinks that corruption will yield a higher income than honest behaviour. The expected value of following a corrupt strategy is determined by the size of bribes offered, his salary, the likelihood of detection, the rate at which future incomes are discounted (the bureaucrat risks loosing his job), and the overall incidence of corruption (if caught by a colleague who is also corrupt, the bureaucrat will presumably keep his job, paying his colleague off). Provided that the cost of providing corrupt services to the public varies between bureaucrats, multiple and unstable equilibria easily arise and the economy may gallop from a low corruption situation to a state with a majority of the bureaucrats being corrupt.

Figure C directs our attention towards the fact that once the process of corruption begins with low cost (lower level of bribes) a positive change in it (higher bribe levels) may lure a large number of bureaucrats ready to sell their services (with higher costs). The economy moves to an equilibrium with a high incidence of corruption and even if bribe size is subsequently reduced, it may be impossible to revert to the low corruption state .The reason is simply that the temporary increase in bribe size has increased the number of corrupt bureaucrats and with that, the probability that civil servants will not be punished for illicit acts even if detected.

The prime reason for ascendancy from a low corruption to a 'high corruption level in India within the three decades is amply clear where conviction rate is only six percent, meaning thereby that in ninety four per cent cases the corrupt get acquittal for (manipulated) want of evidence. Rarely any heavyweight politician in free India has been convicted for any crime howsoever big it might have been.

In a state where corruption stems from top, a high incidence of corruption can be expected. Most civil servants act as mere agents for the ruler and the probability of detection is low. Punishments are only meted out if bureaucrat behaviour conflicts with the interests of those in power.

Systemic corruption begets vicious circle of "secondary-corruption" which affects most aspects of daily life in many Less Developed Countries. Customs and police officers demand bribes for more or less imaginary crimes. Courts pass verdict in favour of those who pay most. School children can not pass their examinations unless their teacher has received his or her dues. The personnel in state hospitals only cater to those who pay them directly, etc. All together, the transaction costs involved in providing public service increase, the efficiency of the government apparatus is seriously reduced and with that also the efficiency of private production, to the extent that the latter depends on such factors as public provision of infrastructure. The economy moves from an efficient low cost to an inefficient high cost economy. Indians today are paying more electricity charges, as also more often reel in darkness and face larger hours of power cuts, telephone tariffs are going up but most of the D Ps are ill maintained and unless one pays the linemen regularly he can not enjoy undisturbed services and so on you can add to an unending list of government services.

The prevalence of corrupt public administration has a direct influence on the behaviour of the private sector as well. Producers have to take corruption in to consideration when they plan their activities in a way that tends to distort resource allocation in the economy. In the first place, special resources have to be devoted to the development of "government relations". The public administration may be thought as a monopolist that supplies services only at a premium, over and above the non-corrupt price (Figure B). This adds to cost in private sector.

Inefficiency and theft in public sector (e.g. in railways in India) lead to imposition of ever new proposals for taxes and tariffs which further creates a market for "rent avoidance" with a higher rate of underhand price. In such cases it is cheaper to negotiate a "direct" settlement with the pertinent authorities. When the public sector is corrupt, this also serves as a more or less direct invitation for firms to seek a share in whatever rents are being generated by government action. Lobbying for special favours, e.g., protection easily becomes a more rewarding activity than cutting cost of production or innovation.

These situations entail distortions, since they make companies devote resources to DUP (Directly Unproductive) activities that make no contribution to the production of goods and services. The same is true of situations where power holders acquire a direct interest in production or resource ownership. In this case, both the public and the private sectors may find it convenient to favour firms related to the ruling clique even when this means paying a higher price or receiving a lower one than what could have been obtained in a situation of free competition. Clearly, the efficiency of resource allocation and utilization is reduced in both cases.

A country's level of corruption depends not merely on the potential for economic rent, but also on so many other things including the political structure. As corruption is closely associated with crime and criminals—(all the corruption may not be illegitimate)—it thrives on the strength or weakness of the state itself. How far its laws are unambiguous and clearly defined or in other words how far they don't leave scope for misuse or abuse of power, how efficiently and quickly corruption is detected and judgments awarded, what is the severity (cost) of punishment; the answer to such questions is related with how powerful the state is. When the state itself is weak and disorganized crime and corruption flourish unabated and in the next phase persons in authority themselves are involved in sharing the pie and they present a Bi-lateral Monopoly type of equilibrium. Where the relative strength of mafia group and state personnel decides the distribution of gain or market share.

In some situations we may conceive a state akin to "group equilibrium" under monopolistic competition in the (crime) market in which the corrupt as well as the state personnel form groups. The market is plus with dominating and other competing groups.

We may also conceive a situation of competitive bribery state where many corrupt officials deal with large number of citizens and firms. The corruption of some officials encourage others to accept bribes, thus creating the potential for an upward spiral of corruption.

In literature the prominent term used nowadays is Predatory or Kleptocratic state which is largely associated with dictatorial or military regimes. Harold Lasswel and Abraham Kaplan (1950) coined the term predatory state while Andreski (1966) chose to call it Kleptocracy. Kleptocratic or Predatory state has been defined as a political system where brigandage constitutes the predominant form of power and the ruler or elite are those who are specialists in Violence. In such a state the ruler or the ruling clique uses the state apparatus to maximize his or its private net revenue. Economists like Douglas North even defines the state as a praetorian entity with a comparative advantage in violence and it uses this advantage to specify property rights in a way which favours the ruler and the group supporting him, i.e., the state easily becomes predatory.

Margarate Levy argues that all states are predatory in principle. It is only the existence of a number of constraints on government behaviour that prevents predation from being practiced in some cases.

When the political power of a person increases, so does the number of opportunities to use this political power for illicit purposes. For from all politicians use this opportunity, but very many do, not the least in the Third world. Dictators in particular, who do not have to face an institutionalized democratic opposition, are in an excellent position to enrich them selves by abusing their public office. Stanislav Andreski has observed that in Latin America this has traditionally been "the surest and quickest way to wealth and more often than not the only way".

This phenomenon is in no way limited, however, to the western hemisphere; it has been a recurrent feature of political life in Africa, Asia and Europe as well. Rafael Truijillo in the Dominican Republic, the two Duvaliers (Francois and Jean-Claude) in Haiti, the Somozas in Nicaragua, Jean Badel Bokassa in the Central Mrican Empire, Idi Amin in Uganda, Mobutu Sese Saco in Zaire, Ferdinand Marcos in the Phillipines, Saddam Hussain in Iraq and all the Eastern European Communist regimes are only some examples of a phenomenon which is widespread both historically and geographically. Ceausescu's Romania was a case of "socialism in one family", with Nicolae and Elena at the top and other relatives below them.

Kleptocratic tendencies are not exclusive to dictatorial or military regimes they have acquired phenomenal proportions even in democratic countries like India which has been designated as one of the most corrupt countries by the Transparency International and other International Business Groups.

In democratic countries prolong period of corruption converts the state from developmental (or welfare) to predatory one. Politics begets power and power begets money. Hence politics becomes the coveted profession. One of the main problems of politicians in these countries is how to remain in power, for without power there is no income. In such an environment bureaucracy will virtually always be corrupt. There are various reasons for this. The most important one is that corruption is sanctioned from the top. Public offices are turned into rewards for political favours at the top levels of polity. Extreme varieties of spoils systems are created. When one kleptocratic clique is substituted for another in government this often means that almost the entire previous administration has to step down, and those who enter do so in order to take up paid sinecures, which in addition leave room for further income through private initiative. The entire public administration is turned into a mechanism for effecting transfer payments to its own members.

The election process too has little to offer as people have no alternative but to choose either of the evil incarnate, for during the process uncorrupt are eliminated by money or muscle power. It may also happen that uncorrupt or lesser corrupt once ejected start playing to the tune of time harmoniously, and the system moves on un-interrupted. Elections in such situations are fought by the parties or individuals on an agenda whereby "real" intentions are always never revealed and high sounding and appealing 'misnomers' or ideologies are created for the purpose. Usually ideologies are created to fight and win the elections, These ideologies entail norms and values which run counter to self interest and, what is more, ideologies are often created with this very purpose in mind; to make the citizens of a country loyal to its rulers and their officially proclaimed goals (seldom the real ones). In that context, ideology serves to make the citizens do something contrary to what they actually want.

Framing the things in an ideological get up can easily be done by the 'elite' which is subservient to the ruling class. The group of intelligentsia in and around the government machinery and administration can easily make the things 'presentable' and 'marketable'.

A functioning ideology increases the legitimacy of the sitting regime in the eyes of the public and there by reduces the cost of maintaining the loyalty of the citizens. Their behaviour becomes uniform and predictable. Rites, symbols and an efficient propaganda apparatus have to be created. Typically, cultural life—be it art, music or literature—as well as research, education and sports and popular and civic movements are all subservient to the interests of the regime. Examples abound in India and abroad. Be it 'garibi hatao' of Indira Gandhi, Mandal divide in the name of 'social justice' and the emergence of caste based politics or Marxist class theory, real intentions are to cling to power, more often than not for self-interest.

Sometimes the step from ideology to religion is not a long one. Evita Peron systematically worked on portraying her husband as a god sent and godlike ruler. Duvalier consciously identified with a voodoo deity: Baron Samedi, the guardian of the cemeteries. Macias Nguema suppressed the catholic church, substituted the slogan No hay mas Dios que Macias (there is no other god than Macias) for it. Kwame Nkrumah had the people of Ghana call him Osagyefo (the Redeemer). Indira Gandhi in India was taken as goddess Durga after the Pakistan war 1971 and many of the leaders of the day now pose themselves as messiahs of the poor and downtrodden *(dalits)*.

In traditional economic theory competition is good, when judged according to Pareto Criterion. What is usually not so good is when competition is shifted from the economic to the political arena, when instead of competing by means of low cost production producers try to outdo each other in lobbying for politically determined favours in order to avoid economic competition. Then we enter the world of rent-seeking or Directly Unproductive profit seeking (DUP) activities, where resources are spent for purely re-distributive purposes without yielding any corresponding goods or services wanted by the citizens in general (Bhagavati 1982).

In populous less developed countries where unemployment abounds and supply side pressures out compete demand side adjustments, sale of public offices is one of the common forms of rent seeking. In many Asian and African countries it is virtually impossible to get a government job without paying for it. In India, seventies onwards, every lucrative seat in almost all the government departments is auctioned to the highest bidder; every lucrative police post is auctioned. There are rates of appointment for different cadres of public office and a system of "percentage" has developed in almost all the offices involving monetary transactions. In such situations attributes like honesty and sincerity are discounted jeopardizing healthy development and growth of economy and society. In a recently concluded Press meet one of the Director General of Police in U.P. remarked candidly about increasing political interference and corruption in the Indian Police Service cadre. "Honest police officers are being systematically sidelined while the corrupt are getting crushy postings", said the D.G.P. "When I joined the cadre, only five officers out of one hundred and seventy five were known to be dishonest. They were singled out and ostracized. But now there is a dramatic rise of this tribe and this is cause of concern." Relating this to the law and order problem in the state, he diagnosed. "Law and order in U.P. is deteriorating over the last one decade and this can be attributed to social and political changes. The nexus between student leader and criminal has contributed to this and politicians are also responsible for the phenomenon."

Police patronizing criminals and criminal activities and then political leaders patronizing police and criminals through political interference in the working of combative machinery have become common practice in India. Researches have shown that many of the criminals themselves have become politician and many elected leaders and ministers in parliament and state assembly have criminal cases pending against them. Even Election Commission acknowledges it.

Even educational institutions are now not free from the menace. There are operating rackets from admission to the award of degree. Even the Vice Chancellors—the God of academias—of many reputed universities have been indicted for being involved in money rackets and appointments scandals. Not only this the situation has gone so low that even the Vice Chancellors are appointed according to their political affiliations.

What Went Wrong?

What prompted the country from a relatively lower corruption level to a higher one is an enigmatic question? Has the value system changed over time and more and more people decided to go the wrong way; have the things changed with the change of generation; have, the forces reckoning for economic development created avenues for short-cuts of material progress; has the leadership quality of the nation deteriorated over time and visionary leaders -are nearly absent; has western philosophy or development and information explosion' of new age paved way for consumerism and high living standard consciousness and ideals; has political development in the country during the last few decades given birth to new ambitions and aspirations in the politicians in the wrong direction?

Coining close to economic questions we find things like this: has development created a situation of jobless growth; has choice of technique gone in favour of 'capital intensive' and reduced employment elasticity of growth; why 'head count' poverty not been reduced and 'trickle down' not worked; are staggering unemployment and widespread poverty responsible for rising crime and corruption!

In social fronts we face questions like: has social transformation in free India given birth to new aspirations among different classes of society; have virtues like hard work, honesty, sincerity and the like become suddenly unrewarding; have people dithered away from the norm of "simple living and high thinking" to "high living and no thinking" stage; has demonstration effect in society generated signals for going ahead by fair or foul means?

Answers to these questions are not simple.

Line of demarcation in Indian scene could be 1967 election or early 1970s when the old guards changed. Though the Indian economy showed resilience in the wake of 'food' and 'foreign exchange' crises after the Second Five Year Plan the rationing and 'control' that ensued is held responsible for black marketing and black money generation. Food rationing created a whole chain of inspectors and supervisory machinery which found it easy to meddle with the rules and get easy buck. This could be the start of systemic corruption, which even after the food crisis was over after Green. Revolution, could not subside (refer Figure C).

Indian economy had been prone to disturbances. The refugee problem after Independence, War with Pakistan in 1948 ,the China war 1962, again Pakistan wars in 1965 and 1971, the two consecutive droughts in 1966 and 1967, and persistence of Inflation in the wake of two oil crises of seventies created avenues for those who had a tendency for fishing in the troubled waters.

In political circle weakening of congress party and its thinning majority after death of Pt. Nehru, rising aspirations of the farm lobby which gained materially as a result of land reforms and Green Revolution and their wish to share the fruits of power resulted in coming to power of Janta Dal in 1967 and in seventies. Let us have a quick look towards realities of economic development and progress of political democracy in India.

In the early 1950s, India was a role model for the developing economies and the optimism extended beyond those who had a dream for India. For some its mixed-economy was an answer to the challenges posed by communism in China, for others its strategy represented a non-capitalist path to development, for yet others who recognized the problems of industrial capitalism, India was on the road to their ideal of a social democracy arid a welfare state. It is another matter that by the-find 1960s there was a change in perceptions.

Soon it was realized that the benefits of planned economic development accrued mostly to the rich, while the growth process largely bypassed the poor. Available evidence suggests that there was a sharp increase in the incidence of poverty during the 1960s as both the absolute number of the poor and proportion of population below poverty line registered a substantial rise.

The political scenario that emerged during the time was characterized by two discernible changes. First, the ideology of nationalism had begun to wane. This was partly a consequence of the passage of time as the second generation came to the fore in the Congress Party. It was also related to the regionalisation of politics that surfaced because the central leadership, after Pt. Nehru was weaker. Second, there was a slow but steady erosion of the consensus in favour of any single party. It is possible in retrospect however, to discern a qualitative change in the interaction of economic and political forces in Independent India which surfaced around that time.

While economic development led to the distribution of gains in favour of the rich, that simultaneously resulted in a large number of population slipping below the poverty line facing exclusion from the market, the democracy required this very majority of the poor to vote them to power. Consequently, exclusion of the poor by market had to be reconciled with the inclusion of the poor by democracy. There was, indeed, a conscious attempt by the state to reconcile the process of economic development (in the form of poverty alleviation and employment generation programmes) with the compulsions of political democracy. How far the mediation help resolve the problem is another issue.

The management of the political process during the regime of Indira Gandhi had profound long-term implications. Winning Pakistan war 1971 raised the status of Indira Gandhi to goddess and she became unequivocally supreme leader of the country. However, this also turned herself into an authoritarian personality which was not consistent with checks and balances needed in a democracy. We find that even though the central government became stronger, the centralization of authority and power at the apex weakened the institutional base of the pyramid, so that the ability of the government to mediate between conflicting interests was much reduced. Next, the same culture spread rapidly to institutions and structures in the political process so that there was no room to dissent or debate within political parties. In this situation, the choice was to stay but accept authority without question or to leave the mainstream and strike out on your own. In the process many of the Chief Ministers lost their voice to dissent and became the yes man of the center or were removed and replaced.

It is good to have good politics and good economics separately but when politics comes in economics or economics (to be explicit money) comes in politics the things go worse. By 1970s the role of money extended beyond the economics of markets to exercise profound influence on the politics of democracy. To begin with, votes were purchased at the election time, not everywhere but in close contests or important constituencies. The practice spread. Those with money power progressively acquired an advantage, over those without money, in the battle of ballot. This created barriers to entry in politics, which are by now, formidable. It was soon realized that, after elections, even legislators could be bought and sold. If the price was right a legislator conveniently forgot the mandate on which he was elected and crossed over to support a programme, a party or a government, in direct conflict with the interests of those who elected him in the first place. It did not take very long for such practices to spread from legislators to parliamentarians. Soon it became a tool to stabilize or destabilize the sitting regime as is evident from infamous

J.M.M. bribery case under Narasimha Rao regime.

There are, of course, vote banks mobilized on the basis of caste, religion or ethnicity, but these can also be swayed in this or that direction, at critical moments, by the lure of money. Similarly, the scenario after elections, now when there is no clear cut majority and there is a state of 'hung parliament' or 'hung council house', is predictable as money-bags or suitcase with money descend upon state or national capital, to make or unmake coalition governments. Of late, regional parties galore is vocal where these parties with three or five members command respectable balancing power. Even one vote balance led to the fall of B.J.P. government in the center not quite long ago. Never before in the history of any country democracy had been at such knife-edge balance as it is in contemporary India.

In a country with mass illiteracy, particularly in rural India, transgression from money power to muscle power or its alliance is not far-off The uprise of local goons and mafias dates back coincidentally with the period of early seventies when criminalisation of politics began to surface. With the prominence of Sanjay Gandhi, who was given the charge of consolidating the Congress party another story began. Subsequent caste based politics started by V.P. Singh and others and the Mandal divide compounded the problem.

To sum up we can say once 'profit maximization' becomes an important motive for political acts or deeds, the conflict between economics of development and politics of democracy could neither be reconciled nor resolved. What comes out of it is the exacerbation of corruption nom normal to systemic proportion further giving birth to vicious circles of 'secondary' corruptions engulfing all walks of common life as described in the text earlier. In such situations democracy fails to contain corruption, for, its pillars had already been weakened by these very forces.

What is the Solution?

Yes every problem has its solution provided one has the

will and determination to do it. And the determination come nom the top leadership—the President or/and the Prime Minister—of the country. Further, the circumstances which gave birth to and fanned the things in the wrong direction had to be deeply looked into and analysed, particularly the weaknesses or the weak points of the system. The analogy goes to the Planchette where the invited spirit of the dead is always weaker than that of the Jiving being. Every corrupt system has its loopholes. They have to be identified first and demarcated.

We have already mentioned in first part of the paper about consciousness raising and maturity of public opinion against corruption. We have found that in many countries elections are increasingly being fought on the issue of corruption itself. Researches, now, are moving beyond perceptions of corruption to studies of wherein governments and markets the vulnerabilities to corruption lie.

But from where to start in India is a big question. Again we find that the compulsions of alliance politics in democracy deters governments, even good intentioned ones, from practicing 'general-will' or the political will owing to their delicate position and their 'short-termism'. Nayyer has talked about the long term impact of this short termism and used the term 'hysteresis' to explain it both in economy and polity. For long economists have presented arguments for imposing agricultural income tax, particularly on rich farmers, according to the 'ability-to-pay' principle of taxation, but no government, be it Congress, Janata, Marxist or Coalition could gather courage even to present it in the council houses or in the parliament for fear of loosing the mandate. But that is another issue.

Our analysis has shown that the start of the problem had been with authoritarianism, that is, the negation of democratic functioning, which silenced the voice of opposition and suppressed avenues of debates and independent opinions within and outside the party. This created a whole array of dummies and yes-men. The period was sufficient enough to have its long- term impact on the functioning of the party and the nation itself. And then the new entrants with no background of public work and even with shady backgrounds got hold of the positions in the party which was by then the single most largest party. This have had profound impact not only in eroding the image of the party but in ruining it to nought after the regime of the party supremo was suddenly over owing to her unfortunate tragic death meted out by her own guards. This also indicates, how the signs of the wan could not be read and people's voice could not reach her unadulterated due to excessive encirclement of her by the yes-men and coteries.

In our analysis, we find that those very forces or actions which were weakening the institutions or pillars of democracy then are also responsible for the later plight of the nation. We have no choice but to strengthen the democracy itself by strengthening its institutions in the true sense of the term. And their our focus points towards Electoral reforms under which it should be insured that persons with shady background and/or known criminal record could not stand for election be it of parliament, council houses, or local government as also they should not be eligible for any public office. Many suggestions could be given on this subject but it is not in the purview of this paper.

The war against corruption must be fought on the following fronts: one, as stated earlier commitment by political leadership; reduction of the demand for corruption by the private sector; reduction of the supply of corruption by the public sector officials; and finally, increasing controls and penalties for acts of corruption.

The war against corruption must begin with an explicit commitment by the top leadership of the country that it wants a 'clean government' and is willing to pay the price to achieve it. This commitment must be accompanied by visible action. Leaders should not only declare that they are against corruption, but they should be seen as not tolerating any form of corruption, whether it involves family members, political associates, other members of government. They must be particularly vigilant and strict especially vis-a-vis those closest to them who use their positions or their special relationship with the leaders to extract rents from the private people.

Political leaders in some countries, have not been considered personally corrupt or, at least, no acts of corruption have been traced to them, but they have, at times, tolerated (or at least have closed their eyes to) questionable practices by family members, political allies, and members of their government. These sins of omissions are as important as sins of commission. The fight against corruption requires that neither of these practices be committed.

War against corruption must start with the pruning of the regulatory framework at central, state and local levels, to eliminate redundant or unnecessary regulations. Attempt must be made to see that regulations that are retained must be unambiguous and clear and more transparent to reduce the possibility of conflicting interpretations. Also, if possible, strict time table should be set by which a given request must be accepted or rejected in order to reduce the chance that public officials may invite bribes by simply sitting on requests. The deregulation of economic activities which is characterizing the economic policies of many Less Developed Countries, including India should in time lead to a reduction in the demand for acts of corruption.

The point that liberalization leads to reduction in corruption is borne by the fact that in India, we find, more exposures of corruption in the post reform period starting 1991. Narasimha Rao period which is said to be the beginning of liberalization at length, was itself the period of exposure of some of the largest scams. As the rigid rules led to inefficient economic systems and sluggish growth, liberalization and global competition may progressively reduce corruption.

Now it is being understood that widespread involvement of the government in the economy, especially when carried out with non-neutral and non-general instruments, creates conditions, which lead some individuals to want to bribe public officials. In other words, it increases the demand size of the corruption equation. However, as for equilibrium in the market to be attained, the other side of the scissor must be there. It is conceivable, as stated in the text earlier (part 2), that two countries could have the same instruments for government intervention, but one might end up with more corruption than the other. The reason might be that the willingness of the public officials to accept bribe could be very different. In this case, one reason for the difference might be the relative level of public sector wages and the status of a civil service job.

Recent empirical work carried out within the I.M.F. has supported what one could believe intuitively, namely that there is a positive correlation between the level of wages in the public sector and the level of corruption. Countries that have low corruption tend to be those where the status of a civil service job is high and these jobs are relatively well paid. In this case, there is less pressure on the public employee to accept bribes (to make ends meet) and there is a higher cost to them associated with loosing their government job. In some Less Developed Countries, however, public employees are paid so little that they are pushed, or even expected, to get additional income, either by having part-time second job or by compromising their integrity. In these countries, the low levels of wages are often also accompanied by little differentiation in salaries across the ranks which creates additional pressures for some employees and especially for those with more discretion on decisions.

Although the level of wages is far from being the only factor that determines the supply of acts of corruption, it is a very important one. We have examples in history where attempts to reduce corruption were made on these lines. In Imperial China under the Ch'ing dynasty district magistrates were paid an extra allowance caned Yang-lien-yin ('money to nourish honesty'). Klitgaard (1988) cites a quote from historian Macaulay's account of Robert Clive's attempt to reduce the corruption rampant in the British East India Company in 1765 wherein Clive planned for liberally remunerating the civil servants of the Company. Clive saw clearly that it was absurd to give men more power, and to require them to live in penury. He justly concluded that no reform could be effected, which should not be coupled with a plan for liberally remunerating the civil servants of the Company. Singapore and Hong Kong, in recent times, have followed an incentive wage policy for public officials.

The next line of action must be related to establishment of better controls and heavier penalties. The controls would be aimed at increasing the chance that a corrupt act will be discovered and punished. Heavier penalties would make it more costly for those who engage in corruption to continue to do so. This was the reason Kautilya prescribed constant vigil on the behaviour of government servants and awarded exemplary punishments to them who were found involved in corrupt practices.

Concluding Remarks

We have discussed at length the problem of corruption, from normal to systemic, systemic to secondary in the Less Developed Countries. We have also discussed the start of systemic corruption in India and its staggering proportion. We attempted analysis in economic framework of market and market price. We also attempted to analyse the interplay of political corruption and economic corruption. A brief account, of economic scenario in India, its planned development approach and the interplay of democratic forces, has also been attempted. The uprise of the 'expectations' of the general people, particularly the rich farmers after Green Revolution, to share political power and its aftermath, the rise of caste based politics, the compulsions of coalition governments to fight corruption, the impact of globalization in reducing corruption by assigning lower role to state in production process and freeing the economy from excessive regulations have also been discussed. But in the ultimate analysis we found that corruption could be contained through strengthening the institutions of democracy itself. It is only properly functioning democracy, which could lead the country towards freedom from corruption'. Non-democratic societies, without a free press and freedom of expression and an. independent judiciary, are less likely to be free from corruption.

It has to be understood that corruption lies in the human nature and its driving force is one of the six instinctive evil elements (defects) in human beings namely greed. Therefore, it is independent of the systems of economy or polity, it is ubiquitous, hence, with autocracy military or non-military (kingship) or democracy; as also pervasive with communist or free market systems. It is only the constraints within or outside the system that make the difference, for example, absence or presence of potent institutionalized opposition. While it is in-built in democracies, its absence in dictatorship makes the things worse. Hence military dictatorships—by nature—have the tendency or potency of high corruption. But even when democratic institutions are non-functional or weak, democracy itself could not deliver goods as is the case in India or other Asian democracies. Strong and vocal opposition in the west makes a lot of difference where democracies are founded on high literacy rate and maturity where as in the Less Developed Countries where mass illiteracy abounds democracy may function but not with fun esteem or vigour. However, as we have seen in recent cases in many countries the uprising of public opinion made the things to change and bow-down of corrupt in high places.

High regimentation, of military or communist system may not serve the purpose as the suppression of basic human freedoms, for long, for example, abstinence from comforts and a bit of luxury for the commonality of standard' of living, makes human beings to revolt as their basic nature desires not an arduous single line path but change, sometimes. This had been the reason that Ceaucescu and Marcos or Idi Amin were no different howsoever their economic or political systems differed. Demonstration effect of high living standard of the developed countries in this age of information explosion may never in all likelihood, let one's desire contained in the idealisms of simplicity. Thus rising consumerism is also one of the factors fanning corruption in the poor countries where demand is unusually made or kept high without any backing of rightly earned purchasing power. There we may consider or discuss the reasonability of one's demand in overall social context and scarcity of national resources.

We have to keep in mind that corruption originates not in any system but is an integral part of the mind set of the man himself And, therefore, we shall have to create conditions where we could keep intact the basic attributes of the people. It will take care of corruption itself.

Note:

An earlier version of this paper was presented at the Indian Economic Conference on the theme Crime Corruption and Development in the Indian Economy, at the University of Jammu, Jammu, India in December-January 2000-2001. I am grateful to Dr. Rameshwar Tandon, Professor Emeritus, Dr. Mohammad Muzammil, Shri A.K. Bajpai, Professors in the Department of Economics, University of Lucknow, India. I wish to thank my son Rajiv K. Gupta, Vienna, Austria for helping me in preparing this paper in its present form.

REFERENCES

1. Andreski, S. (1968) "Kleptocracy or Corruption as a system of Government", in *The African Predicament: A Study in the Pathology of Modernisation,* Michael Josheph, London.
2. Andvig, J.C., and Moene, K.U., (1990), "How Corruption May corruption", *Journal of Economic Behaviour and Organisation,* Vol. 13.

3. Bardhan Pranab, (1997) Corruption and Development a revision of Issues, *Journal of Economic Literature*, pp. 1320-1346.

4. Bhagavati J.N., (1982) Directly Unproductive Profit seeking (D.U.P.) Activities, *Journal of Political Economy*, vol. 90.

5. Kautilya, *Artha Shastra*.

6. Kltgaard, Robert. (2000), Subverting Corruption, *Finance and Development*, volume 37, number 2, The I.M.F.

7. Krueger, A.O., (1974), The Political Economy of a Rent-Seeking Society, *American Economic Review*, 64 (3): 291-303.

8. Leff, N.H., (1970), Economic Development through Bureaucratic Corruption in A. Heindenheimer, (Ed), *Political Corruption: Readings in Comparative Analysis*, New York, Holt, Rinehart and Winston.

9. Levi, F.T. (1985), An Equilibrium Queing Model of Bribery, *Journal of Political Economy*, 93(4):760-781.

10. Lundahl, Mats., (1997) The Economics of Kleptocracy, in K.C.Roy , et. al.,(Ed.), *The Development that Lasts*, New Age International.

11. Mauro, P. (1995), Corruption and Growth, *Quarterly Journal of Economics*, 110:681-712.

12. Nayyar, Deep (1998), Economic Development and Political Democracy, *Economic and Political Weekly*, December 5, 3121-3131.

13. Shleifer, A. and Vishy, R. (1993), *5 Quarterly Journal of Economics*, 188(3), 599-617.

14. Swart, K.W., (1980), *Sale of Offices in the Seventeenth Century*, H.E.S. Publishers, Utrecht.

15. Theobold, R., (1990), *Corruption, Development and Under Development*, Duke University Press, Durham NC.

16. Tanzi, Vito, (1997), Corruption, Government Activities and Policy Instruments—Brief Review of the Main Issues, in *Fiscal Policy ,Public Policy and Governance*, Shome, Parthasarthy (Ed.) N.I.P.F.P., New Delhi.

PART SIX: GLOBALIZATION, DEMOCRACY AND DEVELOPMENT

9

Democratic Policy, Governance and Development in the Less Developed Countries: An Indian Perspective

Polity as a science of governance is a system of managing the resources of the state to serve the best welfare of the people of the state. Polity and economics went in conjugation since the beginning. Kautilya composed Arthashastra, long back, which is a treatise on governance of the state affairs. However, as the subject of economics grew bigger, particularly after the Industrial Revolution and Classical's theorizing on various subjects of economics, Marshall attempted to separate this branch as Economics. Similarly political science too developed into an independent subject. The apparent dichotomy, notwithstanding, the close linkage between the two subjects can never be denied upon.

As to which form of the governance makes its subjects opulent and happy is being deliberated upon since the time of Plato and Aristotle. In the Indian history and literature there are examples of successful Republics in the more developed states like Vaishali, and Magadh. There are examples of several republics in Mahabharata, five thousand years back.

The subject matter of "good governance", to make fruitful and rapid economic growth in the Less Developed Countries, is still on the panel of discussions of the world forums. These areas are still suffering with deprivations and degradation, economic as well as social and political. As a matter of fact about two-thirds of the human race is suffering as a result of low level of equilibrium trap. According to the World Development Report 2000-2001 ' of the world's 6 billion people, 2.8 billion—almost half—live on less than $ 2 a day, and about 1.2 billion—a fifth—live on less than $ 1 a day, with 44 percent living in South-Asia.

Jan Tinbergen—the Nobel Laureate described the pitiable situation of the poor in his book *Reshaping the International Order* thus: " we have today about two-thirds of mankind living—if they could be called living—on less than 30 cents a day. We have today a situation where there are about one billion illiterate people around the world. We have nearly 70 per cent of the children in the world suffering from mal-nutrition ...we have a situation where in the Third World, millions of people toil under a broiling sun from morning till dusk for miserable rewards and pre-mature death without ever discovering the reason why?"

As to how to manage the affairs of the state so that almost all the persons of the population could share the fruits of development and could live 'a long, healthy and creative life' with self-esteem and dignity had been a question of search and research since ages. Which form of the government could bring the ideal or best results were discussed in Greece at the time of Plato and even earlier.

In the history of development of the state Kingship is supposed to be the oldest form of government since the beginning of civilization. The King was taken as not only the "God-sent" but the son of the God himself.

Later on Herodotus, Pindar and Plato recognized the difference among governments in the hands of one, a few, and of many. Aristotle's classification is more exact and has 'remained without essential change to the present day'. He classifies government on the basis of:

1) The number of persons who hold or share the sovereign power in the state.
2) The end to which the government is directed.

His classification is as follows:

> A state governed in the interest of all by one man is monarchy. If that one man or the absolute monarch governs arbitrarily for his personal benefit, this type degenerates into tyranny.
>
> A state governed for common good by a few is called aristocracy. If the aristocrats use their power selfishly then it becomes oligarchy.
>
> A state governed by the whole people for the greatest welfare is a polity. If, however, the majority of the people, realizing their distinctions, govern in the interest of the poor alone, the polity in its corrupt form becomes a democracy.

Aristotle believes that monarchy and aristocracy are the best forms of government. But taking human nature into consideration he is inclined to favour of a "moderate democracy" or polity.

Aristotle sums up the evils of the bad forms of government in these wor :: "Tyranny is a kind of monarchy which has in view the interest of the monarch only. Oligarchy has in view the interest of the wealthy, democracy of the needy."

However, Aristotle, living on this planet earth in 384-322 B.C. with a meagre population size of a few millions could have never imagined that two thousand and five hundred years onwards what could be the shape of democracy and its degeneration on this earth, beaming with a population size of over six billion.

While monarchy had been established in major parts of the civilized world for a long time, and agriculture was taken as the major activity for life sustenance in economy the Industrial Revolution and the modern era changed many of the perceptions of the intellectuals and the common people.

Economic objectives and political objectives were not separated from each other rather they reinforced one another in the later phase. And in actual practice they cannot be altogether separated as they represent different aspects of the personality of the same man. Karl Marx in his *Communist Manifesto* (1848), interpreting materialistic interpretation of history reveals that, " the material life determines the general character of the social, political, and spiritual process of life".

The Industrial Revolution gave birth to Capitalism and at the same time the Classical thinkers in economics formulated theories for smooth functioning of the system to the common welfare of the people. They advocated freedom from state intervention in the market to optimize the results. They denounced Mercantilist logic and asked for 'laissez-faire' or the least interference of the state in economic matters. In foreign trade the policy of 'free trade' was advocated.

Market economy system was developed by them to take care of economic decisions. As per the Classical thinkers a purely competitive perfect market, by optimizing the results can best serve the 'greatest good of the greatest number'.

Although industrialization brought tremendous change in the life style and living standards of the European economies and its people, at the same time the capitalist system gave birth to exploitation of the weaker at the hands of the powerful and the whole society was divided into two classes—one of the rich and the other of the poor. The concerns were expressed over anarchy of the market behaviour and its anti-poor instances both in the commodity as well as in the labour segment (market).

Marxism developed as a reaction to capitalist exploitation and Karl Marx developed theories on the lines of bourgeoise exploitation of the proletariat class and gave a revolutionary call to banish capitalism to banish poverty and exploitation. What Marx suggested was state control of the total resources of the country or the system of a 'totalitarian planning' and the government of the workers or the labour class. What came out was a Communist system of governance, that is, the government of the labourers or the labour party. The emphasis shifted to distributive justice and equality in income and wealth distribution. The state would be catalyst in the system. Thus the dichotomy between politics and economics was resolved in the communist system in a queer manner. In the system state takes direct command of economic resources and takes decisions of production and distribution.

Notwithstanding, its equality emphasis, by and large the communist system in practice (the USSR since 1917) developed into a system of regimentation. And it broke down owing to ignoring the basic human values of freedom and liberty, the right to choose occupation, living style and commodities for consumption from the market. With the disintegration of the USSR during the eighties the fall of Communism was complete.

The point of domination over the world resources gave rise to two World Wars within a span of thirty years of the early twentieth century. So, while the nineteenth century will be remembered for Industrial Revolution and a new insight into wealth creation and production away from natural and agrarian system, the twentieth century will be remembered for mighty clash of power in the form of two World Wars for domination and sharing the wealth of the other nations. As per the materialistic interpretation of history behind every event in history there had been an economic configuration.

Economic imperialism and freedom from imperialism had been the prime phenomenon of previous centuries. Political independence, during the forties and fifties, of many of the Asian and African countries from the Europeans brought out a new era in world history. While countries like India in Asia adopted democracy in polity and mixed economic planning in economics for development of the poor economy, the others took shelter in monarchy or the like in Africa. Peoples' Republic of China with its massive population adopted communism for transformation of the economy.

Later half of the last century with full networking of international institutions like the UNO, the ILO, the WHO, the IMF, the IBRD, the GATT and so on tried to establish an order, economic as well as social, in the post world war. However, the period also evinced a Cold War between the capitalist and communist forces or between the USA and its allies and the USSR. Consequently the world was divided into three worlds: the first world of capitalists, the second world of the communists, and the third world of other remaining countries having clear-cut allegiance to none of the above. They remained the gray areas to be attracted by both through its aid programmes and grants and military or moral support.

With this brief background of economic and political history, to our understanding, the following points emerge for discussion with regard to democracy and economic development or governance and development:

1. Can democracy better serve the humanity and raise the level of economic and social development?
2. Can autocracy, military rule or totalitarian governments, rapidly develop the backward economies through regimentation and could they prove better alternatives to free market functioning?
3. Could democratic transformation reform the African political corruption and kleptocracy?
4. Issues related with unholy alliance between economic and political forces in India and the degeneration of democratic institutions itself.
5. Issues related with transformation of erstwhile Communist States to market economy.

The paper will make an attempt to discuss the issues raised above with particular reference to Less Developed Countries of the world like India, Pakistan, Nepal, China, and Russia and other East European countries.

PART 2

Democracy—the people's government—is an evolution in the epoch of history, which best serves people's interest, as against the tyranny of monarch and evils of oligarchy. As per Lincoln's famous saying it is "for the people, of the people and by the people".

Democratic republics were highly taken as an ideal form of governance in the past. They are taken as ideal even today. For they care for the basic human values of liberty, equality, and fraternity. French revolution was fought for these values of humanity in 1789 and since then they are recognized as basics of the civilized society. The crusade of Abraham Lincoln against slavery and the consequent civil war in America (1776) had already given credentials to people's fight for freedom of man from man. Equality before law, and one-man one vote principle, the basic tenets of democracy, was unthinkable till that date.

With our Constitution makers during the pre independence period, the examples of British parliamentary system, Swiss parliamentary system or American Presidential form were on the fore of discussion. And an ideal mix was attempted in the form of Parliamentary Democracy.

That was the time when India was faced with gigantic problems of partition of the country, large-scale migration and settlement of the refugees, besides rampant poverty and war with Pakistan over the Kashmir issue. In reality we transcended a poverty-ridden economy with multiferous scars and problems. Normalization was not an easy task.

The ideological predilections of Pandit Nehru, the then Prime Minister, paved way for establishment of a 'Socialistic Pattern of Society'. Nehru was considered a modernizer par excellence and he attempted for planned development of the country on the pattern of Soviet Union with the help of vigorous industrialization. Land reform measures were introduced to take care of raising land productivity and alleviating injustices from the agrarian system. Zamindari abolition, ceiling on land holdings, providing ownership rights to the tenants, abolition of privy purses etc. were major steps to establish democracy in the country.

At the same time, the Non-aligned status of the country, with its massive population was sufficient enough to tilt the balance of political polarization in the worlds in favour of either capitalism of socialism. And India became a center of attraction for both the groups. While as a poor economy we were exposed to aids of the rich, as a populous country we were considered a big potential to become either communist or capitalist. A change to communism like in China could have changed the shape of today's world in a considerable manner.

However, the moderate path of mix of the economic systems with democratic pattern in polity became an ideal option for the country. And we started growing, though slowly, with our massive problems and setbacks for about three decades. The rate of growth of the economy is counted around 3.5 per cent and that of population around 2.5 per cent, resulting in a very sow growth in terms of per capita.

Had Indian nation adopted totalitarian planning for the economy and Communism for the polity could she have attained high rate of growth as attained in Peoples Republic of China of around 10 per cent per annum and had it been successful in substantially reducing birth rate and there by population growth, which is considered a big road block in rapid development, is still languishing in the minds of some intellectuals in India.

It is not that Communism did not flourish in India. The Communist party formed governments in West Bengal and in Kerala but the central lever was in the hands of the Centre and the guiding principle was not totalitarian but socialist democracy, therefore, West Bengal and Kerala could not become outposts of the USSR or China. However, despite a long communist rule in the state, West Bengal could not bring opulence in the state and still a substantial part of the population there live below the poverty line. West Bengal is still counted among the poorest states like Orissa, Bihar, and Uttar Pradesh.

Even Kerala, distinguishing itself in Human Development record with high literacy rate and health care could not surpass Punjab or Haryana in income generation.

Change over from democratically elected government to military rule in neighbouring Pakistan too could not banish poverty from the land and raise the rate of growth of economy to a level of sufficiency. It is noteworthy that taking population size, Pakistan is not even equal to a state like Uttar Pradesh of India. And even with such a small population the governance could not manage to set in the process of economic development in a span of more than half of a century.

The military rule in Pakistan has had spells of rapid economic progress but the benefits of the progress have not percolated beyond a narrow establishment. The military rule could not establish a well-equipped framework of development for industrial, agricultural or the services sector. Can Democracy do better in Pakistan in terms of economic growth? The answer is not very clear. The reign of democratically elected Pakistan Peoples Party too had not given better results. So is it the short-termism the villain or something else? So when we talk of good governance, the stature and vision of its leader besides the tenure becomes important. The records of human development, viz., the level of education and health care, the level of investment and the investment climate, level of technology development, too have their role. Economic development does not depend only on economic factors; non-economic considerations too are of great importance.

The experience of Nepal with Monarchy has another

story to narrate. Being land-locked and rich in natural heritage it is one amongst the poorest of the poor countries in the world. The infighting for Kingship and then fighting between Maoist Communist forces and the forces of the Monarch are taking the tiny country far behind the development path.

Russia and the other erstwhile Communist economies of Eastern Europe are in a phase of transition from Communist to a market economy system, after the breakdown of the USSR in the eighties. Soviet republic, which had erstwhile been a super power of the world, broke down in the name of 'reforms'. To our mind, the suppression of liberty and basic human values at the hands of the government of the Communist Party, neglect of the consumer economy, and inequality of income among the different cadres of the Party could be the possible causes of the breakdown besides the attempts of the Capitalist forces. And with this the era of Communism passed away having failed in history to create an amicable life of dignity and liberty for masses and fulfill its objectives of equity and equality.

It is not that in poor countries all are poor. Rather there are groups or a particular segment of the population, which match well in their life style and income levels to those in the developed western countries. Many of the industrialists in India are counted amongst the richest in the world. So is the case in Nepal, where Monarchy dominated establishment paved the way for prosperity for those in the center (of establishment) while others in the periphery are reeling in destitution. Ceausescu's Romania was a case of "socialism in one family", with Nicolae and Elena at the top and other relatives below them. The Dominican Republic during the era of de Trujillo provides another good example of a family enterprise.

The development experience of African countries, tell sad stories of Monarchs becoming kleptocrats. In Africa, the relevant line of division tends to be tribal, and within the tribe, kingship ties are once again a decisive factor, as in the case of Mobutu of Zaire, Tubman in Liberia in 1960s and Macias Nguema in Equatorial Guinea in the 1970s. In other cases, however, such as that of Porfirio Diaz in Mexico in the late nineteenth and early twentieth century, ruler security has been ensured, by allowing a wide and balanced group of interests to share the riches of the country.

In different areas of the under developed world, the rulers or the governments have developed devices to systematically employ their position to extract money and resources from the citizens without providing very much in return. The strategies to be developed and deployed are: how to exploit the population without being removed from office. The theories in economics (development economics) are in the making over such behaviour patterns of rulers be it in Monarchy or in other forms of autocracy or communist governments, boasting equality and justice, or in democratically elected governments. The underlying pinning is the same. It has been named kleptocracy by one and predatory state by the other resembling the same phenomenon as that of imperfect competition or monopolistic competition in the market in economic analysis.

While Harold Lasswell and Abraham Kaplan (1950) coin the word predatory state to define the phenomenon Andreski (1966) chose to give it a label of kleptocracy—defined as a political system where brigandage constitutes the predominant form of power and ruler or the elite are those who are specialists in violence.

Douglas North (1981) even defines the state as a praetorian entity with a comparative advantage in violence and argues that it uses this advantage to specify property rights in a way, which favours the ruler, and the group supporting him, i.e., the state easily becomes predatory.

Margaret Levi (1988) argues that all states are predatory in principle. It is only the existence of a number of constraints on government behaviour that prevents predation from being practiced in some cases. A predatory state is defined as one in which the ruler or the ruling clique uses the state apparatus to maximize his or its private net revenue. As a rule, predatory states are established in a step-wise manner.

In the beginning small groups constitute themselves for collective action to control a given territory for collective good. The territory controlled initially is likely to be small. Even small groups, however, have to face the "free rider" problem, and this bears directly on the creation of the predatory state, assuming that people prefer a higher material standard of living to a lower one. Thus, political entrepreneurs—people who for selfish reasons provide collective good to relevant groups—are likely to appear on the scene. These are likely to be those who have a larger stake in the establishment of territorial control than others. They are the typical chiefs (or Caudillos) who also easily respond to whatever special incentives the group is likely to offer in return for its organization and who take the advantage of what the situation may offer.

The next step in the constitution of predatory state is likely to be one of competition. The power centers established in the first round are all very local in nature and none of them are likely to possess any absolute advantage in the exercise of violence. In this process, different local power holders will compete with each other and coalitions will be formed which lead to the establishment of larger interest groups and domination of large territories. With the passage of time, obstacles to collective action are gradually overcome. Simultaneously, economic life becomes more complex. Transactions tend to be even more impersonal and division of labour increases. For this to be possible, a different type of credible threat of violence is necessary: a large scale one which can guarantee property rights to the extent required by a diversified economy. Then the last obstacle to the formation of large territorial units is overcome.

However, no guarantee exists that this will happen—least of all in the short run. The competition for power easily turns into a long and drawn-out one, especially if none of the contending factions is strong enough to either defeat the others or form a wining coalition with other groups. Groups and coalitions keep blocking each other. This was not only the case of many Latin American economies (during the nineteenth and early twentieth century) it is a living example of what is happening through elections in several states of democratic India today.

We cannot argue in an unqualified manner that democracy is a panacea for all the ills of polity and it overcomes the deficiencies of either monarchy or oligarchy, or for the purpose military rule. And also that the spread of democracy, with a viable opposition, free press, and independent judiciary can transform the economic future of many of the African, Latin American, and erstwhile communist East European economies and ensure justice (egalitarian distribution) and higher quality of life commensurate with high values of a decent civilized society.

Democracies may also degenerate to a level of mobocracy or "tyranny of the majority" and perhaps that was the reason that Aristotle calls it a perverted form of the government and denounced it. It is a system where head are counted and not weighed. It makes an intelligent and a fool equal. This is the reason that a critic calls it "a government of fools".

In economic theory competition is good as it ensures best efficiency through competition. But when competition is shifted to political arena for economic gains and an unholy alliance is created between those in politics and the influential people in economy and when instead of competing by means of low cost production producers try to compete away rivals through lobbying for politically determined favours in order to avoid economic competition the system enters the world of rent-seeking or directly unproductive profit seeking (DUP) activities. One of the main characteristics of the predatory state is that the ruling clique systematically devotes itself to creating and capturing rents of various kinds with the aid of the government machinery. In an economy prorogued with multifarious rules, regulations and red-tapism, the situation is ripe for such a situation.

PART 3

Indian Experience

India became politically independent on 15th August 1947. Establishment of Democratic Republic was the ideal form adopted for India's overall development. And India occupied a dominant position in the world with Prime Minister Nehru. Nehru, Nasir and Khrushchev were the stalwarts of world politics during the fifties. None stood against the towering personality of Nehru and his Congress Party commanded unequivocal support of the masses for about two decades. The atmosphere was abuzz with patriotism and nationalism. And every body had a dream for India's future. As a longest serving Prime Minister Pundit Nehru was in a unique position to shape the nation's destiny. And he did to his might.

As stated above in the text, problems were gigantic due to country's partition and subsequent large scale riots, large scale migration and the refugee settlement problem, war with Pakistan in 1947 over Kashmir issue, besides an exploited economy and massive poverty. The nation tried to cope with the problems and put it on the path of development with the help of planning.

However, after the death of Pandit Jawaharlal Lal Nehru in 1964, the central leadership became weaker. At the same time, politics in India, witnessed the first revolts of the young, manifest in the Naxalite movement and the stirring among the dalits. There was a slow but steady erosion of the consensus. The general election of 1967 established that electoral outcomes could no longer be taken for granted and that the Congress Party could no longer assume the support of the people.

At the same time, by early 1960s it was also realized that while economy is growing at the rate of 3.5 per cent per annum in real terms, poverty, particularly rural poverty too is escalating and the benefits of growth are not reaching the poor. Several studies of that time reveal that the deprived classes especially the people belonging to scheduled castes and scheduled tribes, landless agricultural labourers, small and marginal farmers, village artisans, and others in self-employment in the rural and urban areas remained throughout poor.

The sixties will also be painfully remembered for Chinese aggression in 1962, Pakistan war in 1965, two years of consecutive drought in the years 1966 and 1967, after the death of Jawahar Lal Nehru, which developed into food shortage of a massive scale, rising prices, large scale black marketing, and rising income inequality and so on.

The queer situation was that while economy ignored the poor, the polity had to count it for coming into power. What Deepak Nayyar says, "the exclusion of the poor by market had to be reconciled with the inclusion of the poor by democracy".

However, the new strategy of agricultural development, popularly called Green Revolution of the late sixties yielded results and in a few years economy became self sufficient in food. Green Revolution favoured the rich peasants. The emergence of this new class had ambitions to share the political power as well, and they stated deserting the Congress party, which was already losing its base, and new coalitions were formed. It was this that led to the defeat of Congress Party in general elections of 1967 in almost every north Indian States. Then there was a split in the Congress Party in 1969 and a separate Indira Congress was formed. The old Congress Party lost sight in the race. It is quite possible to discern a qualitative change in the interaction of economics and politics in India around this time.

Indira Gandhi, the then leader of the Congress consolidated the position and soon came back to power.

The 1971 war with Pakistan and its bifurcation and emergence of Bangla Desh, raised the status of Indira Gandhi very high in the Indian minds. However, the state of bliss could not last long. The economy again came in the grip of severe inflation due to the quadrupling the petroleum prices by the OPEC cartel.

The interaction between economic and political forces gathered momentum throughout 1970s and the scenario changed substantially in politics as well as in the economy. Nationalism and old values began to erode in the hands of the new generation, born and brought up in free India, by that time. Fertile ground was prepared by the state of crisis in the economy since the last two decades when regulation and control was evoked at a large scale in the economy to fight out shortages of essential commodities. Rationing and too much of control at the hands of the government officials paved way for black marketing and black money generation. And as the time passed by and the crisis deepened the size of the black economy became substantial.

By this time the role of money extended beyond the economics of market to exercise a profound influence on politics of democracy. To begin with votes were purchased at election time, not everywhere but in close contests or important constituencies. The practice spread at a rapid rate. Those with money power progressively acquired an advantage, over those without money, in the battle of the ballot. This, created barriers to entry in politics.

Soon it was realized that, after the elections were over, even the legislators could be bought and sold. If the price was right a legislator conveniently forgot the mandate on which he was elected and crossed over to support the party, which was in direct conflict with the interests of those who elected him. Soon the practice spread from legislators to parliamentarians. It became a known practice, if after the election there was no decisive mandate 'money bags' descended upon State capital, to make or unmake coalition governments. Regional parties with small numbers with them suddenly became important in the matter. These attributes now almost characterize the political system in India.

It is to be understood that "once profit maximization becomes an important motive for political acts or deeds, the conflict between economics of market and politics of democracy in neither reconciled nor resolved".

The following trends are evident in current politics and social life in India:

1. Polarisation around caste and appeasement of minorities in politics.
2. Black money and violence threat playing an important and decisive role in elections.
3. Rampant corruption and selfishness prevailing in elections and in later life in government.
4. Government administration playing hand in glove with the sitting regime to make them elected for plus posting rewards.

Waning of nationalism and prevalence of selfishness for the last three decades had been the biggest catastrophe for the nation. To day the Indian economy is a leaking bottle in terms of resources. And much of the leakage owe to the present political system. In contemporary analysis the concept of power has shifted to political power. As political power generates economic empowerment as well as social empowerment, it is the quickest and sure way to opulence and status. And in an economy where labour market is abuzz with excess supply of labour, particularly the educated unemployed—the most vocal segment of employment market—the situation is ripe for a switch over from economic market to political market. The outcasts of one market are the hero of the other market.

Political empowerment not only provides them with economic security, it also provides criminal security, i.e., security from being caught after committing any criminal offence. And the prevailing principle is, the bigger the offence the bigger the political empowerment. Hence the person on the top is most likely the apex offender (of the past), either economic or criminal or both. The political camouflage provides him all the security and power. Once the ruling politician is replaced by an equally competent other group, the other one attempts to unearth the history-sheet of criminal and economic offences committed by the person or the persons, it is termed as political vendetta and vilification. By the time any enquiry takes shape, the short-termism of today's political scene, throws out the present regime and then the earlier villain becomes hero of the day, and he in turn starts opening the files of the thrown regime.

As in the present political scenario in India, none of the group is clean enough and every party has its own heroic records of criminal and economic offences and offenders, the public is left with no option to cleanse out the system (criminals). It is only a matter of irony that one is supposed to be better than the other at the time of the election. And there is no guarantee that once the party with slightly clean image coming to power, its members would not run for looting the resources from the official treasury of the government, and the public. Swindling of public money is not taken as offence. And it is relevant to quote Chanakya here, who has found forty ways of swindling of public money by the government officials, in his 24th prakaran of 8th chapter in Arthashastra. And even if swindling is an offence there are no chances to be caught and punished as long as political "paternalism" is there to defend their own lieutenants.

As the legislators and the ministers are the supreme authorities to take care of transfers and postings of the executive machinery—the bureaucracy and the police—the chances of being caught rarely exist. And even if caught, the judiciary, which in itself is not so clean, as it is moved by 'power' (money or influence) rather than conscience in many cases, chances are rare for the award of punishment.

Rarely any big politician in the past has been punished in free India by its free Judiciary. It is a matter of record that in 94 out of one hundred cases brought before judiciary in India acquittal is granted for want of evidence. And as the judicial process is so long drawn out and public memory is so short, people forget the old heroes as the newer ones appear on the scene with bigger excellencies.

Economic policies and economic development are strongly influenced by compulsions of political structure. And probably this had been the reason that vast resources allocated for rural development, poverty alleviation and employment generation in the past several decades could not reach the targeted persons. The intermediaries developed in the system usurped almost the whole flow to make their own-self and family developed. The only development seen in the planning era had been the development of groups or particular segments in society who were near the power center of politics. While in the industrial sector the fundamentals of development too veered round big politicians. And big industrialists were the class who make and unmake the governments by their money power. As elections these days have become costlier affair, winning election on its own resources is rarely possible for a common man. And when there are donors to give large enough donations to party funds could it be possible that economic policies and practices would not be manoeuvred in their favour after winning election and formation of government.

To sum up we can say on the basis of the above analysis that it is a misnomer that democratic polity has the answers for the ills of monarchy or military rule or the oligarchy and it has the potential for facilitating and encouraging rapid economic, human and social development. Democracies too may degenerate to a level of kleptocracy as it has in practice degenerated in India within last thirty years or so.

In cases where public opinion is not informed and matured enough for want of education and knowledge, and poverty is all-pervasive and the country is reeling in unemployment and under employment, how can one think of successful functioning of democracy. It is the reason that Andréski (1966) says that "democracy can only function in a society which is relatively opulent and where privileges obtained through political influence are no longer indispensable for a decent life".

As a last word we can say that:

Man is the object as well as author of all activities and unless he is reformed the social, economic and political order of high values can never be established. It is not only a message for India alone it is a message for the whole world community.

10

World Economy at the Crossroads in the Post-Socialist Era: Emerging Issues before the Socialist and the Less Developed Countries

The objective of this study is to look into the world economic scenario in the post cold war era. The disintegration of the USSR during the eighties marks the end of Communism. The ideology of (capitalist) market economy system is now dominating the scene and the World economy is overflowing with the current of privatization, liberalization, and globalization. It is liberalization and freedom against regimentation and control. The air is in favour of 'Liberty' over 'Egalitarianism' of socialism, 'Efficiency' over 'Equality'. However, the transition faced by the erstwhile socialist economies presents a big challenge. The underdeveloped countries not subscribing to socialist ideology, too present similar challenges of unfavourable terms of trade, slow growth, poverty, inequality, unemployment and poor standards of living. The present paper is an attempt to analyse the factors behind these problems and suggest the remedy from the viewpoint of the Communist and the other Less Developed Countries of the world. This is so because the situation among the developing countries and the erstwhile Communist countries are almost the same. They all are facing social and economic tensions and are struggling with widespread unemployment and poverty problems.

Socialism emerged as a reaction to exploitation in-built in the capitalist system and its (free) market economy system which ignored the 'have-nots'. Besides it created an uneven distribution of income and wealth in favour of those who already had in the society. The Classicals legitimized minimum return to labour in the form of Subsistence theory of wages in order to favour the philosophy of maximizing profit by the capitalist entrepreneurs while at the same time propounding Labour Theory of Value and declaring that it is the labour content in the commodity that determines value. Karl Marx challenged this anomaly in theorizing and the then practice and in his Communist Manifesto (1848) called for revolution against the Capitalist system and the creation of 'surplus value' and exploitation. 'Workers of the world unite; you have to lose nothing but the chains. You have to win the world'. He declared. It was a fight against injustice embodied in the system. It was a fight against inequality in society. And experiences have shown that whenever injustices prevailed social and economic tensions generated and revolutions took place.

Systems fail and become obsolete over time as the reality keeps on changing. The fight against Capitalism took shape and in 1917 in Russia the regime was overthrown and Communist philosophy prevailed after the end of Czarship. Its initial success spread a message and many of the East European countries and others in the Asian world followed the path adopted by Russians. Eventually the USSR too was formed. It was central control of the (scarce) wealth of the nation against private ownership of resources. Planning was introduced which was a thumping success.

The situation after the Second World War was that of a run for dominance by the two ideologies by the two super powers. However, where as the market economy succeeded in giving results the 'regimented society' of the Socialists out of their misplaced priorities lagged behind on economic frontiers. Several reasons could be found behind the disintegration of the USSR besides the efforts of the US to weaken it, however, widespread poverty and discontent could be the major cause of disintegration. It is suppression of basic freedom and liberty, which appears to be another basic reason behind revolt against Socialism.

Nevertheless, issues remain before the transformation of Socialism to the New Capitalism—the issues of injustice, exploitation and inequality. The role of State in development has to be redefined. Whether it would be a producer state, a facilitator state, or a welfare state in the new form.

The Performance

Now a brief review of the conditions prevailing in the former socialist countries is presented. According to a study presented by the Hungarian Academy of Sciences*, the Gross Domestic Product of the former socialist countries rose by 4.5 per cent in 1988 and 2.3 per cent in 1989. The average annual growth in the 1980's was 2.9 per cent. It then fell by 4 per cent in 1990, and by 10 per cent a year in 1991-94. However, the whole area did not behave in the same way. The decrease was less in the Central East European (CEE) countries, where slow growth resumed in 1993. According to the European Bank for Reconstruction and Development (EBRD) data in 1995 GDP in the CEE and Baltic states reached 88 per cent of its 1989 level, but only 48 per cent in the successor states of the Soviet Union.

Industrial and agricultural production (and so national income) fell by still more. Industrial output decreased by a third in the 'Vise grad' countries (the Czech Republic, Hungary, Poland, and Slovakia), and by 50-60 per cent in the rest of Eastern Europe. Agriculture in these former socialist countries is producing about a third less than it was in late 1980's. Industrial and agricultural output has stabilized in Eastern Europe since 1993-94, but remains 20-30 per cent below its all time high.

Meanwhile the rate of inflation in most countries in the region remained in two or three digits even in 1995.

Real wages have fallen rapidly, and the number of unemployed is 15-20 millions, which mean an unemployment rate of 12-14 per cent. Household consumption has fallen by 20-25 per cent in each country.

Decidedly the countries of East Europe arrived at the transition with their economies not in healthy state and the recession, which followed, was not unconnected with the transformation of the economic model and heightened integration into the world economy. The probable reasons for such a state are as follows:

1. COMECON had different criteria of production efficiency from the capitalist market (e.g. due to lower prices for raw materials, often less developed technology, and special rules governing the international division of labor). When COMECON came to an end, most of the production by its members tailored to each other's markets became superfluous, which also affected the efficiency of production for the home market. The economies of scale decreased, and Eastern sales ceased to act as the cover for overhead costs.
2. The decrease in cheap raw material deliveries from the Soviet Union and the need to buy these on the world market instead caused the region direct losses of several billion dollars. Hungary, for instance, switched to dollar accounting on January 1, 1991 and the transfer of trade to western markets was even encouraged by administrative measures. This brought 20 per cent deterioration in the terms of trade almost overnight. The loss came to US $ 1.5 billion in annual terms, equivalent to a loss of 5 per cent of a year's GDP.
3. Uneconomic (or not directly economic) production had been maintained in order to safeguard supplies, and above all to prevent unemployment. Despite severe social consequences and high consequent budgetary costs, this was not continued during the

transition, as the emphasis shifted to maximizing capitalist profits.

4. Privatization has not stimulated production to the extent predicted by many economists. In many cases, firms have decreased production after privatization, and efficiency and profitability have declined. Only parts of the small business sector have expanded, which has proved insufficient to drag the economy out of mire in Hungary.
5. Eastern European governments, under pressure of liberalization from the international monetary organizations, tried to introduce a free-market model that existed nowhere in the world. The role of state as a factor organizing the economy under 'modern' capitalist conditions was ignored and undermined. The markets were opened, almost without restriction, to the products of strongly capitalized western companies, even though they were not always of higher quality. The promotional muscle of these MNC's left local producers at a severe disadvantage.
6. When foreign capital acquires (usually at fairly low cost) more important Eastern European companies producing for the world market, the real intention of the new owners in many cases is not to maintain production but to acquire market for its own product. So production at many companies that pass into foreign ownership has decreased, and several have closed altogether. Domestic products of foreign companies are increasingly displaced by products produced abroad, even though these are more expensive and not always of better quality.
7. Eastern European countries has no Marshall Plan type of avenue to support them in transition, as was the case after the second World War, and their economies succumbed to the heavy debt burden which has become a drag on the economies.

8. Consumer demand has sunk because of the rising unemployment, the considerable fall in real wages, and the differentiation of incomes that serves the primary accumulation of capital. This prevents economic recovery being generated on the demand side.
9. Declining individual and corporate incomes, coupled with tax regulations that allow non- wage incomes to be concealed, has led to a fall in budget revenues. Meanwhile budget expenditure is high, due to support for education, health services, art and science and so on. Social pressure makes these difficult to reduce. In many countries, the budget deficit is being financed by generating inflation, or by bond issue in some cases. Both these tactics tend to curtail domestic savings devoted to investment.
10. Investment for restructuring and accelerating economic growth is lacking, due to the siphoning effect of the budget deficit and unreasonable levels of foreign debt payments.
11. And finally, despite European Union integration, the developed countries remain very reluctant to open their markets to Eastern European goods owing to recession in the world market.

The natural, initial economic level of East Europe after the transition, as it integrates into the capitalist market economy, has been much below its previous level. The situation in Russia and the other CIS states has been far worse.

Recent Trends

After subdued performance for years together, however, global economic activity finally showed distinct signs of revival at the turn of the new millennium. The optimism about a buoyant global economy emanates largely from a turn around in the United States and the satisfactory growth outlook for emerging Asia, particularly China and India.

The International Monetary Fund's World Economic Outlook (April 2004) projected world output growth at 4.6 per cent and 4.4 per cent for the years 2004 and 2005, respectively. The Commonwealth of Independent States (CIS) showed distinct signs of improvement for the last few years, which indicates their economies are growingly adopting the new situation and have started performing. As per the IMF data, the performance of the CIS countries was even better than those of the other developing countries of the world. Russian economy too has shown resilience over the years.

TABLE 1
WORLD OUTPUT GROWTH

	Annual per cent change			*Projections*		
	2000	*2001*	*2002*	*2003*	*2004*	*2005*
World	4.7	2.2	3.0	3.9	4.6	4.4
Advanced Economies	3.8	0.8	1.7	2.1	3.5	3.1
United States	3.8	0.3	2.2	3.1	4.6	3.9
EuropeanUnion	3.5	1.6	0.9	0.4	1.7	2.3
Japan	2.4	-0.3	-0.3	2.7	3.4	1.9
Other Advanced	5.3	1.6	2.8	1.9	3.2	3.5
Developing Countries	5.7	3.9	4.6	6.1	6.0	5.9
China	8.0	7.3	8.0	9.1	8.5	8.0
India	5.4	4.1	4.7	7.4	6.8	6.0
CIS	6.6	5.0	5.1	7.6	6.0	5.2
Russia	9.0	5.0	4.7	7.3	6.0	5.3

Source: World Economic Outlook, volumes 2002 and 2004, the IMF.

Emerging Issues

Following issues emerge in the new situation:

1. Issues relating to Privatization and Decontrol, i.e., Liberalization.
2. Issues relating to free market economy and free trade (uncontrolled trade).

3. Role of State in the new situation.

Privatization of the economy is one of the most important aspects of the reform, taking place in the post-socialist countries. It occurs in each of them under different socio economic conditions. The intentions behind privatization has been, raising efficiency and emancipating the economy through private entrepreneurship, helping to create a competitive environment and reduce monopoly, establishing a powerful stratum of owners and producing a revival of investment, including FDI.

A study relating to the Russian economy shows that privatization in Russia has been remarkably ruthless and swift. However, among the disturbing features are fragmentation of property rights, a high level of criminalization, and the purely formal nature of much privatization of ownership. The bulk of the property transferred into private ownership has gone to the employees of the enterprises concerned, although a closer look at the quality of the property being privatized shows that much of it is too run down to attract other buyers. Where enterprises are making substantial profits, own valuable property, workers have often failed to win control against a combined onslaught by bosses, racketeers, share speculators and crooked officials.

The architects of reform sought to carry out the privatization project in the minimum time. Therefore, in most cases, the big sums of capital have been amassed in the shadow (parallel) economy, or through speculation, bribes and embezzlement. So persons closely involved in the shadow economy, such as corrupt officials and well informed enterprise managers, have come to hold the key positions in the economy.

One channel of privatization concerns the accumulation of individual's savings deposits and vouchers by financial institutions, where the situation and the patterns of property relations are highly confusing. Hundreds of voucher funds and investment agencies resembling mutual funds in the

West in name have sprung up to utilize the vouchers of Russians who lack confidence to invest on the stock market for themselves. However, they still have to pick the right voucher fund. In a number of cases, a fund has proved to be a bogus structure set up by criminal or near-criminal elements to take advantage of the lack of state supervision.

A look into the Russia's shadow economy reveals that it differs radically from its counterparts in Western and Eastern Europe. Some authors believe that the scope of Russia's shadow economy has been determined by conditions that arose under State Socialism. Others claim that the features of shadow business in Russia are determined by present conditions, the product of the model chosen for restructuring the economy and society. According to the Ministry of the Interior, there is an economic crime committed every four minutes in Russia. Of these, theft (including misappropriation and embezzlement) occurs every 14 minutes, crime connected with privatization every 19 minutes, cheating of customers every 35 minutes, and violation of foreign exchange regulations every hour.

In the period up-to March 1994 Russia privatized 9342 firms, Poland 80, and Hungary 140. By July 1994, about seventy per cent of Russia's enterprises were in private hands. However, the mass privatization project in Russia has degenerated, according to the study, into a momentous speculative operation, criminalizing the economy and causing unwarranted wealth differences in society. It further states that privatization has left an unclear picture of property rights in Russia.

The Russian economy erstwhile ridden with monopolies and fraught with shadow economy and criminalization under transition phase, unlike other countries undertaking large scale privatization, has seen very little revenue from the sales passing to the State exchequer. This has radically limited the state's capacity to carry out selective investment in modernizing the economic structure. Further, the change of ownership form has led to the elimination of budget financing for industrial programmes. This coupled with the high interest rates, has left many privatized firms in the dire financial crisis.

Marketization and Freedom in International Trade

Yet another issue arising out in the new era pertains to Free Market. In the Classical system it is the market that decides the basic issues of economy, that is, what to produce, how to produce and for whom to produce. It is the interaction of the demand and the supply forces in the market that decide these issues. The Classicals believed in the operation of "invisible hands" which bring about equilibrium in the market. Market, at the same time, in the Capitalist system, best allocates the resources in a free and pure competitive economy. The expansion of this logic extends to international trade where on the basis of the Comparative Advantage and specialization "free trade" (according to Ricardo) best allocates the resources of the world and thereby maximizes welfare. Obviously, Consumer is King in the market economy system. To maximize welfare, there should be no state or any type of interference and *laissez-faire* being persued in letter and spirit to best subserves the optimum.

Notwithstanding, the unanswered questions are that of "market failure" and of "good and bad" in international trade. Market failure is perceived as the inability of the market to optimally allocate resources over time, that is, for investment because of the "myopic" nature of markets. Besides, market always favours rich and discriminates against the poor. Downfall of socialism may be a case of "Government failure" to withstand up to the expectations of the people, but what about the failure of the market to cater the poor and the downtrodden. The question stands even in the capitalist First World and in almost all of the Third World countries of the world even today.

Those who do not "have" are denied entry in the market. They cannot enter the commodity market as they have no money in their pockets, and they are also denied entry in the labour market or employment market as they have no education or training and have poor health. This is how market discriminates the "have-nots", the poor.

Good and Bad in International trade

Ideas die hard. They live longer than warranted. Economic theorizing and consequently their policy prescriptions work in a certain situation. They become obsolete and unwarranted when situations change. And the situations change over time. That was the reason why the Classical prescriptions failed during the Great Depression of the Thirties. As, by that time the pure competition model had failed to comply with the reality of the situation. Pure and perfect competitions were no more as Joseph Chamberlin and Mrs. Joan Robinson declared independently through their works and brought to the public the reality of imperfect competition and monopolistic competition situations. When the master was no more where would stand its offshoot the "Free Trade"? And if we repeat the same logic today in the Twenty First century then we are decidedly at mistake.

"Produce whatever sells" is the theme behind the Market. But how the freedom in trade has led to tremendous growth of trade in "unwarranted and harmful goods" is a matter of enquiry.

In general, voluntary trade has major consumer benefits. But it is little naïve to assume that no policy intervention is required. The early history of domestic markets included egregious examples of "lemon markets", ranging from the adulteration of food to the marketing of snake oil as a cure for all ills. The rationale for creating food and drug administrations rests in the frequent adulteration of beer and bread back in the 1700s. Many nations developed market institutions to lessen the payoff from cheating. At one point India had 44 brands of non-steroidal anti-inflammatory drugs on the market and no fewer than 20 of these were products banned or not approved in OECD countries. In the 1960's one major study found that more than 25 per cent of all the over the counter pharmaceutical products on the market in the UK were dangerous, ineffective or useless. Faced with disgraceful market practices, The United Nations passed a resolution requiring the collection of trade names of products that were banned or not approved by countries for those products still being sold internationally (UN, 1985). The UN list contains no fewer than 12,000 trade names (UN 1995). The substantial volume of 'dangerous exports' is well documented in published consumer research.

The second threat is embodied in the huge number of counterfeit products traded internationally. Things were never as simple as trade theory expected. Knock-offs, copies and fake products grew at a phenomenal rate after 1980. According to European Report, (1992:6) the amount of counterfeit goods on the world market has grown by 1,100 per cent over the past ten years. According to an industry estimate, pirated cassettes account for 70 per cent of sales in the liberalized markets of Eastern Europe. Software piracy accounts for more than 20 per cent of the market in richer countries (more than 50 per cent in the U S) with lost revenue estimated at billions of dollars worldwide.

While some knock-offs operate to increase consumer welfare, others threaten health. The World Health Organization has observed that in some countries, counterfeit drugs account for 60 per cent of the market. For consumers, the consequences can be more serious than an economic loss.

From about 1990 on, technology has produced yet another threat in trade to legitimate traders and to consumers. The web has opened new window for those who intend to market fraudulent or unsafe products. It presents a lucrative opportunity to scam artists and sellers with miracle cures. The chuck wagon seller of snake oil has gone electronic. The probability of being apprehended for engaging in a scam is far lower on web. And nowhere is this more true than in the international dimension.

Role of State in the New Era

One among the emerging issues in the post socialist era relates to the role of the state. Whereas socialism heavily depended on the state to perform production and distribution both, to maximize welfare of the masses, and through total control over resources, the rest of the world defined its limited role as facilitator of the growth process. However, after the Keynesian revolution and in the light of the Great-Depression of the 1930's, expanded role of the governments was recognized to meet the challenges of widespread unemployment and put the economy on higher growth path. The State took over the greater responsibility of a Producer state and the role of budgetary spending was enhanced to meet the challenges of a welfare state. Indian statesmen and leaders bestowed the responsibility of the 'Commanding Heights' of the economy over its Public sector and the role of private entrepreneurs was to supplement the total efforts of higher growth rate. The situation of India and other developing countries are very similar to those in the erstwhile socialist countries, which remained poverty ridden and infested with widespread unemployment and low living standards.

State has played a decisive role in economic development of Japan. State has still to play a very vital role in the new era in the Post Socialist and in the Less Developed Countries—the Third World countries. It is not just a "police state" concept. The time has bestowed upon the State the responsibility to play a catalyst role in performing the duties of a welfare state—to raise the living standards of the people through appropriate income and wage policies and social security; to provide health care and education to the people; to provide efficient and cheap infrastructure—transport facilities, roads, power and communications; to safeguard its citizens from unemployment and destitution; to provide opportunities and empowerment to those who are denied the basic needs coverage; to provide consumer protection against egregious practices of trade and the market; to control effectively crime and criminals and save the interests of the civilized society; and so on.

Governments also fail. And then people want a change. But as Mrs. Joan Robinson said governments and markets both may fail but one's failure is no argument to favour the other in an unqualified manner. The civil society have has to find the solution then as to how make a better combine and make the systems functional and efficient. Government failure and its inefficiency has have disillusioned the citizens in many of the Less Developed Countries like India itself and that is the reason why privatization is currently becoming popular, besides other reasons, but the State has definitely functions to perform. The government failure is taken as failure of the regulatory state not only resulting in massive losses due to misallocation of resources arising from faulty investment decisions, but also from diversion of resources to "rent-seeking" activities because of the very regulations themselves. Besides, it may also fail to effectively control economic, political and other types of crimes to safeguard the basic interests of the citizens. For example, in Russia, as mentioned above, the conditions under State Socialism itself are held responsible for criminalization and mafioso manifestation in the country.

The Governments may fail as a producer state as the motivational forces under the government and private sector employees are very different but definitely State has definite roles on the lines mentioned above. It has to be powerful and alert in safeguarding the interests of its people from the market limitations and such type of freedom culminating to the level of anarchy. But it is as to how to improve the quality of the governance is for the civil society to consider.

REFERENCES

1. Bob Kerton, *Consumer Policy As A Strategy For A Sustainable Market Economy,* Paper presented in Conference in India International Center, New Delhi.

2. C. Rangarajan, Economic Reforms: An Assessment, *The Indian Economic Journal,* Vol. 49, No. 1, July-September 2002-2003.

3. Government of India, *Economic Survey, 2003-2004.*

4. Government of India, *Economic Survey, 2002-2003.*

5. Peter Farkas, Transition from the Socialist to the Capitalist Model, Working Paper, No. 67, Institute for World Economics, Hungarian Academy of Sciences, Budapest, Hungary, June 1996.

6. Svetlana, Glinkina, *Unofficial Ways of Expanding Private Sector in Russia,* Working Paper No.61, Institute of World Economics, Hungarian Academy of Sciences, Budapest, Hungary, March, 1996.

PART SEVEN:
SUSTAINABLE DEVELOPMENT AGENDA

11

Developmental and Environmental Imperatives of Sustainable Development: India's Options

The development dialogue in recent decades is moving ahead of quantitative aspects of merely 'more growth' to encompass the aspects of quality of life embodied in the Concepts of Physical Quality of Life Index and Human Development Index. In view of the problems created by 'over heating' in some of the industrialiazed economies and consequent alarm over depletion of natural resources and environmental pollutions and hazards visualised in the form of damage to ozone layer and resultant global warming the Concept of Sustainable Development has assumed importance. The Stockholm Conference. 1972 and the Earth Summit held at Rio De Janeiro in 1992 enlisted the growing concern of nations towards these issues.

Sustainable Development is broadly defined as that development which meets the needs of present generation, without compromising on the needs of future generations. In Less Developed Countries SD, before projecting on futuristic scale, should ensure poverty alleviation, provisions for clean water, air, surroundings and a wholesome life for the humanity. Sustainable Human Development should enable human beings to enrich and enlarge their capabilities not only in economic but also in social, cultural, political and administrative fields.

A concept of development which embraces the major economic and social objectives and values that societies strive for is being discussed for quite some time. For instance, Goulet distinguishes three basic components or core values, in the wider meaning of development, which he calls life-sustenance, self-esteem and freedom. Life sustenance is concerned with the provisions of basic needs. No society can be regarded as fully developed unless it can provide all its people basic needs as fooding, clothing, housing, health care and minimal education. A major objective of development is to-raise people out of primary poverty and provide basic needs. Freedom refers to freedom from the three evils of want, ignorance and squalor. It highlights towards health, hygiene, cleanliness and decent standard of living. Self esteem is concerned with the feeling of self-respect and independence.

All three of these core components are interrelated. Lack of self-esteem and freedom result from low levels of life sustenance, and both a lack of self-esteem and economic imprisonment become links in a circular, self-perpetuating chain of poverty by producing a sense of fatalism and acceptance of the established order—the 'accommodation to poverty' as Galbraith has called it.

Using the above concept, of development, we may answer the question like development for what. We can say that development has occurred when there has been an improvement in basic needs, when economic progress has contributed to greater sense of self-esteem for the Country and individuals within it, and when material advancement has expanded the range of choice for individuals.

The attempt in 1990 by the United Nations Development Programme (UNDP) at constructing Human Development Index (HDI) for each country in its Human Development Report attempts to give development a "human face". The dimensions and indicators for estimating HDI are chosen with a view to identifying the basic capabilities that people must have to participate in and contribute to society. These includes the ability to lead a long healthy life, the ability to be knowledgeable and the ability to have access to the resources needed, for a decent standard of living. The statistics selected to capture the above percepts are: longevity, as measured by life expectancy at birth, educational attainment as measured by combination of adult literacy and combined primary, secondary and tertiary environment ratios and the standard of living as measured by the per capita real GDP.

According to the concept of human development, income clearly is only one option that people would like to have, though certainly an important one. But it is not the sum total of their lives. The purpose of development is to enlarge all human choices, not just income. Choices, highly valued by many, range from political, economic and social freedom to opportunities for being creative and productive and enjoying personal self-respect and guaranteed human rights. In this way HD thus has two sides. One is the formation of human capabilities—such as improved health, knowledge and skills. The other is the use people make of their acquired capabilities for productive purposes, for leisure or for being active in cultural, social, political affairs. If the scales of development do not finally balance the two sides, much human frustration can result.

The exponents of HDI state that in conventional development theories economic growth models deal with expanding GNP rather than enhancing the quality of human lives. Human resource development treats human beings primarily as an input in the production process. Welfare approaches look at human beings as beneficiaries and not as agents of change in the development process. The basic needs approach focuses on providing material goods and services to deprived population groups rather than on enlarging human choices in all fields. By contrast human development brings together the production and distribution of commodities and the expansion and use of human capabilities. Encompassing these earlier concerns HD goes beyond them and analyses all issues in society—

whether economic growth, trade, employment, political freedom or cultural values—from the perspective of people.

Sustainable Development

To social scientists and thinkers sustainability of economic growth has been a point of search and research for a long time. However, renewed interest and, alarm caused by environment pollution brought into focus the agenda of "limits" to growth. The Club of Rome study by D.L. Meadows et. al. underlined the finiteness of our natural resources (in sustaining growth). This study projected population growth and also extrapolated the technological capabilities as they were observed over 1950 to 1970 period. Environmental pollution has become a global issue since 1960s. It first arose in the developed societies where affluence and high degree of effluents co-existed, where technology and economic growth defiled the atmosphere; discharged poisonous fumes ravaged the beauties of nature. The fouling of rivers, through 'the effluents of the paper, oil, sugar industries and tanneries, and 'smoggy' atmosphere caused by the thermal power stations were the first citadels to be attacked by ecologists, economists and socially conscious citizenry.

The alarm of the environmentalists resulted in the Founex report submitted in 1971 by a panel of experts to the Secretary General of the U.N. Conference on Human Environment. Subsequently in May 1972, a full fledged UN Conference was held at Stockholm to discuss plans for environmental preservation and it is said in popularizing the concept of sustainable development this Conference played a significant role. The world Conservation Strategy (IUCN, 1980) and the Earth Summit (1992), referred to earlier, places additional emphasis on the concept. The former suggests that "the maintenance of essential ecological processes and life support systems, the preservation of genetic diversity, and the suitable utilization of species and ecosystems" is needed to achieve "sustainable development through the conservation of living resources".

Historically, views of economists about sustainability of growth have altered over time. while Mal thus and Ricardo believed that supply side constraints would prevent sustained economic growth, a more optimistic, view prevailed by the end of the last century as a result of technological advances and industrial revolution. However, following the Great Depression, demand side factors (rather than production limitations) were seen as the main influence on economic activity and its sustainability. In the post second World war years during mid 1960s optimism prevailed. Mathematical neoclassical economists, such as 'Solow developed models in which there is no fundamental constraint to perpetual economic growth in more developed countries. It was, however, recognized that less developed countries would need to break out of their 1m" level equilibrium trap to participate in such growth.

Towards the end of 1960s a group of economists raised new issues: whether continuing economic growth in DCs is desirable (Mishan, 1967) and began to suggest, as stated earlier, that there were limits to economic growth arising out of possible global pollution from production and from depletion of non-renewable natural-resources especially energy resources (Boulding, 1967, Georgescu -Roegen, 1972). A number of non-economists also developed this theme combining it with the Ricardian principle of diminishing marginal returns and stressing the population problem (Ehrlich et a1; 1967, Ehrlich 1970, Forrester, 1972). Daly (1980) proposed that in order to ensure the longest possible period of survival of human race use of minerals should be restricted, a zero rate of population should be aimed for, and consumption per capita should be held to a minimum acceptable level rather than maximised. Gorgescu-Roegen (1972) suggested that actual human population may need to be reduced rather than stabilized to ensure maximum period of existence of human species. He bases his view on the Entropy Law of Physics. Economic growth relies on high entropy (concentrated) energy which it uses and disperses. Eventually the stock of such resources will be completely dispersed and no longer available for production. In his view unlimited economic growth is in principle impossible and there is no possibility of human invention making it so because of the operation of the basic principles of entropy.

The possibility of sustaining unlimited economic growth has also started to be questioned from an ecological view point, including the preservation of biological diversity. Much of economic production relies on biological or living resources. Not only are many of these resources being reduced in quantity or bio-mass, but species and varieties are disappearing at a rapid rate primarily due to economic growth and activities of man and increases in the level of human population. The loss of this genetic diversity could make it increasingly difficult to sustain production from domesticated plants and animals. In the past, wild relatives to domesticated species have been used through cross-breeding and other methods to circumvent diseases and other threats to domesticated species. If this 'wild' gene bank should disappear as a result of economic growth, economic growth itself could eventually become unsustainable. This is one of the messages of the World Conservation Strategy (IUCN, 1980) which also highlights other ecological or biological factors that need to be taken into account in planning for sustainable development, even if only relatively short planning horizon in considered. However, as suggested by Barbier (1987) sustainable economic development is likely to require simultaneous account to be taken of at least three systems, namely, the biological system, the economic system and the social system.

Barbier contents that sustainable economic development "is indistinguishable from the total development of society and cannot effectively be analysed separately as 'sustainability' depends upon the interaction of economic changes with social, cultural and ecologically transformations". Human ascribed goals apply in relation to each of these systems and must be taken into account simultaneously in determining a path or paths of sustainable developments. He suggests that goals in relation to each of these three systems must be:

1) For the biological system: maintenance of genetic diversity, resilience and biological productivity;
2) for the economic system: the satisfaction of basic needs (reducing poverty), equity enhancement, increasing useful goods and services;
3) for the social system: ensuring cultural diversity, institutional sustainability, social justice and participation.

Conventional economists have been very narrow in their approach for they have only taken into account of economic systems, he says. Marxist economists have had a somewhat wider perspective because they have tried to take account of both economic and social systems. Nevertheless, both groups of economists, in his view, failed to take account of biological systems in considering development issues.

In view of Tisdell (1988) Barbier's assertion about neglect of biological systems when applied to economic thought in this century by economists does have foundation but Barbier has not produced an operational concept of sustainable development. In particular, the issue of how trade-off between goals is to be, handled and the nature of interaction between the three systems needs more attention. Yet it is clear that an economic system that abuses biological resources and creates or depends on a social system which itself is unsustainable fill in turn become un-sustainability. The interdependence of systems cannot be ignored if we are to avoid the possibility of serious mistakes about optimal development policy.

Choice of Technology and Environment in LDCs

In the developing countries like India the issues of discussion are not limiting but raising rate of growth, poverty alleviation, illiteracy, unemployment and provisions of bare existence. Obviously in an iniquitous world economy divided by 'poverty curtain' the agenda for discussion would be different. Yet what is present for the DCs is the future of the LDCs in some respect. And hence the lesson to be learnt, in this phase of fast expanding communication of knowledge, trade and technology, is to avoid committing those mistakes which inflicted the industrialised nations most, viz., environmental pollution, and transfer of pollutive technology.

At this point the importance of Sustainable Development Strategy for Less Developed Countries is to be evolved commensurate with the needs and values of the countries concerned and not merely ape the west and import technology unsuitable to the country and people.

The problems posed by transfer of technology by the MNCs to the Less Developed Countries are well documented in the texts. However, little attempt has so far been made to take into account the environmental damage and abatement costs which are involved in TT to the LDCs. Such environmental costs (Economic and social) are involved both in the TT as well as in the transfer of final product. The relationship between TT by the MNCs, growth and environment can be represented by the following diagram. In the diagram quadrant shows he

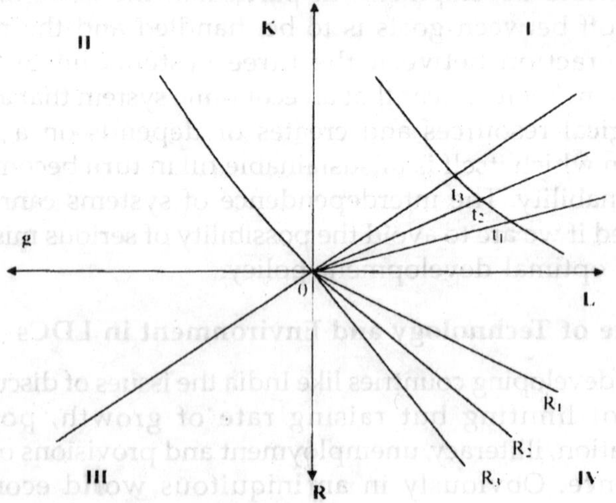

production isoquants against inputs of labour (L) and capital (K). As we assume substitution possibilities between labour and capital, isoquants are convex to the origin. This assumption is made because we must assume that some range of substitution exists in the technology imported by LDCs.

Technological progress and an increase in capital intensity will lead to movements of the kind shown in the diagram— e.g. t_1 to t_2 to t_3 in quadrant I. Quadrant II shows the relationship between output growth (g) - capital and an increase in intensity, the curve bending backwards due to lower productivity at high capital stock levels. Quadrant III assumes a linear, direct relationship between output growths and pollution (R). However, the precise nature of this, relationship is not always known. Quadrant IV postulates relationship between pollution and population growth (demographic pressure). In general, we can expect high population levels to be associated with high pollution due either to increased waste disposal in absolute terms (assimilative capacity being fixed) or to congestion type of externalities. However each capital-labour ratio in quadrant I is associated with a different pollution function since the amount of pollution is determined by the choice of technology as well as curve R in quadrant IV, t_2 with the curve R_2 and so on. The point emphasize is that an increase in capital intensity (without environmental safeguards) is likely to increase pollution (a social cost) and reduce the choice in favour of capital intensive techniques to maximise 'surplus' and growth. The size of social surplus is likely to fall given a rise in social cost.

It may be noted that technical progress could be both 'embodied' and 'disembodied'. The technological gap of, 'embodied' type between the developed and LDCs can be due to differences in the vintage of respective production functions; when the technological gap occurs even when the same amount of inputs say, L and K, produce higher amount of output in an advanced country in comparison with LDC, the gap is 'disembodied'. The 'disembodied' gap can be measured by observing the difference between the two iso-products as at a given L/K ratios. The size of the 'embodied' technological gap is given by the difference in efficiency of capital use in two countries. The 'disembodied' technical progress is usually reflected in superior knowledge better quality of management, administration and marketing and greater strength in negotiations and bargaining.

In our analysis, it has been implicitly assumed that the TT mainly takes the form of transfer of capital goods from the DCs to the LCs. Moreover, it may by emphasized that a TT which is 'disembodied', i.e. which consists of the transfer of knowledge or skill in rather unlikely to add to the problems of pollution. This explains why the transfer of 'disembodied' technology has not been taken into account in the analysis of environmental problems.

Sustainable Development and Agenda in LDCs: India's Case

As stated earlier the problems in the LDCs like India emanate not from 'over growth' or 'over heating' of economy but from 'slow growth', population pressure, mass illiteracy, poor quality of governance and rampant corruption. It cannot be explained only on the basis of economic parameters. We will have to analyses the things in a social perspective where value system of society, attitude towards work and philosophy of life governs the behaviour of a person. Any talk of sustainable development far exceeds the concept of only an 'economic man'.

When we talk of health of eco-system or SD in a country like India we visualise the threats arising from three factors: lack of development, the very process of development and the action of others.

Lack of development or 'pollution of poverty' is the foremost issue before the nation. Poverty is related with unemployment and under-employment which is due to high population growth (and consequent demand for food and work) and low level of productivity which in due course is due to lack of capital, low quality of population and lack of work culture and discipline. I Pollution of poverty' has a direct cause and effect relationship with the level of education. It is directly related with squalor and disease, which again is due to lack of knowledge (literacy) and income. Such type of 'vicious circle' cannot be broken only by economic factors and certainly it--will have to encompass social, political, psychological and institutional parameters as well.

Excessive population and its rapid and continued growth is a prime threat to sustainable development in countries like India. Every extra mouth must be fed, every extra body clothed and house and provided with minimal of health care and education and subsequently employment. At a minimum this leads to the immediate need to increase the production of food, fibre, wood and other materials. Since, like in most poor countries, there is little unused cultivable land left in India to expand into, this forces to rely on successively more intensive agriculture, and the consequent use of fertilizers, pesticides, and other modern techniques which cause increasing strains on the ecosystem and can, in absence of sufficient care, lead to a deterioration in the quality and nutrients of the soil.

The quality of water suffers from the disposal of large quantities of untreated human wastes, and the forests get denuded by being indiscriminately cut down to provide essential fuel and construction material. The demand made on such resources-termed renewable--are more or less proportional to the size of the total population. On the other hand, the lack of financial capital and the urgency of the problem often make it a difficult to protect these resources. It is in the poor countries that such a deterioration of resources most significantly jeopardizes the future health to the environment. Predictions of doom have often concentrated on the rapid depletion of "non-renewable" resources arising from high consumption levels, particularly in the industrialized countries. However, the loss of productive resources in countries like. India is potentially a far more catastrophic problem.

The production of waste, and therefore the pollution present, is also proportional to the size of population. At low levels of industrialization pollution arises primarily from the disposal of human wastes which have a high organic and bacterial content, and often leads to disease and ill-health. A second type of pollution, which is addition to threatening the resource base as described above, can lead to problems of toxicity, comes from the residues of chemicals used in agriculture.

High population density accentuate the problem, not only because of generation and disposal of large quantity of wastes in a small area, but also because the ability of the environment to clean itself breaks down. Thus, while the total size of the population is a major problem, highly concentrated habitation leads to still further environmental degradation. Problems of slums and fouling of atmosphere can be seen from any big city in India.

The second type of pollution is "pollution of affluence" causal-by technological factors and excess of growth. Industry, modern agriculture, urbanisation and means of transportation all produce a vast array of wastes, which when dumped indiscriminately into air, water bodies or soil, present hazards, not only to health but sometimes to life itself. Toxic gases and smoke in the atmosphere, pesticide residues and dangerous chemicals in water sources, excess salinity in the soil are just a few examples of the pollution problems being faced today in the industrialized countries like Japan, the U.S.A and Western Europe. They are also present in newly industrializing developing countries like India.

The largest body of literature on the 'trade-off between economics and ecology' has emanated in recent years from these countries. According to an estimate U.S.A.'s 210 million people and their highly productive system use more resources and do more damage to the environment than the 2.5 billion inhabitants of the less developed countries.

As one writer puts it "the Americans are sheathed in the mass energy nimbus which produces paper, plastics, ash, soot, dust, sludge, slag and fume which on a per capita basis exceeds by many times an individual person's own bodily wastes".

According to a study there is hardly any fresh water lakes or rivers worth the name. "Garbage flows, and the effluents of industrial activity have effectively ensured that the waters are fresh only in nomenclature. The prairies have been polluted by overdose of pesticides. There is, in fact, the entire mix of air, land, and water polluted coupled with eternal jet engine noise." To use a Galbraith phase, in the cities "private effluence coexists with public squalor".

Alvin Toffler remarks, "pesticides and herbicides filter into our foods. Twisted automobile carcasses, aluminum cans, non-returnable glass bottles and synthetic plastic form intense kitchen middens in our midst as more and more of our detritus resists decay".

In Japan, according to a study air pollution in many towns is very serious. Tokyo has a perpetually thick petrochemical smog. The small scale metal processing industries handled poisonous substances like cyanogen and chrome without treating the waste water. Apart from Itai Itai and Minimata diseases food pollution also resulted from Polychlorinated Biphenyl (PCB).

To quote a *Newsweek* study "everyday Italy dumps more than 2000 tones of toxic titanium-soaked mud, 178 tonnes of phosphorus and 44 tones of nitrogen into the mediterranean the result of all this pollution is a steady backup of toxies, hydrocarbons, and particles that are throttling the mediterranean at a terrifying pace".

Big cities and industrial towns in India; present similar problems of slum, garbage, noise and air pollution created by automobiles and smoking chimneys. Effluents emanating from tanneries and sewage disposal has polluted the rivers.

Thirdly, one of the basic threats to humanity is from nuclear pollution. Enormous nuclear tests by bigger countries is a direct cause-of global warming, and derailment of eco system. Nuclear non-proliferation treaty and ultimately nuclear weapon free world is the only solution of the problem.

Policy Prescription and Conclusion

Indian economy in the phase of globalisation, marketisation and privatisation since 1991 has given rise to new controversies by importing materialistic philosophy of consumerism and diluting with the 'order' of Nehru-Mahalanobis model of development based on public sector primacy for developing and maintaining core sector of the economy. Under the massive pressure of large unemployment, mass poverty and slow rate of growth disenchantment with planning arose by the 1980s. Mounting losses in public sector undertakings arising out of weaknesses of decision-making and disappearance of work culture among those in; permanent employment and lack of discipline gave rise to a self-defeating new culture in Indian society.

Another contributory factor for globalization came from external sources. The disintegration of the U.S.S.R.—the citadel of planning and socialism—and emergence of the U.S. as a single superpower brought in the renewed era of capitalist philosophy of market economy and supremacy of private entrepreneurship. Then propagation of the philosophy of globalisation has been a natural outcome to let the industrialised countries of West enter the giant Asian economies to ease their own pressure of unemployment and stagnating growth.

Internal as well as external compulsions and the intellectual kick-backs' led the Indian leaders which were not of the genre of their earlier counter part like Nehru and Gandhi and were Jacking in foresight and strong will—succumb to the external pressures of the DCs and their ally agencies Fund-Bank WTO.

The opening of the Indian economy has, no answers to the perennial questions of capitalistic exploitation of consumers and labour. Arid then the basic questions are still unanswered producing for whom. And what type of goods and services to be produced? To whom, the new form of planning is going to cater? To top 10 per cent or 20 per cent of the population or to lowest 20 or 40 per cent or to middle 30 percent? Have we not lost in the quagmire?

Decidedly the 'new planning' appears to have lost direction in deciding to whom it is going to cater—to 'classes' or to 'masses'. The Jaguars, the Cieloes, the Mercedes, the Esteems, are catering to whom and what in the philosophy behind it when country is suffering resource crunch and burgeoning petroleum import bill is raising the cost of energy and living? Can we afford this luxury?

Development 'for what' and 'for whom' becomes the most relevant questions at this juncture of the economy. Do not we need some kind of discipline in decision making and direction of the economy?

The criterion should decidedly be based on rational principles of whether "most people" can get what they "need most" within the limits of material resources available. In deciding and redirecting the consumption pattern of Indian economy we will have to distinguish between "legitimate consumption" and otherwise.

From a social point of view too "economic philosophy" is not sustainable. By perpetuating inequalities it is going to disturb the social fibre and generate social tensions (echoed in the form of abductions, loot, dacoities, murders, militancy and naxalism).

On the basis of above analysis we may draw certain conclusions. For India. For sustainable development we need a comprehensive strategy.

1. First and foremost the country needs to raise the rate of GNP growth to around 7-8 per cent, to bring out about 30-40 per cent of the people living below poverty line out of primary poverty, without compromising on the environmental front.

2. Limiting the rate of growth of population is a matter of utmost urgency. This may be done through deliberate decline in the birth rate either through educating the couples in reproductive age group or through a package of coercive methods to bring it down at the rate achieved in China.

3. Efforts should be made to improve the quality of population through mass literacy programmes so as to inculcate awareness towards pollution of poverty and population. Awareness towards the ills of unhygienic atmosphere, unclean water and air should form part of the programme.

   Investment in human capital and proper utilization of the available human and non-human resources of the country will go a long way in raising productivity and bestowing refinements in living standards of the people. By making a civilized citizenry most of the environmental problems can automatically be taken care of and avoided.

4. Production of non-necessary consumer goods and copying the western consumerist life-style should not be encouraged so that scarce resources of the country could be utilised for production of "most desirable" consumer goods and services for the masses.

5. Import of pollutive technology and inviting MNCs in consumer goods sector should not be encouraged.

6. Research orientation towards solar and non-conventional sources of cheap energy and search for appropriate technology pertaining to now necessary requirements of the country should be developed.

7. Strict enforcement of environmental laws and adequate safeguards towards polluting and dirty industries should be taken.

8. Attempts should be made at the global level to spare man and his environment from further nuclear

holocausts, e.g., Hiroshima, Nagasaki and Chernobyl.

In conclusion we may say that the question of human needs has also to be viewed in the perspective of man's symbiotic harmony with the natural environment, which is a deeper source of stability and enrichment of man' s vital life and his higher nature. The quality of life in the future will be deeply coloured by what happens to our effort to repair the damaged to our environment and conserve its beauty and balance.

ANNEXURE-I

Pollution & Pollutants: A Survey

The major pollutants of land, air and water are:

1. Carbon dioxide is normally the result of energy consumption in power production, in industry and domestic use. The accumulation of this gas goes on at the rate of .2 percent per year and could significantly increase the earth's surface temperature with disastrous ecological results.
2. Carbon monoxide is the outcome of incomplete combustion in the steel and petro-chemical industries and in the running of motor vehicles. This gas is highly detrimental to human health and its inhalation may cause fatalities.
3. Sulphur dioxide originates from energy production, from the use of coal and running of motor vehicles. It causes respiratory diseases, damages limestone buildings and contributes to the acidification of lakes.
4. Nitrogen oxide comes from aircraft, excessive fertilisation of soils, forest fires and waste disposal. The harm caused by this effluent ranges from blood diseases to smog, loss of fish and 'entrophication' of lakes.
5. Residuals discharged into water courses which can be divided into degradable and non-degradable materials. Domestic sewage contains phosphates which contribute to loss of aquatic life. But food processing, petroleum refining and paper industries produce large quantum's of degradable organic residuals. Such organic residuals produce "aerobic

degradation" and the oxygen content in streams is exhausted.

Carbon dioxide, methane and hydrogen sulphide are poisonous by-products. The foul odour and black colouring of water pools can be attributed to such causes.

6. Mercury from mining, paint manufacture, fungicides and slimicides contaminates seafood and has a cumulative effect on the nervous system. Cadmium also originates from the paint and metallurgical industries.
7. The heavy metals have stirred public opinion in Japan. Poisoned fish through mercury poisoning caused a number of deaths from Minimata disease; cadmium poisoning through contaminated rice caused deaths from Itai Itai disease. In Canada the consumption of fish from Lake Erie and Lake St. Clair has been forbidden because of feared mercury poisoning.
8. Lead, as an additive to smelting, in pesticides, inhibits metabolism and marine deposits and water automotive fuel, in lead is another poisons which enzymes. Its content in marine deposits and water is dangerous.
9. Oil from tankers and refiners fouls beaches, causes Cancer (technicaliy is carcinogenic), destroys marine life and threatens tourism.
10. Organic, or "exotic" pollutants are produced in abundance by the modern chemical industry. They enter water as effluents and are 'persistent' as stream biota cannot effectively attack their complex molecular chain. Detergents, pesticides (DDT) and phenols (from the distillation of coal and petroleum) are the most common form in this category. They are toxic and reduce the population of beneficial insects, apart from medical suspicions that they are carcinogenic.
11. Radio-nuclides might also be included in the category of persistent pollutants. They are produced 99 per cent by nuclear fuel-processing plants and the rest by nuclear accidents, weapon testing and nuclear-powered vehicles. These contribute to genetic mutation.

Annexure – II

TABLE – I
MAGNITUDE OF AIR POLLUTION

Constituents	*Estimated annual global production from material and human activity (metric tonnes)*	*Portion attribute to some form of human activity*
Carbon dioxide (CO_2)	8.5×10^6	20% due to human activity
Carbon monoxide (CO)	2.0×10^8	60% from automobiles
Sulfur dioxide (SO_2)	1.5×10^8	70% from combustion coal
Nitrogen Oxide (NOx)	1.2×10^9	5% industrial
Dust, Smoke	2.5×10^9	20% due to human activity

Source : S. Venu, Environmental & Economic Growth, Commerce Pamphlet 64, 1973, p. 7.

Land Pollution

TABLE – II
WASTE GENERATED – PER CAPITA, KG/ DAY

India	*Switzerland*	*U.K.*	*USA (Philadelphia)*
0.27 – 0.50	0.60	0.80	1.20 – 1.60

Source : S.A. Ali, *Resources for Future Economic Growth*, 9. 69.

TABLE-III

ROUGH ESTIMATES OF ADDITIONAL EXPENDITURE IN DEVELOPING COUNTRIES REQUIRED TO ACHIEVE SUSTAINABLE DEVELOPMENT BETWEEN 1990 and 2000

(US $ billion)

Year	*Raising energy efficiency*	*Developing Renewable*	*Reforesting the Earth*	*Protecting top soil on Crop land*	*Slowing population growth*	*Total*
1990	1	1	2	3	13	20
1991	2	2	3	6	18	31
1992	3	4	4	4	22	42
1993	4	5	5	12	26	52
1994	5	6	6	16	28	61
1995	6	7	6	16	30	65
1996	7	9	6	16	31	69
1997	8	10	6	16	32	72
1998	9	12	6	16	32	76
1999	10	13	7	16	33	82
2000	11	15	7	16	33	82
TOTAL						648

Source: Lal Jayawardena (1990), *The Macro Economics of Sustainable Development*, Quoted in WIDER, Study Group Series 7, p. 22.

REFERENCES

1. Goulet, D, The Cruel- Choice: A New Concept on the Theory of Development, 1971, quoted by A.P. Thirwall, *Growth and Development*, P.B.

2. Galbraith, J.K., *The Nature of Mass Poverty*, 1980.

3. *Human Development Report, 1990*, Chapter 1.

4. Meadows, D.L., et.:al, *The Limits of Growth*, Universal Books, New York,. 1971.

5. Report of the United Nations Conference on the Human Environment, held at Stockholm 5-6 June, 1972.

6. Georgescuf Roegen N., The Entropy Law and the Economic Progress, quoted in Tisdell, Clem, *Sustainable Economic Growth*,

Production and Development, Economics Discussion Paper, University of Otago, Newzeland, 1988.

7. Barbier, L.B., Development", 101-110. "The Concept of Sustained Economic Environmental Conservation, 14 (2):101-110.
8. Tisdell, Clem, *op. cit.*
9. Ganguli, B.N. The Future Quality of the Population, in *India's Economic Development 1947-2000,* Ashish Bosh, et al, Editors, Vikas Publishing House, 1974.
10. Toffler Alvin, *Future Shock*, p. 429, Quoted in Environment & Economic Growth, Commerce Pamphlet 64, S. Venu, 1973.
11. Ali, S.A., *Resources for Future Economic Growth,* Vikas Publishing House, 1979.

12

J.K. Mehta's Economic Philosophy in the Globalised World Economy of the New Millennium: Lessons for India

Professor Jamshed Kaikhusroo Mehta, University of Allahabad, is renowned for his path breaking philosophical interpretation of economics. He was a student of Herbert Stanley Jevons, who was professor of Economics at Allahabad University. Later he joined the same university as Lecturer in 1927 and rose to the position of Reader and Professor of Economics in 1951. He wrote about sixteen books to his credit. His book *A Philosophical Interpretation of Economics* came out in 1962. Mehta was known in the thirties for his discovery of marginal revenue. Later he developed the theory of wantlessness which became very popular. This paper attempts to deal with that.

Development depends on the actions taken by the people. And every action has its origin first in mind. Thoughts emerge in mind and they inspire action. Thoughts are governed by the philosophy one follows. What is true for a man is true for a nation. The policy a country follows is guided by the philosophy it adopts. Capitalist, Socialist and Communist systems have had their own philosophies. Capitalism emerged with the industrial revolution. The contemporary thinkers in changing society interpreted the things in their own way and Classical school of thought came into being popularizing market economy system, *Laissez faire*, and free trade. The ideology of Mercantilism became obsolete and industrializing countries followed the path suggested by the Classicals. Industrial society's guiding force profit maximization produced a counter in Marxist philosophy and the words exploitation, bourgeoisie, proletariat and others like that were used to indicate inequality and exploitation inherent in the capitalist system that emerged from industrial revolution. However, the communist or socialist challenge with its emphasis on equitable distribution of wealth could not last long and within seventy to eighty years of its life it lost its steam and nations, which followed it, remained poor. By the time the USSR was disintegrated it was near final retreat of communism. The new reality of Twenty-First century is far ahead of the phase of "isms". It is the phase of globalization. However, ground realities are much different in developed industrialized countries and the poor developing economies. Scarcity of resources and its distribution has a different meaning in the two worlds. India being a developing country facing poverty problem and slow growth rate has a different meaning of scarcity and she cannot follow the ways or the consumption pattern of the DC's who are in a stage of high mass consumption. Hence our actions seek different direction and J.K. Mehta presents the solution where he distinguishes between desirable and undesirable wants of individuals and group of people and recommends "wantlessness" as the way for achieving happiness. The path suggested by him is decidedly based on Indian view of life and culture.

In the present paper an attempt has been made to show the relevance of J.K. Mehta's economic philosophy in the globalized world economy of the day and particularly the Indian economy. The first part deals with current realities of the world economy and the experience of the last five decades in India. The second part deals with J.K. Mehta's economic philosophy of wantlessness and regulation of wants. The third part tries to trace the roots of Mehta's philosophy in the ancient Indian texts. And the last comes out with the appropriateness of J.K. Mehta's philosophy in guiding current economic scenario of India.

The new millennium started with the outbreak of information explosion and technology, which has changed the old perceptions regarding Economics and economic development. More inter-connectivity and dismantling of geographical boundaries have converted the world economy into a Global Village. However, the world economy is still divided between the rich and the poor or the haves and the have-nots. And unfortunately while the new wave of technology is enriching the already rich of the North around two thirds of the mankind of the Southern hemisphere still reel in poverty, hunger and economic sufferings. The information age, technology and globalization has not reached them. What ideal or the economic philosophy is to be followed by these countries is an important question. Indian economy is facing an ideological dilemma as to which path is to be accepted in this new situation? Its vast 1050 million population of which even according to official figures 26 per cent are below the poverty line, whose Mixed Economy has lost its glamour after initial good start and intentions. The country, which has been a role model for the poor economies of the fillies with its Nehruvian concept of Socialistic Pattern of Society, is in doldrums in the face of poorly performing public sector and new capitalist market economy challenge. Should we accept the pressure and go for centralized path or find out our "own way" of development?

The disintegration of the USSR in the eighties has changed the world scenario as the communist challenge ended and that meant the triumph of the capitalist philosophy. Whatever may be the reason Marxist philosophy failed to deliver prosperity to the nations which followed it and they were outpaced by market economy countries. Although modern form of Capitalism too is modified with the adoption of welfare state concept by the countries.

Indian economy has its own development experience of five decades. Although planning process started in the country in the early fifties the performance has been poor and most of the plans never achieved their growth targets. The growth rate during the first three decades had been merely 3.5 per cent per annum. Faced with a high population growth rate of 2.5 per cent per annum the per capita growth rate remained nearly one percent per annum for a longer period of time. Many setbacks, e.g., China war, four times Pakistan war and recurrent droughts too were accountable for the poor performance. And by 1990's when the economy went into deep foreign exchange crisis it was realized that there is something seriously wrong with our policies and our overemphasis on public sector and expectations with the government to do businessman's job is not going to yield results. And a fresh debate started over the modality of our Mixed Economy and Socialistic Pattern norm. With the coming of Narasimha Rao a vigorous programme of dismantling of license and controls was undertaken partly due to the new realities faced by the country and largely due to the overwhelming pressure of the international agencies. Although liberalization process had already started earlier during Rajiv Gandhi regime the momentum to it was given in 1990's.

Notwithstanding all the fanfare of globalization the stark reality in India is that the country's economy has lost its direction. We cannot clearly answer the question if we have left the socialist path and have redirected the economy towards capitalist path where market will decide our decisions. In reality Indian economy presents a picture of paradoxes where along with information technology basic problems of poverty and economic sufferings co-exist. Corruption, black money and other such things have their own way to play, which has been well recognized by the agencies like Transparency International and other overseas business groups. In the situation a direction is required and J. K. Mehta presents the answer, which is relevant in solving the problems of the day.

J.K. Mehta's Wantlessness

Economic science has been concerned with maximization of satisfaction and choice of man with reference to scarce means at his disposal. The fact that we choose to satisfy some wants and not to satisfy others imply that the satisfaction of former wants give one greater utility than the satisfaction of the latter ones. Now that Economics is a science of choice and the end of all choice is maximization of satisfaction, Economics studies human behaviour as concerned with the making of choices in such a manner that maximum satisfaction is achieved out of them in the end.

Now the question arises whether maximum satisfaction, which happens to be the end of human behaviour can be more fully, achieved when a large number of wants is satisfied or when the wants is cut down to the minimum. Western economic thinkers are of opinion that maximum satisfaction is possible only when the greater possible number of wants is satisfied out of the given resources. And this has inevitably led men in the west to multiply their wants and make life more and more complex. The economies which have achieved the age of high mass consumption like the USA and the Group of Ten via industrial revolution and take-off are supposed to be the role model for the lesser developed ones. The problem before them is how to maintain those levels of high mass consumption.

J.K. Mehta developed the theory of wantlessness as a counter to the western economist's theory of ever-expanding wants as the prime mover of economic activity. According to him instead of it's (wants) adding to the sum total of happiness it subtracts from it a good deal. In fact he thinks that maximization of satisfaction is rather completely inconsistent with the maximization of human wants. Wants emerge in the minds of people as desire and when they emerge become a source of pain for not being able to satisfy them. Samuel Johnson once "Tote" every desire is a viper in the bosom, as long as it is chilled it is harmless, as it gathers warmth it makes one restless". And not only this but as soon as a want gets satisfied it looses its charm and begets newer and newer wants. A want is a painful experience. This is evident from the fact that we wish to satisfy it and get rid of it as soon as possible. We would not have bothered to remove or satisfy it had it not been painful. So the removal of a want means removal of pain and procurement of pleasure. And this pleasure is the same thing as satisfaction or utility. If one wants to get maximum utility or pleasure or satisfaction one should see to it that all pain is removed and no pain is experienced in future. Thus every desire or want leads one from equilibrium to a disequilibrium situation. Its fulfilment gives temporary satisfaction only to be challenged by a newer disequilibrium situation with the emergence of newer wants.

Alfred Marshall had referred to economic activity as flowing from the urge to satisfy given wants. He had also pointed that as societies develop in material endowment new activities would create new wants. Thus according to him in the early stages wants create activities and at the later stages activities create wants. Mehta's approach was slightly different. According to him maximization of satisfaction is better achieved when the wants are at their minimum.

In the situations when resources to fulfill wants are limited or scarce and one want leads to other and wants can never be taken as given, the process of want satisfaction leads to encroachment on other's resources. For, the whole process of economic behaviour here means conflicts to obtain command of resources of others. It is only when resources are unlimited that the disequilibrium process inherent in the satisfaction of wants will not lead to clashes and conflicts based on jealousy and limitation of resources. In fact the whole process of exploitation and feeling of inequality can be traced to individual's crossing the border of wantlessness to that of want maximization.

Indian view of life and its spirituality has long been taken by the materialist society as the basic cause of poverty in the country. There is a danger to misconceive the context of wantlessness and happiness by those who do not really understand the core of Indian view of life and philosophy.

Kabir the noted saint of middle ages has given the message in his famous couplet that wealth arising out of herds of cow, elephants or horses and other miscellaneous jewels has no meaning at all when "contentment" comes. There is no limit to one's greed. But the simple way to happiness is containment of desires.

The ultimate of every economic activity is attainment of happiness. But the materialistic route to happiness via multiplication of wants can only lead to individual tensions, frustration and unhappy end of life besides giving rise to social tensions, exploitation, inequality, unrest and wars which are destructive to peace and happiness. This is probably the reason why individual psychological problems abound the rich nations while the poorest Bangladesh counts for the highest in happiness index. It would, however, be a distorted interpretation that for being happy one has to be poor. Rather the key to happiness lies in containment of desires and contentment.

Basis of J.K. Mehta's Philosophy

What J.K. Mehta has presented in economic philosophy is a reflection of Indian culture and philosophy. In true sense Economics developed in India much before Adam Smith wrote his *Wealth of Nations* in 1776. Kautilya's *Arthashastra* writtend during Mauryan age has defined Economics in terms of man's well being on this planet earth when he says:

Manushyavati bhumih ityarthah;

Tasya prithivyah labhpalnopayashastram arthshastram.

The land inhabited by men is called *Artha* (wealth) and the science *(shastra)*, which depicts the way to upkeep that land for the benefit of mankind, is called Economics. This definition while incorporating land, labour and capital in the realm of economics keeps mankind's welfare above all. Not only this upkeep of land points towards modern concept of maintaining environment. And Kautilya was not the first to develop treatise on polity and economics. Our Vedas and Upanishads preach the original and ultimate message to man as how to attain higher levels of opulence and well being. The very first of the Upanishads *Ishopanishad* in its very first sloka narrates the real meaning of wealth.

Ishavashyam idam sarvam, yatkinch jagatyamjagat;

ten tyakten bhunjitha; ma gridiah, kasya swiddhanam?

All that is in existence in this world is surrounded, internally as well as externally, by the Supreme, the Isha. All the wealth thus created by Him should be utilized with the spirit of sacrifice. He has given it to the man. But no man should be greedy, for, this wealth is not theirs. Then there is a question whose wealth it is? And the answer is it is His wealth and the man is mere trustee of God's wealth. A true realization of this message changes the whole meaning of life. Even in Rg Veda there are prayers for the wealth and opulence.

'.....Vayam syam patayo rayeenam'

O God! Make us lord of wealth and Aishvarya. He is the 'Hiranyagarbha' the richest of all.

Gandhi took this principle of trusteeship and sacrifice and preached all his life for containment of desires and the right way of earning. For the real happiness springs from sacrifice and contentment.

The Indian philosophy of life takes the present life as a path of larger cycle of lives. which is based on the principles of karma and rebirth Lord Krishna in *Geeta* says:

Jatasya hi dhruvo mrituah; dhruvam janm tmi.tasya chao

It inspires one for good karma do good to all and that is the only way for salvation from this life cycle.

There are four *'purusharthas'* for men; *dhama, artha, kaam* and *moksha*. And there should be proper balancing in life of all the four. Happiness lies in this proper balancing. And this makes life successful. The message that emerges is that materialistic path if not properly balanced is not going to bring pleasure- the ultimate desire of everyone in life.

Lessons for India

In this fast changing world Indian economy is facing an ideological vacuum. Its Nehruvian policies dreamt of a Socialistic Pattern of Society and adopted Mixed Economy that was supposed to be an ideal mix of good things of capitalism as well as communism. It tried to keep at bay exploitation of the first and regimentation of the second to give it a human touch and anchor. However, the experience of the last fifty years defied that dream. We the people today are fed up with inefficiency of the government sector. And it is being increasingly realized that governments cannot do businessman's job. It is mainly because motivating force of businessmen and government is different.

Now after the disintegration of the USSR and disappearance of Communist challenge capitalism triumphed. Globalization is an outcome of that. With the technological advance and spread of information technology inter-connectivity among nations has increased and geographical boundaries are slimming. Cultural invasion is a part of the phenomenon. Hence the ideologies of socialistic pattern and equality are fast loosing their strength before globalization's economic and ideological forces. It is an era of the end of "isms" as well. We are facing new realities. And in facing newer challenges we have to be cautious that core values of our culture and character are not lost. As they suggest the ways for development, happiness and success in life in true sense. And here J.K. Mehta has its own distinguished role to play.

Economics does not stand on its own feet, says Schumacher. It is derived from a view of the meaning and purpose of life. Economics means a certain ordering of life according to the philosophy inherent and implicit in it. And the only fully developed system of economic. thought that exists to day is derived from a purely materialist view of life. The path is dangerously leading people towards unhappiness and frustration particularly in the LDC's like India where people have left their own Indian way of peace and happiness long derived from ancient wisdom of our sacred texts and sages and are adopting the value system of materialism, of *arth* and *kam (bhog)* keeping in oblivion *dharma* and *moksha*. And this cultural confusion is not going to bring real success and happiness in life at least in Indian society where still scarcity of resources has a particular meaning and pinch.

Let us first define the meaning of development and its purpose. Certainly development is for maintaining 'core values' of the society. And development and success is to be counted in terms of end result of peace and happiness. The illusion of keeping up with the Developed Countries of the west and throwing away the philosophical and spiritual roots has made J.K. Mehta's ideas as non-relevant in the current Indian context. It appears that in a poor society like India most of the population is effectively forced to be incrementally wantless. This is probably because of lack of incomes and/or employment or empowerment—social as well as economic. India is continuing in this state even after fifty years of freedom and planning. The disequilibria created by the policy of globalization have made the situation even more difficult. And globalization like industrial revolution is a phenomenon that has come to stay, says Bimal Jalan . It has its plus and minuses and the country have to adjust it and tilt the policies to reap its advantages and safeguard its people's interest. And there is the scope for our 'own way' of development and ideology.

In realizing our own way or Third way as Tony Blair calls it, we will have to prescribe certain "limits". Material things are of real importance for a person, a family, or a nation—only up to a point', says Schumacher. We can distinguish three economic conditions, he says, misery, sufficiency and surfeit. Of these, two are bad for a person, a family or a nation and only one, sufficiency is good. Economic progress is good only up to a point; beyond that, it is evil, destructive, and uneconomic.

Limits to the wants of upper segment of population for the benefit of the lower strata of society orients a wilful transfer of excess resources as is contained in the theory of Bhoodan of Binova in making a true socialist or egalitarian society.

J.K. Mehta brings about the end result of an ideal society through individuals exercising control over wants. If the top group becomes incrementally wantless, then the other groups in hierarchy will gradually attain satisfaction of the same level of wants as those of the top groups. The process of class conflict has no place in this system. Nor there is a requirement that all means of production should be owned by the State. It is clear that logically his approach would lead to an egalitarian society without the Marxist routes.

13

Gandhian Economic Thinking: It's Relevance in 21st Century India

At the outset we should acknowledge that Mohandas Karamchand Gandhi was not an Economist as such. He was much more than that. He was a saint, a Mahatma and the Father of the Nation. His economic ideas were a part of his general crusade against exploitation, poverty, social and economic injustices prevailing in India. His whole approach is rooted in human dignity. He wanted to elevate economic philosophy from its materialistic base to high spiritual plane where actions are by social objectives rather than self considerations.

Gandhi is not a name. It is a philosophy. The philosophy which is firmly rooted in Vedic philosophy. He gave the world message of truth and non-violence. In economics he presented the approach of trusteeship. The message of trusteeship emerges from Ishopanishad where it has been established that whatever is there in this world is the property of God. And He has created all this for all His creatures. There is plenty for every one's need in this world. Man should consume things with the sense of sacrifice and he should not take other's share. Upanishad says one should not be greedy and should always remember that it is not his property. This has been given to him for proper utilization. He is only a trustee of God's property.

Gandhi gave the message to the humanity that sacrifice in consumption and non-possession of material wealth is the basic thing to be understood. There is enough for everyone's need in this world but all the wealth of this world is not sufficient for one man's greed. Had this been understood properly World wars would have been avoided and Hitler has not come into being. In the world community ridden with terrorism, violence and racial strife, today in the Twenty first century, Gandhi's message of Non –Violence in resolving the problems has become much more relevant than ever before.

The present paper is in three parts. The first part seeks the original roots of Gandhi's spiritualism and *Satya* (Truth) and *Ahimsa* (Non-Violence). The second part makes a brief review of development of Indian economy during the past sixty years and the rise and decline of Gandhian economic ideology during that. The third part is concerned with the developmental issues before world economy and India in the post reform period. This will deal precisely with issues of market economy and consumerism, excess of industrialization and its sustainability, the issue of rising disparity and its repercussions in the form of rising crime and naxalism in the country. And finally an attempt will be made to evaluate Gandhi's economic thinking and its relevance in the new millennium.

PART-1

Gandhi regarded economics as a moral science and laid tremendous emphasis on its ethical aspect. Economics that hurts the moral well being of an individual or a nation is immoral and therefore sinful. Its goal is not pure material benefit but advancement of humanity on its road to progress by strengthening the character and the development of personality of each individual engaged in such activity. He formulated economic principals in the context of his design of an ideal social order: a non-violent, non-exploitative, humanistic and egalitarian society.

Today the economic thinkers are trying to find out the meaning and purpose of economic development. Economic development was defined in terms of growth of gross national product and per capita income not so long ago. During sixties Physical Quality of Life was the basic concern. Then came the Human Development approach. Mahbubul Haq and others in the World Bank found out in nineties that Man is in the centre of development and he should live a long and healthy life. As in most of the poor countries life is short and miserable the concept was well attended.

Years later it was found out that the purpose of development should be happiness and happiness index was prepared world over. Then it was found that people in Bangladesh, one among the poorest countries, are the happiest people in the world. Some more attempts are made in recent time to give credential to this approach. This is akin to defining an elephant by the four blind-fold persons.

The basic question still stands what is the objective of economic development. Western view has no answer to it. Money, more money then still more money. Then what? Life of stress, frustrations and miserable death. The example of happiness attained by the poor people living in an underdeveloped country like Bangladesh, and not in possession of material wealth, disapproves the very basic tenet of this materialistic approach to happiness in life. As happiness is a state of mind, it does not have much concern with accumulation of money after a point. Rather more and more of income and wealth make life more miserable. Here money commands man rather than man commanding money. It is slavery.

So the western economic philosophy becomes indeterminate.

Here comes Mahatma Gandhi who proclaims: the root of happiness is righteousness,

Sukhasya mool Dharmah.

Dharma is righteousness in action, thought and words.

The basic criterion of judging what is right and what is wrong is, what you considers not good for yourself, do not do that to others. That is the basic test. *Dharma* prescribes the duty of a man.

In *Manusmriti* Manu has given ten characteristics of dharma:

Dhriti, kshama, damoasteyam, shaucham, indriya nigraha;

Dhirvidya, satyam, akrodhah dashkam dharma lakshanam.

Dhriti is patience, *kshama* is forgiveness, *dam* is controlling own mind, *shauch* is purity of body and thought. *Indriya nigraha* is controlling the five *jnan indriyas* (sense organs) and five *karma indriyas, dhee* is intellect and *vidya* is acquiring knowledge, *satya* is truth and *akrodha* is not to be angry. These are the ten elements or characters of dharma.

In *Yogadarshan* Maharshi Patanjali has suggested eight steps to realizing happiness and God, who is happiness *(Anand)* incarnate, vis-a-vis *Sat* and *Chit,* truth incarnate and the very basic source of life (Chaitanya). The first and the second steps of this *Ashthangyoga* are *yama* and *niyama*. The discipline of *yama* is five fold: *ahimsa* (non-violence), *satya* (Truth), *asteya* (not to steal), *brahmcharya* (celibacy) and *aparigraha* (non-possession).

Niyama, as per Maharshi Patanjali, too has five disciplines: *shauch* (purity), *santosh* (contentment), *tapa* (to brave difficulties in fulfilling duty), *swadhyay* (knowing ownself), and *Ishwar pranidhana* (to delve in Him through meditation).

Purity *(shauch)* has three dimensions—*kayik, vachic* and *manasic*—physical purity, purity of words and purity of thought. According to Maharshi Manu, physical purity comes through water, source of mental purity is truth *(satya)*, and *jnana,* knowledge, refines intellect, by *tapa* and *vidya* together 'self 'is refined.

Adbhir gatrani shudhyanti, manah satyen shudhyate·

Vidya tapobhyam bhutatmah, budhhir jnanen shudhyati.

Gandhi's derivation of non-violence, truth, purity of body and thought, contentment, hard work, non-possession, and celibacy owe to these sources of Vedic philosophy.

The core of Gandhian philosophy is grounded in non-violence and truth. Truth—*sat*—is an attribute of the Almighty. Truth is eternal. These are the norms which are for man's benefit for all time. They are based on dharma. Gandhi's interpretation of dharma is truth-bound—*satya-moolak dharma.*

According to *Nyayasutra:*

Pramanyenartha parikshanam, (1/1 *Nyaya Bhashya*)

What stands at the alter of justice is truth. This also interprets what is unjust can never be true.

Maharshi Manu describes three forms of truth: *satya bhava* (true attitude), *satya vachan* (true speech), and *satya acharan* (truthful action). This represents three things—mind, speech and action—*man, vani* and *karma.*

In Vedic philosophy the three basic attributes of God are *satyam, shivam* and *sundaram.* What is to the benefit of all (read 'welfare') is *shivam.* That which incorporates 'welfare of all' (Pareto optimality) is *shiva tatva.* Here *shivam* —welfare of all—is attached with truth or the sence of what is just and what is not just or unjust. Then these two attributes of godliness are attended by the concept of beauty—*sundaram.* That only could be beautiful which is true and beneficial to all. This "Trinity" concept is the crux of the Vedic philosophy wherefrom dharma has been derived.

Economic ideas of Gandhi flow from the perspective of *satya, dharma* and *ahimsa.* It puts man and his overall upliftment in the centre. Dignity of man was in the centre of Gandhi's movement against untouchability, which had divided Indian society for hundreds of years.

Another word attached with Gandhi is *Ahimsa*—to desist violence (even at the cost of physical sufferings). *Ahimsa* according to Maharshi Vyasa is:

Sarvatha sarvada sarvabhutanamaanabhidrohah ahimsa gyeyah. (2/30 *Yogadarshan)*

Ahimsa is not only non-brutality towards animals, in its wider perspective it is relinquishing enemity. By one's actions the other one should not feel hurt is *ahimsa. Himsa* may be physical as well as mental both says Maharshi Manu. Even thinking of one's harm is violence.

Manasa anisthachintanam,

Satya and ahimsa became the basic tools of Gandhi to fight with rulers in South Africa and the British rule in India. It was new to the world. These were the Gandhian experiments with truth.

Obviously Gandhi's whole life and philosophy and his high order spirituality has drawn heavily from Vedic scriptures, Upanishads, Geeta and Mahabharatha. He had been a firm believer in God. His message was that to achieve anything—swaraj inclusive—the path, the way of doing things, should be righteous. He believed in purity of instruments involved in attaining a right thing. There he was above Bal Gangadhar Tilak for whom "end justifies the means". Gandhi differed.

Among others whose works and who influenced Gandhi was the works of Ruskin's *Unto the Last,* Marxian egalitarianism and Leo Tolstoy's contentment. It is said, Gandhi's *Antyodaya yojana* is taken from Ruskin's concept of *Unto the Last.* Gandhi and Karl Marx both believed in revolution to change the existing economic and social order but they differed in their approach. Marx's revolution was violent but Gandhi's revolution was peaceful. His tools were Satyagraha and Civil disobedience. He wanted to penetrate the heart of the enemy, howsoever mighty he was.

His strategy and approach was new to the world which had been fighting battles and wars to win over the enemy to achieve objectives. Never before the world has seen a frail mortal with immense spiritual power of heart in finding out solution this way. This was something revolutionary.

On his martyrdom Andrew Ewart writes "Thus blind and unreasoning violence ended a life dedicated to denouncing its use in the affairs of mankind, and the world lost the counsel of a wise and selfless being whose deeds and words still guide the destinies of his vast nation and will continue so to do long after those who live by the sword have perished by the sword."

PART- 2

Rise and Decline of Gandhi's Economic Ideology in Independent India

Gandhi dreamt of self-sufficient villages, developed cottage and village industries, co-operation and a life based on simple living and contentment. Country was in poverty and more than half of its people were living a miserable life at the time it became free. In today's terminology they were living below poverty line. The country was divided into two nations. The economy was shattered. As India was the country of villages, more than seventy percent of its population was living in villages. They were dependent upon agriculture. Country was facing big problem of settlement of those who had come from Pakistan after partition. There were no developed industries worth the name except cotton textile and steel industry. There was chaos all round. A daunting challenge was present before the nation builders.

Gandhi never liked machines as they replaced labour and were the basic cause of unemployment. He was not in favour of industrialization. Industrialization gives rise to Capitalism and exploitation of the working class and consumers in the market.

At the time of Independence in 1947 there were two competing ideologies of economic development in the world. One was Capitalistic market economy model and the other was the Communist or Socialist model. The first was based on private property rights and free market. The other was Communist model where all the property belonged to the state and there was no individual choice. State was responsible for providing employment and every other thing needed to its people. Equity and egalitarianism in distribution were basic to the model. It was a reaction to the capitalistic exploitation and economic disparity created by the system.

Indian leaders wanted to bring an ideal model of development which would be free from exploitation and ensure freedom of choice to its individuals. As the socialist model developed into a 'regimented society' model we wanted to take only its best part, of developmental planning and avoid un-freedom part. India adopted Mixed Economic system for development. In polity we opted for Parliamentary Democracy.

Gandhi could not live long to see his dreams come true in independent India as his voice was silenced by the forces of communal hatred against which he struggled whole life. On 30th January 1948, he was shot dead while going to evening prayer in Delhi.

The Gandhi Nehru model of growth aimed at establishment of a Socialistic pattern of society based on equity, justice and co-operation. The orientation of Five Year Plans since the beginning was rural development and speedy industrialization in the country. Community Development Projects were started and Land Reforms were undertaken. The objective was to raise productivity of the farm sector and remove injustices from the existing system. The motto was land to the tiller. It was hoped that this will remove rural poverty and establish an order.

Soon the departure from Gandhian path became eminent as the country started on the path of large scale industrialization since the second Five Year Plan in 1956. By the Industrial Policy Resolution 1949 and Industrial Policy 1956 the responsibility of speedy industrial development came on the shoulders of the government. The commanding heights of the economy came in the public sector and the private sector was given a supportive role. Nehru was considered 'modernizer par-excellence' by many. He chose the path of rapid industrialization to modernize India. At that time economic development was synonym to industrial development. It was industrial revolution which has brought prosperity in the developed countries of the world.

Realities were harsh, however, and soon the economy had to face resource crunch on all sides. Population was rising at a fast pace and food shortages became perceptible. Foreign exchange reserve of the country was exhausted and private capital—resident as well as overseas—was slow to come.

During the first decade of planning in the country the objectives of five per cent per annum growth rate was not realized. Per capita income growth was slightly above one per cent. Consequently poverty persisted at a vast scale.

Sixties brought insurmountable difficulties in the form of Chinese aggression in 1962 and yet another war with Pakistan in 1965. Death of Prime Minister Jawahar Lal Nehru on May 27th 1964 was another big upset. Years 1966 and 67 were years of drought and the country was pushed into severe food crisis. The lesson of China war drew our attention towards neglect of defense sector. Subsequently the next five year plan's objective became Defense and Development. A large part of the budget allocation was made for defense sector.

Food crisis was the result of neglect of farm sector and low investment in agriculture. Fast growing population and hence rising demand for food was another factor precipitating the crisis. Community Development Projects and National extension Services did not bring desired results and farm productivity was slow to rise. Land Reforms too went in to the quagmire of court cases.

Food rationing was introduced in the country. Wheat was imported in large scale from the USA, Canada, Australia and other countries. With shortages and control of essential items flourished black marketing and black money generation which changed the entire politico-economic-socio scenario of the country in the coming decades. This was the beginning of the downfall of Gandhian values and morality.

By the start of seventies a new generation took command of economy and politics in India and its various offices and institutions. They completely forgot who Gandhi was and what his values were. The institutions of governance came into the hands of people uncommitted to social values. Self- interest in politics and economic fields began to dominate the scenario. Politico-economic forces and institutions were being made corrupt by money power and muscle power.

Yet another war with Pakistan in 1971 further made the economy go back several years. Notwithstanding, rays of hope came in the form of the Green Revolution whose seeds were planted in the form of a 'new strategy of agricultural development' in the mid sixties. W got success in Pakistan war. On the farm front too we succeeded in breaking the food crisis to a large extent. However, much of the seventies faced double digit inflationary pressure, large scale unemployment and rampant poverty. Much of the inflation was owing to quadrupling of petroleum price by the OPEC. The objective of our Five Year Plan attempted to address the above problems.

Early seventies is regarded by many thinkers as the period of sharp decline of Gandhian economic ideology and domination of self interest in public life. Powered by economy of controls and authoritarianism, rampant corruption, and black money a parallel economy was flourishing side by side. The growth rate of parallel economy far exceeded the growth rate of real economy.

While Gandhi regarded economics a moral science and has laid tremendous emphasis on its ethical aspect, the people of new generation, born and brought up in Free India, completely neglected those values of Gandhian era.

The system was fast moving in the opposite direction.

By eighties Indian economy was described as "Tiger in the cage". Attempts to liberalize started during this period and economy picked up. The rate of growth of gross domestic product crossed the barrier of 3 to 3.5 per cent and moved ahead of five per cent.

Political scenario in the country greatly changed after the death of Pandit Nehru and subsequent down fall of the Congress party which erstwhile had been commanding single party majority in Parliament and Council houses of the states. It was partly due to the authoritarian attitude of Indira Gandhi and partly due to the rise of the peasant class which attained economic power as a result of the Green Revolution. They wanted to share the political power too which was by now understood as the 'real' power. The rise of Janata Party and other regional parties could be attributed to this factor. This time will also be remembered for the beginning of criminal's entry into politics.

Eighties will also be remembered for Mandal divide and reservations in government jobs. This was another death knell to Gandhi's way of achieving things. Gandhi and other senior leaders in Congress party wanted elimination of the caste system from the country. Caste system in India had divided the whole population in the country and had given rise to hatred and feelings of superiority and inferiority not based on qualifications but on birth. Untouchability was the result of this very system.

During mid-eighties certain developments in other countries of the world also greatly affected the entire scenario. The USSR disintegrated and the Cold war between Communist and Capitalist ideologies ended in favour of the latter. Arguments of "egalitarianism" faded before competition and "efficiency" of the market economy system. There was a virtual revolt for freedom in so called Socialist countries of the world against authoritarian regimentation, economic inefficiency and widespread poverty.

In India too people were fed up, by the time, with inefficiency of the government sector and performance of the public sector undertakings which had started loosing heavily. "Weariness from planning" had started emerging among people. The country was in the grip of large scale unemployment.

In the beginning of the nineteen nineties Indian economy was in serious foreign exchange crisis and its credibility had dipped. In the circumstances Narasimha Rao government introduced Economic Reforms in the form of liberalization, marketization and privatization. This period is also marked by rise of money power in politics and economics. Money bags started descending upon New Delhi to make and unmake the governments in the centre. Situation in the states was much worse with the large scale entry of criminal elements in Council houses. Even Parliament was not untouched with it. Election Commission of India had got full records of criminal cases pending against parliamentarians and members of legislative assemblies. The situation completely negates Gandhi's social values, economic ideologies and his code of self-less service in public life. Politics is good in isolation. So is economics. But when politics comes into the realm of economics and/or economics comes into politics the downfall becomes limitless.

In the present scenario people come into politics not only for political power or to serve people but mainly for economic power attached with it. Political power generates income. And income is needed to win elections. So the money power propels the political power. It ensures political power. As there is no income without political power it is necessary to somehow remain in power. This politico-economic nexus was unthinkable at the time of Gandhi.

PART-3

Developmental Issues before India in the post reform period and Gandhi's Relevance

In India of 21st century we visualize a dichotomy. The realities are conflicting and much harsh than at the time of Gandhi. The economy is growing at a high rate of eight to nine per cent, the stock market is booming, our foreign exchange reserve is at a comfortably high level, and free trade is bringing to our homes a variety of goods and services simply unimaginable even a couple of decades ago as a mark of the benefit of globalization. We are everyday reminded that India is poised economically and politically as an emergent world power.

Once one step outside the charmed circle of privileged minority expounding the virtues of globalization and liberalization we enter into an India of despair and grief. It is a world of those wretched ones living below poverty line where growth has not reached. It is a world of rising farmer suicides, naxalism, terrorism, hatred, communal violence and widespread squalor. There are families who do not have access to safe drinking water. There are no toilets in the house and the inhabitants are compelled to ease themselves in open fields and around railway tracks. Ladies feel shy and come out only when darkness descends.

Looking at a conservative official statistics, between 2001 and 2006 in four states of Andhra, Karnataka, Kerala, and Maharasthra more than 9000 farmers committed suicide. According to another estimate of the Ministry of Home Affairs, some 120 to 160 out of total of 607 districts in 14 states are Naxal infested. Supported by a disgruntled and dispossessed peasantry, the movement has spread to nearly one fourth of Indian territory. Of the affected districts the revolutionary movement is intense in 90 districts while the remaining districts have seen mass organization activity/ underground squad movement, but not revolutionary violence.

The unrest in society indicates towards large income disparity prevailing in economy. Had the fruits of economic development trickled to the bottom rung of society the crisis situation would not have arisen.

Besides we may address the problems with another angle and include some more issues. Here the problems pertain to three Ps: poverty, population and pollution. Though poverty had come down significantly over the past decades it is still sizeable. Around 260 million people as per official estimates are below the poverty line. And this size matches the entire population of India at the start of the 20th century. It is much more than the entire population of many countries in the world. Hence we find not one but two or three India living simultaneously. One is poor and the other is rich. A poverty curtain divides them. One is poised to jet age the other one still languishing in bullock cart age. One is rural and backward the other is urban and modern. In one India income level is very high and there are problems to manage money. In the other one people are starving and desperately looking for some gainful employment for survival. In one India there is talk about higher and higher quality of life; in other for life itself.

At the same time the excess of industrial growth in the developed countries of the world has presented yet another problem of environmental pollution and global warming. They talk about its sustainability. There is concern about 'limits to growth'. As a result of rising environmental pollution level life sustenance itself is threatened. The developed countries are returning back to nature. Their consumption pattern is heading increasingly towards natural products.

In India we are following western model of economic development and still lean on industrial development to raise the rate of growth and ignore the farm sector. The rate of growth of farm sector is around 2 .7 per cent and there is condition of somewhat stagnation. Rural income is consequently not rising. This is when the dependence on agriculture is still substantial. More than 60 per cent of population still live in rural areas and are dependent upon agriculture and allied industries. But in the wake of our emphasis on industry we ignored this sector. Problem of "food security" is looming large before the country.

Ideologically we are in a state of vacuum. Our Objective of a Socialistic Pattern of Society has already lost steam. Our Mixed economy is dissipating and public sector is increasingly giving way to private sector. And now our policy makers are under the pressure of Crony Capitalism of market. We have not yet developed our own model of development. We ignored Gandhi since the beginning and reached a state of frustrating materialism. We are following the way of consumerism and heading towards the quagmire of materialism. This is a path towards frustration and strife and violence. We can not avoid confrontation and it could be violent whose signals have already coming in.

In the 21st century Gandhi and his economic philosophy is relevant for two reasons. One for showing the path of survival to human beings which is threatened due to miss utilization of natural endowments and disturbing natural order; and secondly, to establish economic and social justice for the poor and destitute living in India and other poor countries of the world.

The world today is threatened by terrorism, hatred and violence. Even the mighty countries do not consider themselves safe. Gandhi is remembered by the world community for his universal message of Non-Violence and Truth. We may not like his tools of Charkha or his emphasis for cottage industries in the changed circumstances of 21st century India. But his basic objectives of "work to every hand and food to every mouth" have to be ensured to check confrontation.

The message of Gandhi can never be obsolete. They are the message from Vedic philosophy whose objective is to upgrade the man itself. Vedas have asked man *"manur bhavah"*. Be Human. And spread humanity. People will return to this ultimate path of peace and happiness when they would be exhausted of consumerism and materialism.

REFERENCES

1. *Ishavashya Upanishad.*
2. *Yoga Darshan*, Patanjali.
3. *Manusmriti.*
4. *Nyaya Bhashya.*
5. Andrew Ewart in John Canning, *100 Great Modern Lives*, Ed. Sixth edition, Rupa, 1972.
6. *Prajna, Gandhi Janmshati Visheshank*, BHU, Vol. 13, 2, March 1969.
7. *Yajurveda Samhita.*

14

Economic Philosophy in Vedas: A Spiritual Based Human Development Agenda

Any society is guided by the philosophy of life given to it by its knowledgeable people, the philosophers, the wise men, saints, rishis and the seers. In India Vedas are the texts of sublime knowledge and they contain a vast treasure of knowledge that has guided Indian society and people for millenniums.

In the Twentieth and the Twenty-first century the process of liberalization and integration of various national economies into a new complex web has begun. So much so with the advances made there is much talk about knowledge based societies. Naturally the geo-political situation is more fluid than ever before in history. What used to be mere social issues earlier have also become economic issues or political issues, under the principles of human rights violations. In economics too development is perceived in terms of certain fundamental freedoms.

In this complex situation, social scientists and economists have a unique role. Because social sciences go beyond the mere hardware or animate beings. It deals with human beings and societies. It deals with how or what human beings think. It captures their joy and agony, pain and pleasure, hopes and frustrations. Thus it is close to finer or subtle aspects of knowledge.

Indian civilizational strength derives from the fact that our intellectuals and seers addressed the questions of human beings and his place in the universe directly. It was not an earth-centric or anthropo-centric view. There was a cosmic unity.

The knowledge from the Vedas are meant for the lower and higher stages of human development, i.e., for the worldly or empirical as well as for the transcendental. The verses from the *Yajur Veda* describes how it is necessary to have a coordination between the two: "One who strives to attain the lower knowledge, while neglecting the higher one is in darkness and one who feigns to show that he would be caring for the higher knowledge alone without due regard to lower one is groaping still more in darkness".

अन्धं तमः प्रविशन्ति येऽविद्यामुपासते ।
ततो भूय इव ते तमो य उ विद्यायांरताः ।। यजु० 40/9

"The blinding darkness go the men who worship nescience. Those proud of little knowledge enter darkness that is darker still".

The central concern of Vedic thinkers is to discover the connections among Ishwar, Jeev, and Prakriti. The assumption then is that the universe constitutes a web of relations, that things that appear to stand alone and apart are, in fact, connected to other things. A further assumption is that these real cosmic connections are usually hidden from the view of ordinary people, discovering them constitutes knowledge. Knowledge that is contained in Vedas. And it is this knowledge of the hidden connections *(karya-karan sambandh)* that gives the person with that knowledge, power, wealth, and prestige in this world and heavenly bliss and immortality after death

It is through the inspiration from Vedas that ancient seers of that age developed positive sciences and made the world worthwhile to live in with comforts and purposefulness; and again inspired by the same Vedic thoughts, they explored the realms of inner life and got an insight into some of the fundamental mysteries of the innermost realms of psychic and spiritual worlds and superb knowledge of the Brahman and His realization.

The objective of the present paper is to explain the knowledge from Vedic texts which prescribe four objectives of human life: the four *purusharthas*: *Dharma, Arth, Kam,* and *Moksha* and let the world derive the message that *Artha* and *Kam* in isolation can bring disastrous impacts on human life and they have already brought havoc in the form of World Wars and innumerable sufferings and material deprivations to human beings. Vedic outlook concentrates on the integrated view that only when *Artha* and *Kam* is prefixed with *Dharm*, the righteousness the man could attain salvation from sufferings of life and attain *Moksha*. And that is the only righteous path the society can move to world and inner peace. It is the Western philosophy of life focusing on only *Artha* and *Kam* and the consequent definition of economic development based on satisfaction of unlimited wants, consumerism and uncontrolled materialism which is responsible for creating most of the deprivations and frustration in economy and society.

PART-2

In modern parlance Adam Smith is called the father of Economics and his famous book *Wealth of Nations* (1776) is treated as epoch-making work of economics. Then a whole array of thinkers Ricardo, Mill, and Malthus etc. constitute the classical school of thought. The period coincided with economic revolutions, first the agricultural and then more importantly Industrial in England and in other European countries that changed the whole scenario of the world. It was the beginning of industrial society and an era of the beginning of Capitalist philosophy. The Classicals perpetuated, validated, and supported Capitalism by their theories of market, demand and supply, wages, rent and profit and foreign trade. They also, at the same time, accepted the inbuilt inequity embodied in capitalist theory.

The Classicals preceded Mercantilists and Physiocrates. However, much earlier in Bhatatvarsha Kautilya has composed the treatise on Political Economy and public administration. Kautilya's *Arthashastra* is not the first but the last of the works of Indian thinkers of the past. Apart from Kautilya our Brahman Granthas: the Upanishads have written vividly about arth, it's meaning and purpose and the happiness of life. The Upanishads are the lectures of knowledge from the Vedic Samhitas.

The four Vedas, *Rig, Yajur, Sam,* and *Atharva* have six parts called *Angas: Shiksha, Kalpa, Vyakaran, Nirukta, Chhand,* and *Jyotish*. It further contains six philosophies, *Samkhya, Vaisheshic, Nyaya, Meemansha, Vedant,* and *Yog* called six *Darshans*. The *Rigveda* has 10522 Mantras, the *Yajurveda* has 1976 Mantras, the *Sam Veda* has 1875 Mantras, and the *Atharva Veda* is composed of 5987 Mantras. The Vedas have four Up Vedas namely, *Aayurveda, Dhanurveda, Gandharvaveda,* and *Arthaveda*. *Artha Veda* pertains to *Shilpa vidya, padarth gun vijyan* and the knowledge of manufacturing and creating things for the pleasure and opulence of mankind.

Vedas explain the *Karya-Karan sambandh:* cause and effect relationship, embodied in man's life, which is the root of pleasure and pain. It is the establishment of inner relationship of Karma and its outcome. It is not only a narration of theory. It prescribes the code of conduct for life and its happiness.

On the other side, the western philosophy has not ascended above the fulfillment of worldly desires emerging out of sensual pleasure. Even after an advance of more than two hundred years modern Economics is unable to define the purpose and objective of Economics and is veering round the study of wealth, to the study of human behaviour, to human welfare, to scarce resources and fulfillment of maximum wants, to human development, to sustainable economic development and so on and so forth.

Simultaneously, the objective of economic development is pondering round creation of material wealth, to raising the quality of life through health care and literacy, to Human Development. Human Development is comprised of indicators of income, health care, and literacy. "Long, healthy and creative life" of people being the objective of development. Thereafter the things are also associated with Environmental Sustenance and Sustainable Development not only for the present but also for the future generations of mankind. It is an acknowledgement of the symbiotic harmony between man and nature and its other creatures. Now it is being increasingly realized that man is not alone on this planet earth rather he is a part and parcel of a greater design of the universe which contain and sustains not only the man but also other creatures and plants. Many of the living and non-living beings also play an important role in deciding the fate or future of man- the living being. Interestingly it is also being realized that much of the harm has already been done by the man's actions in disturbing the harmony between man and the nature through their own endeavour for industrial development. Meaning there by that post industrial revolution advancements in some of the 'high mass consumption' societies has been solely responsible in polluting the atmosphere and depleting ozone layer and there by being catalyst in causing human sufferings for the present and future generations of mankind. One step forward and two steps backwards is the present condition of the so-called intelligent society craving for human welfare without even knowing the real meaning of welfare.

Economics has not been defined since Lionel Robbins and Samuelson in textbooks of economics to incorporate the changed scenario of the Twenty-First century. It has vaguely been associated with scarce means and satisfaction of maximum (endless) wants and human welfare. Does human welfare means targeting a hungry society craving for ever- new consumer good for sensual pleasure. What constitutes a Man and his behaviour? Is he a mind-body-spirit mechanical or chemical combination only? Why has he come? Who has sent him to this planet earth and for what purpose? Is he an economic entity only? No answer is available for many of these curiosities and questions with the Western world.

PART-3

Gita in its Samkhya Darshan Depicts

"Of created beings before death is unknown, between birth and death is known and after death again is unknown;..." Ch.2/28.

Can we explain the connection in pleasure and pain of one's current life, with his earlier life? What is the cosmic relation and reality between present and past lives of a creature? Only Vedic philosophy has the answer.

Man is a visible as well as an invisible entity. He is recognized by his physical body. But a much bigger part of him is invisible. His invisible entity plays much important role in his and others life. He is also recognized by his good or bad nature, and his good or bad deeds He is also recognized by his knowledge and intelligence. How knowledgeable he is. The invisible part of man's life plays a much greater role in his life. Analyzing what constitutes his reactions to a particular situation or action is a complex thing. It is to analyze his behaviour pattern. How he reacts to an economic situation is the subject matter of Economics. Theories of market, demand and supply explain the equilibrium conditions in different market forms and situations. But why he reacts the way he is reacting is a complex thing to analyze. Vedas deal at length with the subtle form of man in a detailed and scientific manner.

Man's Origin, Constitution, Forms, and Determinants of His Behaviour

Vedas declare Man is beyond Death. What vanishes is only his tangible form (body). The body disintegrates into the five elements out of which it was created: *Chitin* (the earth), *Jal* (water), *Pawak* (fire), *Vyom* (sky), and *Sameer* (air). His subtle form is constituted of mind, intelligence, *chitt*—in which his memories and samskars are contained, and the self. This part of man's existence is immortal. And in this way he is immortal. He is beyond death. What changes form is only his body. Why and what for he comes to form or life depends upon his deeds and misdeeds. This is the Karma philosophy contained in Upanishads and the ultimate source the Vedas. Be it known to man that the man's actions alone are responsible for his pleasure and pains the whole scenario will change.

The concept of an 'Economic Man' is only a partial and incomplete view of a man's life and hence modern Economics which is confined only to economic activities of man's life has an in-built limitation. Ancient Indian texts on the other hand present a holistic picture of man's life.

According to Upanishads man's composition has three strata. His one part (body) is tangible *(sthool sharir)*, the other part is subtle *(suksham sharir)*, and the third part is subtle most *(ati suksham Karan sharir)*. The first one is visible while the other two are invisible. Life is in the form of presence of a spirit (soul), which is ageless, timeless and immortal, and it transgresses from body to body. When it (also called *jive*) enters a body one comes to life and when it leaves the body one is declared dead. There is a reason (Karan) why and what for one assumes a particular body form. Life's bliss and sufferings; pleasure and pains are owing to the karma performed by a *jive* in this life as well as in the past life or lives. This *karya-karan sambandh* explains the life cycle and the happenings in life of a *jive*.

Further every man is a combination of three Gunas: *satva, raj*, and *tam*. The sublime, the baser, and the baser most. Their composition in a particular man decides his nature, attitude, and faculties. Men are superior or inferior depending upon the composition of these gunas or bhavas says Manu in *Manusmriti*. Man's actions are decided by the prominence of one or more of these bhavas.

Again the man's composition can be analyzed like this: that man has five koshas in him. The *Annamaya kosh* (the physical body); the *Pranmaya kosh;* the *Manomaya kosh*; the *Vijyanmaya kosh;* and the *Aanandmaya kosh.* The first one, *annamaya kosh* is made up of grains (food grains)—the energy part (*agni* or fire) emerging from food consumption transformed into *rasas* produces *veerya* (semen) in body of a matured man. *Kath Upanishad* mentions the similarity of man's life with that of a grain's life cycle.

The *pranmaya kosh* is composed of five main and five sub *(up) pranas. Pran* makes one a living being. They are *pran, upan, vyan, udan,* and *saman*. The *up prans* are *nag, kurma, krikle, devadatt,* and *dhananjaya. Pran* moves through the vehicle of *vayu* (air). They have different controlling functions in different parts of the body.

Manomaya kosh, the mind, is again a living part, always wavering like electrical waves in the brain. It is the fastest moving object in the world even much faster than the speed of light and sound. It makes one aware of his existence. Its character is most complex and difficult to explain. It is responsible for the feelings of pleasure and pain, agony and ecstasy, sorrow and gloom, greed, love and hate and all that. *Yajur Veda* explains its properties in Chapter by six mantras.

Vijyanmaya kosh is the intellectual part of a man. It is composed of intellect, knowledge, logic, reasoning, power of analysis, and so on. One is knowledgeable or dull headed depending upon the development of this faculty in man.

Lastly the subtlest form in man's composition is his *aanandmaya kosh,* which is supposed to be one of the original and indestructible qualities of the Supreme. His happiness and pleasure depends upon this faculty.

Besides the first one, the *annamaya kosh* the rest are invisible. It is said that power is always invisible. It also explains that many of the things, which are not visible by the eyes, cannot be denied existence. Thus there is a complete scientific analysis of man's constitution, his behaviour pattern, his actions and their governing factors in Upanishads, Smritis, and Vedas. Man's economic life is an important but not all-abounding part in life.

PART-4

Objectives of Man's Life

The very basic question arises what are the objectives and achievements of man's life. It is taught in dharma and adharma part of the sacred scripts. They explain the objectives of life and the way to attain them. They announce the duties of a man: what should be done and what should not be done.

Life's greatest objective is to attain freedom *(Moksha)* from the cycle of birth and death. This is the fourth *purusharthas* of man's life after *artha, kama,* and *dharma* as has been stated in the earlier part of this text. It also prescribes that the essential thing is not to relinquish dharm, righteousness, at any stage with *arth* and *Kama* otherwise the whole thing will be vitiated. This is the very basic message of our ancient scriptures. The superiority of Indian philosophy lies in the fact that while western philosophy of materialism perpetuates sensual satisfaction the Vedic scriptures speak of restraining the senses and sensual pleasure and have attached *dharma* at every stage with actions pertaining to *artha*, and *Kama*. They prescribe a code of conduct for a single individual as well as for group behaviour.

The way to attain this super most objective is by adhering to truthfulness *(satya),* and *dharma*. *Sat aachar* or truthful conduct and non-violence has also been prescribed in Buddhist philosophy.

Manu speaks of ten properties of *dharma*. They are *dhriti, kshama, dam, asteya, shauch, indriya-nigrah, dhee, vidya, satya,* and *akrodh*.

Meaning there by, developing patience, forgiveness, restraint of mind, not to steal other's wealth, purification and cleanliness of body and mind, restraint over sense organs, sharpening intelligence, attaining knowledge, truthfulness in speech and conduct, and not to be angry.

Manu at other point has prescribed the ways to purify body, *manas,* knowledge and the spirit (self):

Adbhir Gatrani Sudhyanti, Manah Satyen Sudhyate;

Vidya Tapobhyam Bhutatmah, Buddhir Jyanen Sudhyati.

The physical body is cleaned by water, while manah-the mind, is purified by satya, the spirit (*jive*) is purified by application of *jyan* and *tapa,* and one's knowledge is refined by *jyan* acquired from *shastras* written and composed by saints and seers.

Manu in chapter 12 has also restrained from doing the following ten wrong things, which pertain to mind, voice (speech), and body. Mental functions are: thinking for stealing others wealth; thinking bad for others, jealous behavior; and wrong determination. Wrong pertaining to voice are: harsh language; speaking a lie; speaking bad about others in their absence; and talking irrelevant. The wrong done by body are: stealing others wealth; violent behaviour; and *vyabhichar—par stree gaman* and all that.

Manu in chapter four of *Manusmriti* has clearly and emphatically stated in *sloka* 176 that only that artha and Kama are acceptable which are righteous. Others are worth rejection:

Parityajtedarthkamoh yo syataam dharmvarjitoh;

That is wealth acquired through wrong means—by stealing, by robbery, by violence, or by deceitful act is altogether to be rejected. In chapter twelve he has warned that by doing the wrong one will reach the baser degrees of life.

Vaisheshik darshan (philosophy) explaining the form of dharma has stated:

Yato abhyudaya nihshreyas sidhih sa dharmah; 1/1/2

Meaning there by, that conduct which brings the higher things desired in life like physical, mental and spiritual upliftment, peace and pleasure and supports in attaining *moksha* is *dharma*.

In *Yogdarshan* Patanjali pronounces:

Yogaschittvriti nirodhah.

That is controlling and containing senses is yog. Yog is the way to union with the Supreme. He has prescribed eight ways to attain the Supreme by *yog*. They are: *yam, niyam, aasan, pranayam, pratyahar, dharna, dhyan,* and *samadhi*.

Kathopanishad in one of the verses pronounces *Aatman* as the chariatteer of this body chariot. The body chariot of a person is driven by five horses, which are very powerful. And they drag the chariot to the gratification of their own pleasure path. They are the five sense organs—the eyes, the nose, the ears, the tongue, and the skin. They seek their pleasure in different directions. The pleasures they seek are called the sensual pleasure. Eyes want to see something to their pleasure, the nose seeks good scent, the ear takes one to sweet music, the tongue wants good taste, and the skin seeks pleasure of touch. These horses drive the mind in their own directions. It is the property of the mind that it runs very fast, even faster than the speed of light or sound. The mind is under the command of Buddha—the knowledge. These are the properties of man. A man who is not wise runs in the directions taken by his mind. And here *Isopanishad* states:

The blinding darkness, go the men who worship neiscience.

This means work without knowledge takes one to darkness. Intelligence or wisdom (*buddhi*) is of three kinds: *medha buddhi, prajya buddhi* and *ritambhara buddhi* according to the degrees of refinements.

It is with this background of knowledge, restraint on sensual pleasure and dharma that *artha* and *Kama* are added to the life of a man for material gratification and physical attainments of his own-self and his dependents.

The Vedic texts have prescribed four ashrams for a man's life. *Brahmcharya, grahastha, vanprastha* and *sanyas.* Out of a programme for one hundred years life one has to undergo the stage of *brahmcharya* (student) for twenty-five years, then he has to attend to his family duties as prescribed in *grahastha dharma* for next twenty-five years. After attaining the age fifty he has to relinquish his grahastha duties in favour of his son and others and lead a life for the welfare of not only his own family but for the community. Then at the age of seventy five he has to lead life of a sanyasi where his endeavour would be welfare of whole society and his own salvation.

PART-5

Meaning of *Artha* and *Arthashastra* in Ancient Indian Literature

In ancient Indian literature Artha has got several interpretations depending upon the situation and the circumstances. It has been used as meaning, objective, and purpose, e.g., objective of life or purpose of life. It has also been used to mean reality—*yatharth.* It is used for knowing meaning and content of words. It discovers and reveals the meaning of words.

In *Vaisheshic dravya, guna* and *karma* are pronounced *artha.*

Kautilya Says

Manushyavati bhumih ityarthah;
Tasya prithivyah labhpalnopayashastramarthshastramiti.

The earth which contains mankind is termed Artha, wealth. And that science which treats of the means of acquiring and maintaining the earth is *Arthashastra,* science of polity. So in Kautilya's view the basic object is human welfare through maintenance and sustenance of mother earth.

In the pre Industrial societies earth or land has been the main source of life sustenance and prosperity hence it was called mother earth. It is the land, which produces grains (food for life), vegetables, plants, medicinal herbs, flowers, and various trees and so on. Besides various minerals in the earth, water and other things from earth makes man's life sustainable on this planet and make them comfortable and happy.

Kautilya has also meant *Artha* in the sense of *Vritti*—the way of earning livelihood. So it is a system by which people get a living. It is the modern definition of an economy or economic system. The chapter under which he has written these things is named *'Tantrayukti'*. Tantra means system, as *artha-tantra,* economic system.

Under chapter four he has treated *artha jyan* under *Varta*. Agriculture, cattle breeding, and trade constitute varta. It is most useful in that it brings in grains, cattle, gold, forest produce, and free labour *(visti)*. It is by means of treasury and army obtained solely through varta that the king can hold under his control both his and his enemy's party.

Yajyavalkya in *Mitakshara* has meant *arthashastra* as *Dandniti* (code of punishment).

Shukraniti too subscribe to this meaning of Yajyavalkya while Kamandak (800 A.D.) took *Arthashastra* as *Nitishastra* (Ethics).

The meaning of *Arthashastra* by Kautilya is superior to the modern definition of economics, which is basically materialistic. Modern Environmentalists are emphasizing the man and nature relationship and are coming to the point that man's actions in the wrong direction of deforestation, excess of industrialization and consequent fowling of atmosphere, rivers, lakes and other water bodies, extinction of birds and other species are creating threat to the life support system of man and other creatures and is a threat to the life itself of the mankind who is threatened with ever new kind of diseases and disorders.

In Kautilya's system *artha* though important has not

been considered in isolation. It is a part of the *purusharthas* as described above. He has given a code of conduct for man and has said that a proper balance among *Dharma, Artha* and *Kama* is to be maintained (1/7/4). In the very next stanza he states excess of any one of the three shall vitiate the two and destroy itself too. He further says, the basis of *dharma* and *Kama* is arth hence artha is important. The message of restraint over *artha* and *Kama* and prefix it with *dharma* and maintain a rightful balance among the three is everywhere in all the Indian texts of ethics, *dharma* and philosophy.

The point of restraint over materialism is being discussed in modern parlance since the Earth Summit and concerns are raised towards "limit to growth" in view of obnoxious impacts of excess of industrialization. It is an attempt to return to nature by man.

Renowned social scientist Schumacher in his 'Economics in a Buddhist country' has stated that Economics under the western impact perpetuated the philosophy of materialism and there is total absence of any idea of "limit or measure" of material wants. The materialist's idea of progress is an idea of progress without limit. In his own words: "Economics as taught today throughout the world—before the iron curtain or behind—recognizes no limit of any kind. It is, therefore, the Economics of Materialism and nothing else. There is implicit in it a purely materialist view of life, and it is inseparable from this view of life." Economics of materialism is not of universal validity. It is the time to (one should) take cognizance and admit that other systems of Economics are possible and necessary and are already available in rudimentary form.

Mahatma Gandhi laid the foundation for a system of economy based on Hindu philosophy of contentment, simplicity, *satya* (truthfulness), and *ahimsa* (non-violence) for the development of all. He emphasized the need for upliftment of the downtrodden—the poorest of the poor and rejected in society. He gave a system of Swadeshi and khadi (charkha).

Pandit Nehru under the greater impact of Buddhism adopted the principle of Panchsheel in his foreign policy. He laid the foundation of mixed economy and socialist path to safeguard people's interest from capitalistic (materialist) exploitation. How far his system yielded results is a matter of debate whether it was a theoretical or ideological wrong or an implementational failure on the part of his descendants.

While it is understood by many (under the western impact) that chronic poverty in India had been owing to her attachment with Hindu philosophy of contentment, and simple living Gandhi was of firm view that "Much of the deep poverty in India is due to departure from swadeshi in economic life. If not a single article of commerce had been brought from outside India she would be today a land flowing with milk and honey". Gandhi's philosophy worked wonders in India under slavery when his Swadeshi Movement (1905) had a formidable impact on the British to consider leaving this country.

'Economics does not stand on its own feet', says Schumacher, 'it is derived from a view of the meaning and purpose of life'. And the western Economics is derived out of a purely materialist view of life. India needs its own development models and theories, developed by its own genius and the rich knowledge contained in Vedas and other scriptures. We need not copy the westerner's path and let our economy open for imperialist exploitation of newer form.

Material things are of real importance for a person, a family, or a nation only up to a point. So we can distinguish three economic conditions—misery, sufficiency, and surfeit, says Schumacher. Of these two are bad for a person, a family, or a nation and only one, sufficiency is good. Economic progress is good only to the point of sufficiency; beyond that it is evil, destructive, uneconomic.

Any system of thought that recognizes no limits can manifest itself only in extremely impermanent creations. This is the great charge to be laid against materialism and its offspring modern Economics, that they recognize no limits and in addition would be incapable of observing them if they did. This is the terror of the situation.

Self imposed limits, voluntary restraint, conscious limitation—those are life giving and life preserving forces. They should constitute the new Economics.

J.K. Mehta developed the theory of Want-less-ness as a counter to western economics. According to him by maximizing wants we would make life more and more complex and it will lead to misery instead of adding to the sum total of happiness.

The ultimate of every activity is attainment of happiness. But the materialistic route to happiness via multiplication of wants can only lead to individual tensions, frustration, and unhappy end of life. This also gives rise to social tensions, exploitation, inequality, corruption, unrest and wars which are destructive to world peace.

In conclusion let the message be spread from the Vedas, Upanishads, Kautilya, and Manu etc. which constitute the Indian philosophy that a proper balance and coordination among *Dharma* (righteousness), *Artha*, and *Kama* is the only ultimate way for attaining happiness in this life and salvation after death. The message is loud and clear that man's life has a purpose, that creator of all wealth is the Supreme and let every one know and follow the righteous path of earning income and wealth and be disciplined in indulging into gratification of sensual pleasure, Kama. The unrighteous path of acquiring wealth shall lead to struggles, misdemnure, frustration, violence and unhappy end of man's life. The *Yajur Veda* in chapter 40/12, as well as, *Ishopanishad* clearly states:

अन्धं तमः प्रविशन्ति ये ऽसम्भूतिमुपासते ।

ततो भूय इव ते तमो य उ सम्भूत्यां रताः ॥ यजु० 40/12

Those who run after nature only (priority or sensual gratification only) go in blinding darkness, and those who decry the sublime knowledge and run after lower knowledge, Neiscience, enter into even more darker worlds.

REFERENCES

1. *Gita*, chapter 2, Sankhya Yog.
2. Gupta, I.D., J.K. Mehta's Economic Philosophy, The Indian Economic Association, Conference Volume, 2002.
3. *Human Development Report*.
4. *Ishopanishad*.
5. Jean Dreze and Amartya Sen, *Economic Development and Social Opportunities*, OUP, 1998.
6. Kautilya, *Arthashastra*, Samashastry and Raghunath Singh bhashya.
7. *Kath Upanishad*.
8. *Manusmriti*.
9. *Satyarth Prakash*, Swami Dayanand Saraswati.
10. Schumacher, Economics in a Buddhist Country, *IASSI Qly.*, Vol. 15, No. 3, Jan-March 1999.
11. Sen, Raj Kumar, *The Indian Economic Journal*, Vol. 51, No. 2, 2003-04.
12. *Vaisheshik Darshan*.
13. *Yajurveda*.

Index